# BORN IS UNBORN

# Anup Rej

Between Heaven and the Brain
# BORN IS UNBORN

www.booksofexistence.no

The book contains excerpts from diaries and philosophical
and literary writings of Anup Rej

# Contents

# Preface

When the author was still a small child (before the school going age) God appeared in his mind. "He" came to give the child the message that God did not exist in the male and female figures of gods and goddesses, which people worshipped around. Instead, "He" explained that God existed in the mind as a mystery, hidden from the world, who could not be seen, felt or touched by any one. The Divine Being made its existence felt as a power which drew the child to look closely at the light, touch with reverence the leaves trembling in the air, watch the starry sky with wonder and awe and feel love for the colours, shapes and movements animating the flowers, insects, birds, animals and all living creatures on Earth. This secret friendship with God led him to take distance from the belief in the existence of gods and goddesses, who the people were worshipping in deep religiosity and faith.

As the child grew older God confirmed his nearness through the artistic and literary activities that the author pursued at that time. While learning to draw artworks on papers he discovered again and again a strange unknown realm of the mind. It felt as if the hidden hands of God were working through him. Many times when he sat down to write about deep thoughts, unusual streams of words flew in the mind filling it with emotions, as if, God was dictating words from a world hidden behind the perceptible world. Thus God became a fascinating experience. However, the child never wished to tell about this encounter with God to anyone, with the fear that his inner friend from the other world may not like this secret to be divulged.

When he reached the age of adolescence this invisible and intangible world started appearing as cosmic visions: First, it appeared as a spiral galaxy flying through the room by waking the boy from sleep in the middle of the night. Then it took the vision of the cosmos strewn with starry constellations vibrating as jewels in the dark night.

Until the author reached the age of twenty, this inner world did not interfere with the ego-bound life. So far the Godly and the earthly realms existed as two separate worlds: The world of God existed as a hidden realm, totally disjoint from the reality where human beings, bearing will and desire, carried out their daily activities. However, this state of happy friendship with the inner being changed as he stepped into his twenties: The ego-bound will and desire started being overridden by the Will of God.

At the age, when he was stepping into adulthood, God started revealing Himself in a different way: In the same physical body two different existences started emerging. One existence was bound to the will and ego-bound mind, with whom the author could identify himself as a person, while on the other side, there existed a Divine Being, who could penetrate the physical state and incarnate in a physical body – a phenomenon which could not be grasped by the human mind. Unlike the earlier days of the childhood, when God remained as a bystander and watched the play of the child and helped him to search and find the Divine Being in the world (though he was invisible) in a playful way, now God started confusing him by overriding time and again the will and desire of the ego-bound mind. At the same time God started explaining about the nature of the human will and the Will of God – how they worked and contradicted – and invited the author to make a journey following the will of the Divine. The conditions for taking the mortal soul to this journey was that the author must cast off the ego-bound will and logic that he had acquired through his education and cultural upbringing.

It meant dissolution of the ego and will and invitation to submit it to the Will of God, who contradicted  reasons and logical arguments, which the author needed in order to function in the world together with other human beings. It became the beginning of a tormented life which soon ignited conflicts, doubts, and disbelief in the existence of

God. In attempting to gain back control over activities of life, which was grounded on the ego-bound will and understanding of man, again and again the author felt frustrated: Every time he was overwhelmed by the Will of God, and His way to control the ego-bound man. Time and again the will was brought to submission; it rose with doubt and disbelief again and again to free the mind from the dictates of God. Thus it continued for many years which affected the scientific career of the author as a Nuclear Physicist. However, no one in the world ever got any hints about what was going on in the mind of the man who called himself an existentialist. At this age too it remained equally secret and hidden as it had been during the childhood.

Then came a catastrophic moment, which turned everything into a great chaos in life: In an accident on the Alps in Switzerland the author lost his beloved son (only child), who was a great source of joy in his life. The extremely improbable accident, which was preceded by a premonition of death, appeared as a thundering rod from God. This death of the one, who meant so much in his life, and whom he loved so dearly, released a shock and a trauma which totally transformed his life since then. He became a new man, who was a part of the universal being, of whom all human beings were parts. Now God appeared as the Guide of the Soul, and took him in a journey through different realms of consciousness. He left scientific pursuits for some years and made this journey through philosophies, mythologies, religions and cosmos. A book, describing the journey of mankind through ages, unfolded while the author was guided by his Divine companion. The writing, which began with no idea about what the content and structure were going to be, took the shape of a profound epic of Man of great complexity in form and content. It took the author in a journey through all worlds of human emotions, creativity and contemplation. In a poetic language the Guide of the Soul revealed worlds inside worlds in a will-bound reality of human existence which was the source of illusion.

The literary-philosophical work culminated in the "Dialogues Between Man and God" where the will and ego-bound man held dialogues with God. He wanted to know from His Divine Guide about the nature of the existence of God which can be understood by man by the use of known human language, and which may be able to remove doubts and disbeliefs about God which had plagued his rational mind. In these dialogues he also wished to know the answers to ethical and moral questions which will-and-ego-bound human beings should follow in life.

After this journey through different realms of consciousness that constitute human spheres – from instinct-bound life to the most enlightened state - the author returned to study the mystery of the cosmos once again. This time, through accidental coincidences, he discovered a universe which is totally different from what the main stream scientists had been professing for nearly a century. He discovered a universe without beginning and end, which hid an eternal cosmic design in all scales – however small or large the cosmic object may be. The universe existed as a complex entanglement where micro structures and macro structures were all entangled inseparably as a whole. In this universe time existed in the background of a timeless design, which never changed and remained hidden behind all cosmic structures.

In this universe the birth, evolution, death are all parts of a great design, a harmonic melody of a great song as described by the Celts known as Oran Mor. It never ceases, never ceased in the past and will never stop in the future. As the Celts conceived, it is synonymous with the creation itself, which never rose in the past at any moment of time, and will never come to an end in the future. The universe continues eternally its great harmonic enfolding and unfolding filling all creation, embodying everything as inseparable parts of the whole.

This great symphony is infinitely deep in structure, unfathomably complex in its arrangement, which reflects an inconceivable intelligence acting behind it. The universe is unbelievably profound, which evokes the greatest sense of awe and wonder one may ever experience. However, this symphony is built in a simple way by following a template.

The Great Melody that contains all existing beings, and puts all things in their appropriate course of the journey of life from birth to death, leads everything in the universe along entangled loops which has no beginning and end in space.

In this Great Music, melodies and notes rise from the interactions of the whole, and the whole brings reverberations in all. It fine tunes every sound, even those lasting for the smallest fractions of time in the tinniest corner of the universe, to create a harmony and beauty of an immense dimension. One may call this song as one wishes. Thus God reveals himself in the orderly harmony of what exists.

It is not someone creating something else. Instead, through the mediation of the triple spiral the micro-structures feed back energy to larger structures to sustain the existence of the macro-world. The macro-world keeps the micro-worlds in existence by supplying nourishment to them. Thus micro- and macro-worlds are existing eternally while supporting existence of each other. Things which create something are created by others in turn. The creator and the created ones are inseparably dependent on each other and tied in an entangled universe. Like every sounds of the harmonic music of Oran Mor, they all participate in the song which is synonymous with creation and creator itself.

God is animating everything everywhere and existing in the same way in all by imaging itself in the similar way in the largest to the tinniest of creations.

This book is an account of the above stories from the childhood till the discovery of the new universe as the realm of God. These varied experiences have led the author to understand the nature of God, and the limitations of human mind to understand the great mystery. However, in spite of all these experiences and search, God still remains an enigma to him. He still wonders about the true nature of God, who has appeared in his mind with such clarity. It is a phenomenon arising through the mediation of the neural network which bring the experience of waves swirling in the mind in a virtual space simulated by the super-super-super computer of the brain. It is also a story of torments when the author has submitted to the Will of God and revolted again and again to regain a ground in the world of logic and reason. He has used scientific knowledge and rational introspection as anchors to find safe harbour on islands ravaged by the turbulent onslaughts of the mind. It is a drama where he has made a journey from shores to shores, while collecting evidences for and against the existence of God. At the end of the book he leaves the questions of the existence of God open to interpretation by the readers themselves.

While still vacillating between belief and disbelief, submission and revolt, faith and doubt about one`s own sanity of the mind, the author fails to distinguish reality from illusion, knowledge from ignorance, and suffering from joy. One has followed the other in his life as unavoidable reality of existence. Similarly, God has followed man, and man has followed God as inseparable dual partner, penetrating the body and mind. Here what one may call something inside the brain and mind, and those that seem to exist outside it, merge as the One who defines the human existence as a part of the divinity. Together with molecules, atoms, and dusts and gases in the cosmos he experiences his human existence as one with God.

Still questions remain unanswered: Who is God? Is "He" the one who is the cause of the eternal recurrence of the forces upholding the death and birth of all – from micro-molecules to the largest structures in the cosmos? Or, one who brings pestilence and disease which bring death in order to return energy back to life? Or, is "He" the force that penetrates the mind and squeezes out chemical from the brain cells generating the experience of love, joy, ecstasy and epiphany?

The book offers new perspectives to both the religious believers and the atheists.

# Chapter 1

# ENCOUNTERING GOD

*K*now that you are never truly born and you will never truly die, because the spirit is immortal in all. Although everybody must change and transform from the living to the nonliving and back to a new life again in harmony with the dance of the forces bringing destruction and new life, know that you are beyond destruction and change. What you put on as a body is like a cloth that you need to change with the changing motions of the material environment burning inside a cosmic pyre in flame. Without this annihilation of the body and its regeneration, everything would be stagnant and there will be no existence and motions that create the universe bound in causal chains. The spirit cannot burn in any flame. It exists as the mind in the universe that is a dual counterpart of the material world, and cannot be separated from matter, which is bound in causal chains. Matter cannot exist without mind and mind is non-existent without matter on which it must reflect to bring consciousness in the mind.

Know that beyond the powers of fire, water and wind you are a part of the Great Mind that is everlasting, omnipresent, and One. You are invisible to your own eyes, unconceivable by your own thoughts, unknowable by your own power of knowing because your true existence is deeper than what you may be able to conceive. Within you there exists another existence, beyond that another existence and so on... They look at each other from the depth and illumine your thoughts. The deeper one gazes within oneself, that lies further away from the material world, one may get in touch with a deeper realm of the Great Mind. The one, who you think you are, is only an idea formed with certain concepts of reality and knowledge about matter and mind that is very limited and incomplete. You have many more levels of consciousness within you, than what you have been able to fathom with the help of language and thoughts at the level where your so-called consciousness operates. Discover in greater depths the different layers of existence lying within you. Know yourself as a part of the infinite being. Meaning of your life is to realize this oneness with the One and experience the Great Love that animates all everywhere, and in all times. More man realizes this unity at every level that lies deeper the greater becomes the experience of living. It can never be fully fathomed by thoughts, because thoughts are moulded by concepts that are defined only at a particular level of awareness, which is incomplete.

Know that you were invisible before the birth, and will remain unseen after the body will be cast off. Do not be touched by sorrows and sufferings that arise due to the incomplete knowledge of the relations of life. With the disappearance of the body nothing disappears apart from the memories of sensation and the linguistic framework with which the memories are stored, interpreted and structured to suit the conditions in which the body is bound in the causal relations of the world. The spirit, that becomes conscious of its existence at a particular place and in a particular time, does not retain these memories after the dissolution of the body because memories refer to the body of the matter to which they need to be associated with. However, there exists a different state of existence, which relates to the matter in the new life, and appears as spirit in which senses may reassemble data and form the power of the consciousness once again. This spirit is egoless and has no separate identity as you, he, or me. All different identities are formed when the spirit is embodied in matter and are conditioned by it. Through the instrumental framework of the sense apparatuses the mind manifests. However, the soul may impart power to penetrate deeper and deeper levels of existence. By concentrating the power of the mind and meditating about true nature of the self, one may discover greater realms of the mind and realize the unity of oneself with the Great Mind.

Leave behind the delusion, and contemplate on the mind that is pure and divine; submit your will to the Great Mind and remain unshaken *by the suffering of life. This is the way to reach perfections. This is how you will be able to see the deeper domains within you that are still unseen. Through trials and tests, failures and errors you will be purified and gain realization of the Great Mind, who can be known by knowing the true nature of the self. However, at each stage of this process, one needs a concept about the Great Mind. Only through living and interacting with others, who are also parts of the same Mind, one will realize that the Great Mind is not what one may have previously thought it to be. Through errors and failure and abandoning the previous concept one will arrive at a new concept which needs to be refuted again and again in order to know the true nature of the self in a greater and greater depth. There is no end to this process of the self-knowledge because the Great Mind is endless, unfathomable and infinite.*

*Recollect the memories of your life, bring them in harmony with the spirit moving with the Great Mind and submit your will to the Divine. Follow the journey without possessing the delusion that you are the one who comes, or goes. Surrender yourself to the Great Mind, and contemplate in the tranquillity and harmony of the whole."*

Messages like this had appeared many times before in the mind as spiralling waves moving through a strange space simulated by the brain. However, nothing similar had happened before like on the day when God said that he would appear before me as a human being wearing a body made of blood and flesh.

Gripped by an immense excitement I was looking around to meet God. Being guided by the spiralling waves I was walking over the bridge across the Ganges that linked the main train station, called Howrah station, to the other bank of the Hoogly River, which is another name of the Ganges when it enters the delta of the Bay of Bengal. The bridge was constructed by the British during the Second World War to facilitate the movement of the soldiers to the Burmese border by trains. It now carries hundreds of thousands of vehicles and innumerable pedestrians every day.

Howrah station has grown to be one of the most crowded and filthy station in the world. It also acts as a place of accommodation for the daily labourers and the beggars in the city, who have no other place to take shelter at night. The footpaths along the bridge has become an extension of the slum of the poor and poverty stricken dwellers, who have set up shanty homes with plastic sheets and jute bags, collected from the main whole-sale market, that lies close by the bridge.

I had to walk because I had no money to buy a bus ticket to come home, which was about ten kilometres away from the station. I had money when I left my room and started the journey. However, when I came to Howrah station, I discovered that I was pick pocketed by a beggar. He had appeared to ask for money when I was paying for the ticket at the ticket counter in the Kharagpur station, where my train journey had commenced. It was a strange whirlpool of events! Before I bought the ticket in Kharagpur station, I had no idea about where I was going. Only after coming to the ticket counter I realized that my destination was Howrah. "Someone inside" dictated the name of the destination.

The whole episode started while I was attending a class on the theory of relativity. In the middle of the lecture the spiralling waves surged commanding me to leave the lecture room. By surprising the professor and the classmates I left. I did not know why? When I came to my room in the Hostel, where I stayed, I realized that I was going somewhere – without having any idea about where that place could be! When I came out of the Hostel I saw a rickshaw passing by. I asked the rickshaw driver to drive me to the railway station. After arriving in the station my feet like a robot led me to the ticket counter. After buying the ticket I understood that I was going to Calcutta. The beggar appeared at the moment I was paying for the ticket. I gave him some money and took the next train. After I entered into a compartment the inner waves gave the message that I was going to meet God in blood and flesh.

The walk over the Ganges revealed a miserable world where hungry women, men and children begged from the passersby. This was a painful confrontation with the misery of the world, that made me emotionally charged. I demanded "If you truly exist, appear before me and explain why these human beings are suffering in such wretched state?"

The next moment the world dramatically transformed. I was no more the man who existed a few seconds earlier: I became "two-in-one".

I got split into two beings belonging to two different realms. On one side there existed a man in flesh and blood in a world immersed in suffering, and on the other side God existed without body and form. When God spoke the head sank, in submission to the Divine power. This strange experience became extremely overwhelming. There was no doubt in my mind that God had appeared in flesh and blood. The mortal ego, whom I know as me, took the role of Arjuna and the Divine power played the role of Krishna in Bhagavat Gita. A dialogue between the mortal, possessing ego and will, based to the experiences of the physical body, and the Divine, who appeared as a mystery beyond comprehension to the mind, ensued. The head sank and rose as the mind changed states between the realms of the will-bound man and the Divine existence. In the same physical body two totally different beings seemed to exist. God answered every question that I wanted to ask.

The ten kilometre walk along the streets of Calcutta, drowned in chaos and human suffering, turned out to be one of the most revealing moments of my life, which transformed my understanding of the nature of the Divinity and its relations to the human. It also helped me to grasp the true meanings of the dialogues of Bhagavat Gita. I realized that Arjuna and Krishna both existed in me as me and also as not me. Since that revelation a new chapter started in my life.

This meeting opened a window to know about things that were not knowable by the human reasoning. I started conducting dialogues about the nature of things, mind and creation with God. Our relationship became so intense and fascinating that I gradually started withdrawing myself from the world and spent most of my times in the company of the Divine. A different reality, that cannot be explained by science, and approached by any philosophical speculations by using logic of the reasoning mind, gradually overwhelmed my existence. It was like an invisible world casting its shadow over the physical existence. The young man, who started his exploration of life as an existentialist and a student of physics, gradually got entrapped in a psychological experience that only the mystics may understand.

Since then ...

*"I feel I carry a duality of existence : One part of me appears as someone who belongs to the one who is the universal and the eternal, while the other part is associated with a carnal existence trapped in the circumstances of temporal events. I am mostly familiar with this later part. It is the source of my knowing and perceiving the world. The other part demands from the human ego complete submission to the Will of God. The carnal body has a strong urge to hold on to ego and will, which is bound to the perceptive world. I do not know which part of these two, constituting me, represents the true nature of me and whose will I should follow in life. This brings constant contradictions and conflicts. I always experience that there is someone who exists outside the physical world whom I can never grasp, and who has no reality that can be described by any language. This other "me" appears as a guide and tries to steer the ego-bound will. Often I discover the presence of this incomprehensible Being, appearing as wave-like movements in the mind, dictating paths that often fall in conflict with rational thoughts. "He" says that I must perform tasks that has been destined for me; I am born to serve a purpose. I should bring the messages of God to the world. The other part, who makes the intellectual and rational me, finds more comforts in believing that the material world is governed by physical laws. These laws should constitute the ground for understanding the mysteries of life and all existence. The supernatural phenomena are only deceptive quagmire of the mind. They are mental concoctions caused by psychological distress. Like hallucination, they have no reality..*

*I tell myself: The man, who wants to erect life on reason, should better not believe in God. This rational man in me share the ideas of the existentialist philosophers and calls himself an atheist. Thus I exist as two individuals: One, who I do not know and comprehend, but who plays the role as a guide; the other one is the human part who does not want to believe in the spiritual existence. On one side there exists one, without whose permission I can not engage in doing and living; on other side there exists a being bound to bodily perceptions, who wants to make the*

12

*conscious mind as the guide of life. This duality has created a crisis of identity. I no longer feel that I am the one who I want to be. I realize that often my acts are not results of my own rational decisions but are arising from the Will of God.*

*Who am I really? I do not know whether I am a scientist, or an artist, or a philosopher, or possess any identity that my activities may define! From what I experience I know that I possess a body on which a mysterious force  acts and drives me to  live in the world. The purpose and goal of living do not arise from the will in the way I know it. I am like a twig floating in a stormy current moving towards an unknown destination. Only my guide knows where I am heading to. The man, who is the bearer of human will and whose consciousness is based on knowledge,reason and perceptions, does not understand the extra-perceptive world.*

*What a psychological mess in living with someone as a part of myself, which I can not grasp! Whenever I fall in despair. I return to God to seek for advice. He has become so inseparably a part of me that I can no longer conceive of an existence without His presence. Everywhere He follows me. He never leaves me alone. Whenever He intends to bring to my notice something I should see and observe, He takes control of mind. I often get overwhelmed by unpredictable surprises revealing the nature of the great mystery embodied in things around...”*

When I wrote this diary in 1974 I was a young man living in Calcutta with my parents in a middle class family of eight children. My parents were atheists and shared Marxist ideology. Books of Marx, Hegel, Heidegger, and Sartre were abundant in our house. Our family fell starkly outside the religious culture of India, where the gods and the goddesses had greater impacts in reality than what the human beings did. My eldest brother was a celebrated guest in the Calcutta Coffee House, a renowned place for the young intellectuals. He made the whole clan of the leftist intellectuals of Paris the favorite philosophers and writers for his younger siblings. While my father translated works of Goethe and Nietzsche from German and novels of Dostoevsky from Russian, my brother fed us with novels of Camus, Kafka, Sartre, Jean Genet etc. In our family there was no place for God.

We lived in an atheist island surrounded by religious people. Most relatives and neighbours were religious – including my grand-parents. My grandfather had often told the story of his encounter with a sage, who had mysteriously appeared on his way along the road passing through the paddy fields skirting the village boundary where he lived. The sage had heralded a message of God to him. After delivering the message the Sage had melted away in the air. According to my parents this story was a hallucination seen by a religious man. When my father was born, my grandfather believed that he was a gift of God and named him Debabrata, which meant "as promised by God". Though Debabrata showed exceptional talent from his early childhood, instead of serving God he became a sympathizer of the communist ideology that denounced the existence of God.

As the fourth son of Debabrata I got entangled with God instead. Messages of love, meaning of suffering from a Divine world, as the example below, appeared in my mind time and again.

*"Love every human being.*
*Know that the love permeates all that exist.*
*Know Him who is the light of all creation and the source of love.*
*Know love and become one with the existence of ALL.*
*Know what is.*
*Love what is.*
*Merge into the existence where you are a part of all.*

*God is bound in you.*
*God suffers with you.*
*With this realize God in you.*
*You suffer as God, in God and with God.*
*You suffer for your separation from God.*

*Offer your will and suffering to the Will of God.*
*The suffering you experience is the suffering of God,*
*that the whole universe undergoes and the suffering that is eminent in*
*the infinite and the whole.*
*Through this suffering love manifests.*
*Know that suffering is love and love is suffering.*

*I face Earth.*
*On Earth I have brought forth my incarnation.*
*In such incarnation I appear as a body embracing human ego.*
*God faces you in the depth of your being and sees you as Him.*
*However, I am not the face of a man in his daily life.*
*I am not the face of reality.*
*But everything that you call real exists in Me.*

*I exist at every point in space and every moment of time as*
*existence entangled with you.*
*Thus I am bound in body and form.*
*This bondage is my suffering.*
*This bondage brings separation from the others.*
*But the universe to exist I need to bind myself in all*
*Because I am love.*
*I am the creator who is bound to His creation.*

*The man, you see is the one who is made and formed the way you gaze.*
*He is a projection of life in relation to all others. To know man is to see*
*him beyond these projections in his true nature as me, who is a thinking,*
*feeling and a reflecting being living in a secret abode where he feels secure*
*and free.*

*Knowing others see you in the context of history*
*and the perspective of eternity.*
*At the end see Me as God.*
*Every man is a door to God - the door to eternity.*
*The way to know man lies in becoming indistinguishable from*
*other human beings.*
*Encounter the man of flesh and blood.*
*Know man through your experience of God."*

Such messages appeared as waves moving through the brain, forming words and sentences and then disappearing from the mind. When the mind was not focused in a meditative state the messages were unstructured and less coherent. But when the mind was focused to discuss an issue it was possible to conduct a coherent dialogue.

15

Below is an example of such a dialogue:

"Who should decide about how should I live and act - God or me?"

*"You should decide what you may intend to do. God will guide you away from the erroneous paths."*

"How can God help man? Is He conscious of human errors and faults?"

*"The ego finds its own path. I face ego as a mirror that exists in eternity. I am a mirror that makes ego see in its reflection the existence of God. Thus I appear in order to correct human conducts.*

*Know me as an ever-present mirror existing in all. I do not actively participate in the living world. Instead I make souls experience my presence in the inner realm, which draws them towards Me.*

*I am not consciousness; I am not thought, or idea. I am serenity. I am love. I appear through human mind as consciousness borne by the human mind."*

"If you are not thought, consciousness or idea, how do you communicate with man? How do I know you?"

*"It is not Me whom you know. It is the image of your own reflection in the mirror appearing as Me whom you experience as Me. The ideas that we are communicating through this dialogue are not arising from a realm who is Me, separate from you. It is you yourself casting an image through your mind, that you call Me. It is a reflection of an ephemeral existence in the mirror that exists eternally. In this mirror you see yourself as an image of Me. We exist as an inseparable Being.*

*It is your vision perturbed by your consciousness and ego, accompanied by knowledge and bodily senses, which is creating this confusion in your mind".*

"Is God communicating with me?"

*"It is your ego realizing the presence of God. It sees its own image in the eternal realm of God.*

*This is a dialogue between two images of the same: One image is present in the world, the other is the reflection of the ego in the ever present mirror of God, not shaped and formed by the physical world."*

While sunk in this psychological quagmire, I received a fellowship to go to Norway in 1971 to pursue research in the field of theoretical nuclear physics.

Amidst research, conferences, teaching, writing scientific papers and handling the practical problems of making adjustments with a totally different climate, food and culture, the existence or non-existence of God became a less important issue for some years to come. Furthermore, wife, family and son added new dimensions to life that demanded more attention to the worldly affairs than what existed beyond.

The dialogues with God again surfaced when I went to live in New York. It surged with my academic down going as a physicist. I had already abandoned research in nuclear and particle physics, and started looking into the theories of the creation of the universe instead. I bought the first IBM personal computer that appeared in New York in 1982. The more I computed with the digital machine, more I wished to get out of the world of reasoning and computations. As the conflict between scientific reason and the presence of God continued I felt captivated inside an existential crisis. I wrote:

*"I feel enclosed and imprisoned in a bubble of emptiness. My yelling and shouting do not reach beyond the surface of this empty sphere. My mind sees itself by reflecting on itself; watches its own image and creates an illusion of the possibility that one day I may be free by getting an answer to the riddles that have captivated me into this void. I am entrapped by my own images in an abyss enclosed by innumerable mirrors – though, all may be parts of myself. I see different images in different mirrors. In some my face appears distorted as elongated and infinite without any real shape; in some it looks as a singular point without any dimension of length, height or breadth; in some it appears fleshy and bulky; in some I look skinny and wispy reduced to an existence dwindling to a point of total extinction. These are some of the images I see circulating on the surface of the bubble of emptiness. I try to make noise in order to get help to come out of the hole that has enwombed me in the universe. However, my voice does not reach beyond the boundary that entangles me in deeper and deeper traps inside the mind. How can I escape this confinement?"*

We had moved to New York from Switzerland about a half a year before this encounter started once again. Now the place, where I found myself, had no similarity with the reality around the room in Calcutta where I had conducted my first dialogue with God. Now I was sitting in a room at 23rd floor in a luxury apartment in a posh area of the most vibrant and famous city in the world. It lay at the Upper East Side of the Manhattan Island on 79th Street and York Avenue. The lobby of the apartment was decorated and furnished like any 4-star hotel lobby in New York with costumed guards at the entrance gate. In this affluent world I was trapped in a psychological crisis of existence.

*"God! Who He could be? With the help of the intellect I cannot form any idea of Him, who may know the reasons why I exist. Is God a mind superior to the mind I possess? How can I understand that great mind? How can I understand His language? He may have a logic and method of reasoning different from the human logic and reasoning! In such case I won't understand that supernatural mind. Moreover, I am not sure if any such supernatural mind truly exists! What I know to be sure is the existence of my own mind that brings the consciousness that "I exist". This mind receives and stores different categories of experiences. From one corner of the mind I see colours in the sky and the beauty in all; from another corner I see the void and the abyss of darkness where I am capti-vated. I never understand how mind exists in such different states!*

In facing the mystery of God every time I felt disoriented and fumbled in the darkness, I returned to the guide again and again with a hope that one day I may be able to comprehend truth if I could penetrate into the enigmatic language of God that He used in the dialogues.

Examples of dialogues :

"Is there anything called truth? Can truth be known?"
*"Truth germinates in the shadow of your knowledge. Knowledge itself is bound to the nature and laws of matter and experiences of events oc-curring in time and space. As knowledge and experience may expand, beyond all that you know, truth has no end to fathom. It is the universe itself."*
"What shall I search then?"
*"Do not search truth with the help of scientific reason alone. Such knowledge is incomplete because it is based on the relations of material things. This knowledge creates patterns which co-ordinate thoughts ac-*

18

*cording to the movement of the material streams moving as perceptions in the mind. They are only shadows of the true essence embedded in things. Remember, I am above the confinement of matter. I am the light behind all that exist. I am not confined in the movements and shapes of things."*

"Why have you entered this confinement of my existence? How do you answer me? Where are You?"

*"I am everywhere. I am within you and outside you. I am a force that makes you search for truth in the depth of things. I am the origin of all sufferings. I am also end of it. "*

"Such answer does not help because I do not understand what you say. They appear as words from a world that is unfathomable by my intellect and impenetrable by my knowledge. Tell me something that I shall understand and which will help me to find the path to come out of this trap where I am imprisoned."

*"Then believe what I say in blind faith."*

"Why blind faith?"

*"Because you won't understand the purpose behind your existence using the knowledge and reason of the human mind. You have to follow the commandments, I send, without questions and doubts."*

"Tell me what do You want me to do?"

*"Understand the mystery of the Cosmos and Me. Carry the fire of heavenly spirit and the messages of the Divine world to mankind."*

"What path should I follow?"

*"Write an epic I have already asked you to write. Explain to mankind the state of the mind that they call freedom of the will and the true nature of freedom that the human beings should seek. Write the universal eternal story in which all are living and dying as parts of me. Illumine human mind with the light that emanates from the light of God, and elevate human visions to see the unseen and the unknown in the visual forms of arts. Work for Me and do not doubt and question the meaning of your acts and my purpose."*

Before coming to New York we lived for three years in Muri bei Bern surrounded by a pastoral beauty lying at the foothill of the Swiss Alps. There was a panoramic view in front of the windows of the Chalet where we stayed. The surreal world, that had followed me and surged through expressions of arts since my childhood, became more intense and closer in this surrounding. From my writing desk I had a view of "Jungfrau" in the direction of Northern Italy. Under this splendid mountainous view the spirit beckoned me to make a journey and write an epic.

I made my first attempt to write this epic after I came to New York. It began as a Dialogue between the Sprit and the Poet, who was standing on seashore of human suffering. The main theme of the dialogue was the nature of God and the way man could communicate with the Divine Being, who was beyond the power of any language and words for human mind to conceive.

## A dialogue between the spirit and the poet

**Poet:**
Darkness covers me like membranes around cells. Like the first cells in the embryo, though I receive blood, warmth and care of the mother universe, which curves like a sphere around the horizon, I am floating as a bubble of agony. I despair why am I born in this colossal sphere of darkness? The rays, that penetrate its surface and reach me, dance like waves on a rough sea, bringing the news that all are transforming and transmuting – all life must pass into death and all death must resurrect as life again. As foam of nothing, transparent to light, I exist in order to be battered by pains of thoughts, passion, lust and will. Other bubbles, similar to me, churn around and scatter light, warmth and agony of the souls that make us mortal creatures. In this abyss moments and instants of love, joy, or hate rise as wanton winds blowing the bubbles to their annihilations: They collide, burst and disperse into the void merging with the darkness. Leaving the body wrapped in layers after layers of saline blood, they fly through the dark in wings of light along indiscernible paths carrying the souls to places we cannot know. Time flows; causations induced by forces, that perpetuate motions of life and death, haul the remaining of the carcasses to lagoons where blood clots jot and pass to feed the corals in the sea. The dead creatures, that once swum in the bubbles, separate from the world that once lived on the beach dance under the veils of light. How can I understand this life

20

and death, this perpetual swirling of foams that churn between the realms known and unknown?

**Spirit:**

*In order to know the nature of God, who enters your mind through the invisible window of the soul you need to abandon the path of knowledge and the will that causes the experience of suffering. I enter and exit your mind through your will. Neither I have any body, nor am I confined in any form. I dance with the wind, breathe with the living world, reflect the light that illumine human souls and make them see the realm that remains unknown. I sing in solitude sharing the voice and emotions of seekers of love and beauty of life. I open in the heart the wings of the butterflies to collect from the weightless light the warmth of the sun that create pleasure, inspire dreams and open the veils of the beauties who dance the dance of light. In a transient sphere I fly as words of fire, in letters that only the receiver of the divine love can decipher.*

**Poet:**

But these are mere words. I fail to understand their meaning. They appear as accidental thoughts entering through the windows of a darkened mind stirred by pain and sorrow. Tell me in a language that I shall understand who are you?

**Spirit:**

*Neither I am knowable, nor am I unknown. I can be known to only those minds where I choose to reveal my presence with the purpose to send messages to the world. Knowing is a process bound to the material world and its laws. The languages and thoughts are confined within boundaries of experiences that are triggered by the senses. When you try to know, your mind falls in the frames of logic and experiences governed by the motions of the material world. But I am not confined to these material laws. Although I can enter and exit your mind structured by patterns, symbols, words and thoughts, I am unknowable by any language.*

**Poet:**

But how do you speak in this mind, in such a language though I experience it as something strange and abstruse?

**Spirit:**

*As I have explained before, I am like a mirror where you cast your own shadow in words and thoughts. I reflect them back as words and shadows of your thoughts. Your doubts, errors, conflicts return to you. In hearing the echo of the sounds that return as reverberation from the mountain chains, you know that I exist as the spiritual mountain that engirdles your mind. By hearing the echoes you hear the voice of the mountain that is Me.*

**Poet:**

Do I hear my own words that entangle me in patterns of thoughts? What is reason? What ignites doubts? Do I ignite doubts in my own mind? Or do you ignite doubts in order to bring me out of the paths laid by ignorance and errors? Is it your weird way of guiding man in finding truth and meaning behind things that cannot be understood by reason? Or is everything that I experience as God, delusive and false?

**Spirit:**

*I am not a mirror that exists in space and time, but a mirror that moves through layers of the mind where I appear as light that disentangles itself from the laws of matter that create visual images. As you gaze, the light from my mind penetrates your eyes to redress the errors of your vision, in order to erase the traces of deception that the ignorant mind may cultivate. The pieces of images and the words that swirl in your mind seek to relate to the light that is not bound in past, present or future. Being scattered by the motions of thoughts they are in a journey to seek the realm that exist beyond space and time.*

**Poet:**

How can I be sure that it is God who speaks, and not me?

**Spirit:**

*The shadows of the world, that are projected in your mind and appear in your consciousness through words, may disintegrate into pieces similar to clouds disintegrating in wind invisible in the clear sky, before reappearing again in another place and time, where they may create new clouds that cast new shadows of light. These constantly parting and join-*

ing shadows, driven by desire and will, bespeak the emotional nature of man. The light, that drives emotions and causes them to move from one state of the mind to another, is the power that bespeaks my existence. As in the case of the clouds, the shadows that reach the eyes do not reveal the true reality existing behind the clouds as light, the words, which you hear as the voice of God, is neither true nor false. They carry the projections of the streaks of light, through severed clouds that reach the visions in the inner world, where the images of the Divine can form.

The way you hear my answers depicts the nature of the inner realm that is disentangled from the laws of the material sphere. The words you hear are the shadows forming and joining in this inner realm. Although they may appear to follow a pattern of thinking based on events and cause, the experiences that I create in the inner world, bring man to realize about the realm that lies beyond reason. The forces that rise in the inner realm from a source beyond reasons and logical thoughts bring the words in your mind that transcend the meanings of words that you understand as a reason-bound man.

The questions you pose and the answers you receive are like music composed by thoughts, that dance with the movements of the wind, that blow through your heart's harpsichord. The voice you hear is inseparable from the voice that you yourself bear, though it is not the voice from the world, where words receive their usual meanings. Your questions and thoughts move in the inner realm, like shadows cast by the light in the mirror that I am. Thus you see your own reflections as awe and wonder of God. My answers emerge through rational pattern of thoughts in the mind, like shadows depicting forms, which are neither true nor false. Though reason is the only way to know, that can be transcribed into words, you should know that I am not knowable through reason and attainable to conceptualization through the law-bound processes of the human mind.

**Poet:**

How would I know that these words are not deceptive constructions of my mind, bringing false conceptions of God that may have no reality at all? You say you are beyond all words. However, words are the only way to conceive things and the nature of beings that exist in shapes and forms. You say you are beyond shapes and forms, and the scrutiny of words that make meanings in the world as we perceive and know. You say you are the Mirror: Man must stand in front of it to receive guidance without associating you with any reason, emotion and thought. How can I be sure that what I hear may be true and not treachery of my own mind? How shall I know that they are not hallucinations created by the brain as a false projection of a world that does not exist? How can I be sure that this dialogue is not an echo of my mind from a deep dark sphere, where there exists nothing but chemical and mechanical laws that generate random arguments and thoughts through accidental associations and chance? Am I trying to create God to find a false recluse?

**Spirit:**

*Do not ask because all you will hear would appear as voice rising from your own mind. You won't be able to resolve the doubts through power of reasoning of your mind. Neither reason can resolve the mystery that I am, nor can the words convey the nature of the light that dwells in you.*

**Poet:**

What should I do?

**Spirit:**

*Listen to Me when I appear in your mind. Do not question what you hear. Do not doubt the existence of God, who resides in your mind. I am you and Me at the same time.*

**Poet:**

Like a ghost you follow me. Why have you brought me to this surreal shore to conduct this dialogue that may appear absurd and insane to any reason-bound man? Why don't you leave me in peace?

**Spirit:**

*I want that you should write about it. Write about the drama of the conflict between human existence and existence of God. As a hidden force I shall help you to see your own image in the Mirror of God, and conceive in words the existence that has no reality and form.*

**Poet:**

24

How can I perform this task while my mind is full of doubts and torn in conflicts?

**Spirit:**

*You cannot escape your destined path. You won't be able to escape the suffering that conflicts and doubts bring because all knowledge are incomplete and reason has limited capacity to unravel the true mystery of life.*

**Poet:**

In this darkened world I hear the voice moving the human soul. I am standing by the beach where the waves, carrying the charred remnants, wash away the remaining of a livid world. As the waves touch the feet in veneration to life, lights glitter underneath, sand sprinkle foams and recede to a motionless world. I see under the flesh an ocean that is carrying me to the destination. I am surrounded by a sphere that rotates and spins. In this part of the universe the waves dash against the mountains made of graphite, quartz, marbles, and other rocks - hard and soft. They sprinkle in the air the caressing touch of the eeriful light that fills the inner world about which I wish to know. Tell me why have you brought me to this shore to face the mystery of God that cannot be known? Why do you draw my eyes to the realm that no eyes can ever penetrate?

**Spirit:**

*I am a tranquil fire that burns in body and mind of all human beings. Though you are born following the laws of nature governed by the codes in the genes – a machine that runs by using water, air, and chemical compounds, know that beyond the mechanical world there exists a soul, that cannot be understood using the laws of things. Though hunger, passion, desire may rise as results of the needs that body may feel to defend the biological existence, know that hunger of the mind for knowledge, love and truth has no root in the world of hunger of the body. They rise in the mind to remind you that you are a part of a spiritual existence.*

**Poet:**

In this beach I hear the shriek and cry of human beings being de-

25

voured by the hunger of nature. Tell me something that may comfort the burning souls.

**Spirit:**

*No one would be able to escape the tongues of fire spreading through water, air and earth. They consume life in order to renew life as new cells. They transfer the codes and messages of life from the past to the future. The fire that you watch engulfing the corpses, swells as waves to bring down life, and shelters built by shores. It feeds the storms that uproot the giant trees, appear as eruption of volcanoes, creates mudslides and cascades that roll down from the hilltops to erode the earth. It opens floods and deluges on settlements and thus massacres animals and humans in great numbers. It is caused by the greed, hate and lust that reside in nature as the force renewing all. Above the burning shore behold the rays, the spectra of rainbows that bend like eyelids above the mists and smoke, hear the sounds of the waves that sprinkle the gems that fire has wrought, lift your eyes to the weightless world where above greed, hunger and tides on Earth I reside in the universe carrying the images of my existence in the realm beyond the images of the stars.*

**Poet:**

Yes! The stars! … They are far.. far …far away bringing the lights from the past! In this space, entangled by enumerable motions of objects, I encounter the light through my mind that does not touch motions but move with them. I want to see this mystery far deeper…beyond the limit that any mind can reach! May be, there is no such end where knowledge may truncate, the realm of knowing may come to a stop, the mind may cease!.....

**Spirit:**

*Language rises as a reflection of the images of the world, that you perceive, mirrored by the mind. The words receive meanings from the world appearing in finite forms bound by the material things. The material relations appearing through languages provide understanding that one needs in order to work, eat, sleep, reproduce and survive as all other animals on Earth. Although these relations are rooted in the mystery of the universe, the world in your immediate surrounding is the mirror in which you see your face. Thus you are bound by the material nature of the surrounding world. However, your mind is boundless and vast. It is not bound by the limits of the objects in which it images and mirrors itself. Though mind has no language of its own without reference to the world, and carries the imprints of the material relations and becomes thoughts that matter dictates, know that these thoughts can be moved by a force that does not obey the mechanical laws. I speak with the help of thoughts that are imprinted by the material world in the mind. Therefore I cannot relate to you about the truth that is beyond the relations of matter, and outside the concepts formed by thoughts. Know that I am not bound in matter, or space and time, or thoughts. I act in the mind to imprint my presence in the material world.*

**Poet:**

How can I be sure that things are really so, as you describe? Neither can I accept this world from where I hear these words by renouncing reason, nor do I find my way out of this ghostly world by walking along the path of reason. I feel baffled and confused.

**Spirit:**

*You are destined to suffer this conflict because being a human being you are reaching out for the realm of God. With the help of human knowledge you won't be able to grasp my true nature.*

**Poet:**

Why does not this mind find comforts in the belief that you may exist! Why does it resist accepting the inner voice that speaks in an enigmatic language whose meaning is difficult to understand? Why is this conflict? Why on one side I am trying to guard the mind from deception and delusion and on the other side sinking in the illusion by believing that a divine being has entered in my mind?

**Spirit:**

*O poet! You are bound to the nature of the material world through your flesh and blood. Knowledge and reason are reflections of your mind in the corpuscles making your blood and nerves where senses stream carrying the perceptions with which you understand the relations of the ma-*

*terial world.*

**Poet:**

From that night, when you first appeared as a voice in my mind you have tried to persuade me to believe that you steer all destiny, and I should submit my will to you. But why have I disbelieved what I have heard? Why does my mind want to escape this mystical nebulous world?

**Spirit:**

*The fire of knowledge, which is kindled by flesh and blood, illumines human thoughts. In this fire you have heard my voice. Though I may appear amidst sensual fire, I touch no fire, and cannot be conceived by knowledge of man. I am above shadows and light of knowledge. I draw mind towards the realm where nothing moves with relations bound to effects and cause. In me, every relation as known by the mind ceases. I want you to write about this drama. By using words understandable to the human mind I have acted in your mind to convince that I am not an illusion. But the nature of the human mind is such that it sees paradoxes in what you hear. You cannot avoid this contradiction. Perform the tasks I have entrusted you to do.*

**Poet:**

Will it bring more suffering if I refuse?

**Spirit:**

*Suffering is inevitable to human life. You cannot escape it. The suffering is caused by the absence of knowledge of God. But this knowledge cannot be attained with intellect.*

**Poet:**

Will you release me from the suffering if I obey you and perform the tasks?

**Spirit:**

*I cannot release human life from relations that it must bear with the material world and its laws. I transmit signals that appear as messages in the mind. As reasons cannot confirm the existence of these signals, and words fail to describe the nature of its existence, your suffering cannot be redeemed. I can never be fully known.*

**Poet:**

I seek liberation from this blind alley, where mind cannot discriminate what is real and what may be false, what could be true or what might be delusion and untrue. Why do you ask me to write? What purpose would it serve?

**Spirit:**

*The destiny of your life cannot be reversed. Like a corpuscle in the womb of the mother one becomes a part of the universe at the mercy of the forces that govern the unity of things and motions in time and space. The clouds of dust that once ignited the stars that now form the material composition of cells, have passed from the birth of stars to Earth where the life like the human being are born. When life is born, matter follows the laws of the universe and encodes messages that give birth to mind and thoughts. Write in order to depict this drama that you experience in the human mind that witnesses the existence of God. Though the laws cannot be undone, the relations in space and time cannot be bypassed, O poet! Know that I am beyond time and space, unbound by the material laws, who keep all living and nonliving beings in motions, and determine the destiny of everything in the universe. I want human beings to know about the nature of this spiritual world. O poet! Through experiencing these sufferings you will know the nature of the force that transcends the laws and time.*

**Poet:**

I am enthralled by the nature of this mind that tries to transcend the limits of knowledge, and moves like fire in the sense-bound world. By opening colourful wings as dreams, phantasies, imaginations it seeks to cross all limits of words and meaning. I can question, doubt, and penetrate layers after layers of this mind. I recall memories of pleasure, love, hate; I can accept and reject anything following my will and disposition; I can distrust, disbelieve, play with words and even laugh and jeer at myself! O spirit! What a wonder is this mind!

**Spirit:**

*This wonder is Me. This is the realm of the spirit through which I transmit the force that can help man to experience a world existing beyond the dictates of the material laws. The freedom, you seek, comes from this world, which remains hidden and unknown. Its power and force cannot be measured by any other instrument but mind. The human mind must cross the shadowy maze along its way. In this maze layers after layers of shadows of different worlds are overlaid, different visions penetrate different time and space, and different levels of understanding are ordered in different levels of consciousness. In every step, man takes, man may step into different realms. Unless one knows where one moves one may lose one's way. You cannot escape this fallible trap of the mind.*

**Poet:**

It is a wonder that I am born to confront this awe, this fire of doubts, this boundless imagination that carries the mind beyond the confinement of words, knowledge, reason and earth-bound thoughts.

**Spirit:**

*This is how the human beings know that I exist. I am the mirror where desire to transcend the world rises, the fire of doubt erupts, and freedom departs the confinement of feelings bound in flesh and blood. O beloved soul! Follow the Will of God.*

**Here the writing stopped.....**

The news of my father's illness reached me in New York. I had to abandon the writing project and travel to Calcutta to look after his treatment. He was suffering from lungs cancer. My father's illness steered my life for the next three years my father lived. Every week I wrote a new poem to him. Since my childhood he had been the greatest source of inspiration to my intellectual and artistic life. He was the only one who could understand the inner world and the stirring in me. He had always encouraged me to go on searching in the unknown territories of knowledge and implanted in me the dream to fulfill an ambition that no normal human being aspires. He was not only father but a friend with whom I could share the  dimensions of life that no one else could share.

From New York we returned to Norway in 1985. After returning to Oslo my academic life as a physicist more or less came to an end. There was no one in the research community with whom I could discuss the problem I was working with. Moreover, I had no academic position any longer. My new interests in cosmology made it even more difficult for me to find an academic foothold in a scientific milieu which was more interested in practical research. However, I maintained a loose scientific contact with the University of Trondheim, where I gave a series of lectures. Then I sank in a period of depression.

My father passed away in the autumn of 1986. After that only one person on Earth, who could cheer me up and lift my mind to see the greatness of human soul was our son Ånun. Amidst this depression and melancholy, he remained a dazzling source of light in my life. He was an exceptionally gifted child, who possessed an amazing creative power and a beauty of spirit that I adored. He started composing symphonies as he became eight years old.

In contrast to the symphony of Ånun my life was sinking in an abyss of darkness. The research work in physics had already come to a standstill in New York. After a short visiting assignment at the Stevens Institute of Technology, I returned to pursue the higher-dimensional theory of gravity that I had started in Bern. While in Bern I had come across the string theory, that theoretical physicist at CERN in Geneva was talking about. The string theory led to higher-order correction terms to the Einstein's equations of gravity. I had been working on this theory for a while with a hope that I might be able to understand how elementary particles might have risen from the void in the universe.

I was sinking more and more in this abyss with the strengthening of the belief that I had been receiving answers from God, whose mystery I wished to penetrate. I relied on the intuitions and inner suggestions more and more in understanding the mystery of the universe. When I thought that I had found mathematical solutions of the model I was working with and went to DESY in Hamburg to present my theory

31

to the experts in string theory, it fetched ridicule from the professors working at that prestigious centre. I returned feeling deeply humiliated and totally broken down in spirit. This raised my anger against myself and God. I understood that I was deluded to believe that I was working as willed by God.

*(from Diary)*

"*A year ago, I was enjoying an exciting mental state believing that I had found the clue to unfold the riddle of the mystery of the universe. Now the darkness had fallen. I felt devastated. The dreams had passed. The reality appeared harsh. All around me I saw the rubble and felt entrapped inside the debris of what I called myself. A catastrophe had occurred while I was dreaming. Now perplexed and puzzled, like a shock ridden victim of an earthquake, I was seeking an exit from the ruin, "What shall I do now? Where shall I go from here?" This shock had been so intense that I had not been able to write for several months. What I had been writing appeared meaningless babbling rising from self-delusion. The primary cause of this catastrophic psychological debacle was the sudden realization that the belief that had ensnared me in the deep roots of my mind was baseless. I believed in God. I thought there was a force who was guiding me. Abandoning reason and scientific path I was following the dictates from the inner world for the last twenty three years believing that they were coming from God.*

*Now that believe was shattered. I woke up to the realization that I was a victim of unconscious mind. God was nothing but myself appearing as self suggestions. The man who wanted to be God now felt trodden and crushed as a foolish dreamer, who lacked the ability to judge the reality of life. All previous failures and sufferings I had interpreted as test of the Divine will. Now the Divine had evaporated from my mind and I was left alone with myself. Tragically the most vital period of life were destroyed by this meaningless dreamlike pursuit of truth. There was no way to reverse the acts and return back to the past to restart life from the beginning again. I felt I was deceived.*

*At the age when most people reach the apex of their careers, I had arrived at the nadir. At no time of my life, it seemed as hopeless as now. There seemed to exist no way to return to start life anew. This tragedy was a consequence of a single mistake: I got fascinated by the possibilities of the existence of a world beyond human reason and knowledge - a mystical realm where God existed. I was deluded by the illusory power of the unconscious mind. More than twenty three years had passed when I first fell in this trap as I encountered God over the Ganges. I believed, I was a part of God, I was born to lead the mankind from darkness to light. I thought I possessed the key to unveil the mystery of the universe. I believed that my ideas would one day replace the scientific knowledge of modern time, my writings would become the highest expression of literary and philosophical work ever made by man, my paintings would reveal in visual form the mystery of the invisible world where God existed, and my acts would free the human beings from ignorance and suffering. I dreamt I was not a man, but one with God.*

*Now God is dead. He is only a delusion of the mind, a reflection of my own desire to transcend the ignorance of human life. It is me who has deluded me. It is me who has created God and brought him down. Now I have come to realize that there is nothing beyond me. There is no power outside me that can decide my life. Creating God is a false way of trying to escape the challenge of human life.*

*Now, everything appears dark. I feel, as a punishment to transcend above all human beings they have stripped me naked and hurled me to a dungeon in Hell. I walk among the crowd carrying abject disgust for myself and the human race. I feel humiliated in the deep bottom of my heart. I am afraid the others may laugh, pity me, think that I am insane and a fool. But there is no escape. Only God, if he existed, could have saved me from this humiliation and suffering. But He is dead. I find no one else but myself to blame.*

*Is it too late? Have life really slipped away from me for all time? Can I ever accumulate enough force again to engage the threatening and the deceptive powers of the mind in a battle once more? Can I free myself?"*

Three months later the destiny struck me with its cruel force, and everything in my life changed dramatically. A new journey of life started.

# Chapter 2
# DEATH OF ÅNUN: WAS IT PREDESTINED?
### (Excerpts from "Dance of Joy in a Labyrinth: Life and Death of ÅnunLund Rej")

I saw Death was whirling its robe amidst a busy crowd in the centre of the main shopping street. He appeared in the disguise of a man - bald and well dressed - wearing a mysterious and sinister mask. His body was hidden under a long winter overcoat swirling graciously with the motion of his limbs. He was moving slowly - once up, once down the footpath -throwing a cunning and surreptitious look at me. He seemed to be waiting for someone.

I thought it was me. The sun was intense. The fear of death was dazzling like a clot of blood in this intense sunlight burning my mind. I felt the sunray was chocking my breath, the air quivering in the light was flitting away from my chest as if I was going to die soon. In fear I stood up, moved haphazardly around in search of fresh air and then came back and sat down again beside the fountain. There seemed to exist no more open place than where I was.

It was the fountain in Place de Molard on Rue du Marche in the centre of Geneva. Time was Saturday morning, 17th of February, 1990. Ånun was constantly moving around this fountain like a bird dancing in joy as if dreaming to fly away with the wings of rainbows. He was moving in small rhythmic jumps with his head bent downwards while his left arm and fingers were dancing in harmony with his inner ecstasy. His right hand kept dangling in joy holding the dear possession he had made during this shopping hour - a plastic bag containing a pad of note papers, a pen he had bought for writing music and the score book of Beethoven's overture, Elonore. He had bought these things from his most beloved store in this town - the music bookstore in Rue de la Cite in the old town - a few minutes ago...

The reality around appeared to be a fabulous kaleidoscope turning inside a labyrinth. It was automatically revolving jittering the ephemeral moments of life - every moment, there were new sounds, new colours, new faces, new associations in the mind. The trams and buses were moving and stopping; shoppers were jostling and pouring in and out of the shops; men and women were appearing and disappearing out of sight waving different colours and forms of fashionable clothes and ornaments like automated manikins of the modern world. Here Death was gazing at me moving to-and-fro along another path passing through the labyrinth. He seemed to be waiting for the moment when my mind would fail to remain alert and he would overpower me with all his forces. And right at this time Ånun was composing the last piece of music in his mind. He was unmindful of what was going on in this busy human world. He was appearing and disappearing from the sight like a small bird appearing and disappearing in between the crowded bodies of the shoppers moving constantly without showing any consideration to the needs of this creature looking for golden corns of music in the sunlight circling around the fountain of light.

We came to Geneva only the night before as Ånun's winter holidays for a week had started...This Saturday morning gave us our first opportunity to come to town. Ånun wanted to fulfill the main purpose of his coming to the town - to visit his most favourite music bookstore.

He loved this store. Immediately after entering he ran to the bookshelf containing the score books of Beethoven's and Mozart's music. Like a butterfly in a sunny full bloomed garden he flitted from one book to the other. Finally the butterfly decided to sit on one of them - it was the score book of Beethoven's "Fidelio" opera. It was an opera dealing with a theme of revolution - a peasant uprising against a reign of terror. It was a thick book. Ånun glanced through the book in a lightning speed and expressing an intense joy laughed, "Pappa, I wish I owned the whole bookstore!" His beautiful smiling eyes flashing love for music filled my heart with a sense of joy too and I also laughed, "So, do I", wondering how did he know about the world of opera too! He had recieved some money from mormor and morfar for buying something from Geneva. For Ånun there was no better way of spending this money than in this bookstore. Ånun wished to buy the opera but looking at mamma's face he could easily gauge that it won't be correct to make such a proposal. It cost more than the money at his disposal. He put back the score grudging, "It is too costly" and as it was within his budgetary means took out the score on Fidelio's overture Leonore,instead. Furthermore, after paying for the overture he would still have some money left to come back to buy something else another day. He needed note papers before leaving the store. He went through all kinds of note papers before finally deciding which one to take. It seemed that before writing a piece everything - even the size, shape and colour of the note papers - were well planned in his mind. Mamma agreed to pay for the note papers in order not to exhaust his limited economic means. And as we left the store, Ånun's purpose of being in the town was fulfilled and he did not wish to enter any other shop. He wanted to go home. Before returning Ragne wanted to do shopping and therefore Ånun and I agreed to wait for her in Place du Molard. It seemed as if apprehending the presence of the evil, a group of invisible ritual dancers emerged beating drums and filling the air with rythm of African tribal dances. As the beatings of drums approached nearer, the Death-man vanished from sight and the intense fear of death came to an end. Soon Ragne also returned. Hearing the rhythm of music Ånun broke his dance and came jumping to find out what was going on. An African group was playing the drums on the other side of the footpath on Rue du Marche to celebrate the recent release of Nelson Mandela in South Africa. After enjoying the rythm of the drums and refreshing the happy memory of the release of Mandela, we went to catch the train for "home", but it had just left and we had to wait an hour for the next train. To cheer him up in this boring situation we bought a few pralines from the famous Mercur shop and went to the waiting room of the TGV trains leaving for Paris to while away that hour. Ragne and I divided the Journal du Geneva between us while Ånun resumed his dance terminated in Place du Molard jumping about the hall of the waiting room chewing a few of the chocolates.

Although whenever we came to this station in the later years his mind was always turned towards Paris and Notre Dame. This time Ånun neither did notice that we were sitting in the waiting room of the TGV trains leaving for Paris, nor talked about Notre-Dame. Instead he was busy designing the musical building of his fourth symphony in his mind. We could "hear" the music in his movements. Sometimes he moved fast as in prestissimo, then leaped in the air as in a crescendo and then fell in a calm pace as if the music passed into pianissimo. As the hall was nearly empty, it made an intricate pattern of movement uninterrupted by any adult intervention. Only a security guard came to check what was going on. But he felt convinced that this jumping behaviour of the child was no security threat and left the music to carry on.

After concluding this ritual dance with a big jump, Ånun came to sit down beside me and took out his note papers and pen from his plastic bag and ushered his plans in with his usual extremely careful way to recieve my attention. "Pappa, you are going to be angry with me", he said. I wondered, "Why?" He revealed that he was going to write his fourth symphony and had already planned to arrange this symphony for piano so that it could be played in the summer concert of his music school. The reason behind this "complicated introduction" was that he was anxious I might not appreciate the fourth symphony because only a few days before leaving for Geneva he had told us that he was writing a piano concerto and working on an opera based on Ibsen's Catalina. Again another symphony! He had already made sketches of so many symphonies! For him to say that he was going to write music was as natural as boys of his age talking about cars. I was only worried if he produced music in such a speed without keeping the papers in order, it would be difficult to sort them out later. Before he started his first movement, I took the opportunity to explain why I thought one needed some discipline and should not jump from one composition to another so fast. He agreed to all I said as quickly as possible in order not to give me any further opportunity to continue my lecture on self-discipline and to be able to continue with his plan of the fourth symphony. He had already gauged my reaction. Now he desired peace and my silence. Asking him to put the date on the paper before he started writing I stopped and the first movement of his fourth symphony started coming out his mind on note papers in a speed of his favourite TGV trains. After finishing the first page he showed to us the instruments he was using in the first movement: 2 Flutes, 2 Obos, 2 Clarinettes, 2 Faggots, 2 Cor-C, 2 Trombones in C, Timpany C-G, Violin one, Violin two, Viola, Violin cello and Contrabass. The movement started with all the string instruments together up to the third bar, then from the fourth bar all other instruments joined the orchestra. He asked my opinion and as usual I gave him my answer, "very good" and dug my nose in the page of advertisement of houses and apartments in Geneva. We intended to buy one if we would come to live there, planning that Geneva would be Ånun's future home base.

Next morning Death appeared again swinging his robe. Now instead of Place du Molard he was moving graciously on the top of Mont Blanc gazing at us once more with his sinister look. He was moving up and down through a chiaroscuro of light and shadow veering round the wind - as if, trying to hide his face from the sun. His face was camouflaged by clouds, his cruel eyes were hidden under the shadows cast by the mountain valleys, his body was hidden under a white robe studded with millions and billions and trillions and trillions of crystals of snow glittering as jewels in the dazzling sunlight of a beautiful morning.

It was a sunny Sunday morning. We were out fishing on Lac Leman with Synnøve and Bjarne. There was almost no mist on the lake. All the mountain tops -including Mont Blanc- were clearly visible in the background. On one side there were majestic Alps while on the other side of the lake the mountains of Jura engirdled us. They were like snow-clad beauties bathing in the sky waving their transparent azure veils and greeting the humans welcome in a world where lights were dancing with joy, winds were whispering in the ears of the mountains, blissful moments of happiness were springing out like fountains of endless joy sprinkling rays of the sun in colours of thousands of rainbows curving and rising over the inner skies of the human souls. Everything was as beautiful and charming as possible to excite strong romantic feelings about panoramic Switzerland. Here, while fishing, Ånun was trying to fathom the depth of the lake pulling the string time and again without being able to hold his curiosity and excitement at a momentary rest. The ripples of joys were dancing over the lake reflecting the warmth and pleasure of smile flowing through his bright brown eyes looking through the depth of the lake extended from Heaven to Earth. "Pappa, how many meters deep do you think this lake could be at its deepest point?"

As Ånun finished his question, I became very nervous. I thought Death was waiting for me. I got preoccupied with thoughts: "What should we do, if the boat sinks?" In the beginning of the journey Ånun was nervous too. But within a few minutes the excitement of the trip seemed to make Ånun feel as comfortable like a seagull riding on the mast of a boat in search of fish. He was flying around the small boat to find out on which side the luck would favour him at last, creating big waves of fears in my mind. My fear became worst when a fish was foolish enough to sacrifice its peaceful existence in the hands of Bjarne to fulfill the pleasure and meaning of the human pursuit. Ånun got so excited about Bjarne's success that the boat started to oscillate increasing the probability of a fall. I was trying to make Ånun sit down but he was irresistible when something so exciting fell in his mind's net. The real excitement was how to keep this poor fish alive in the plastic bucket meant to make room for the day's booty. The fish was badly hurt in man's unscrupulous means of cheating the creatures of lower intelligence camouflaging a dead sharp hook with a fly like bait. The rest of the fishing fun became how to nurse and bring this poor creature back to life again. We picked up floating weed from the lake believing that these pieces would be able to simulate a natural surrounding for the survival of the fish. Each attempt of the fish to turn towards a normal swimming posture was hailed with tributes of joy in honour of life. Whatever Ånun did spread joy, whatever life Ånun touched he revered it with great respect, whatever Ånun did for fun he compensated it with utter seriousness. He loved the harmony and melody of the music orchestrated by nature and therefore he wanted to complement this infatuating act of cruelty with his tender love. He was like a seagull that flew and danced wishing to plunge in nature's mystery in every sea, in every world, in every sky, in every domain of human life with a hope to discover the music of life.

After this success, there was a wish to return home to find a larger pot for the fish where it could find more natural room for manoeuvring. Bjarne found this idea suitable to bring an end to the trip as it was getting difficult for him to row against the wind. However, the shadow of Death followed as an evil spirit disguised in the form of a dog barking at the entrance door of the house. It was Synnøve and Bjarne's pet dog Enka barking to express pleasure in seeing his master. Within one day Ånun had developed a relation of friendship with this animal although by nature Ånun was normally very scared of big dogs barking so loudly. It appeared in front of my eyes as Mephestopheles appeared in Faust's study in the disguise of a dog. I became afraid of the satanic look of death in its eyes "With fearful fangs and fiery, staring brow... a hybrid brood of hell... Hell's old lynx ...", I shouted in my mind, "You spawn of hell! You thoroughly destroy my peace, pray you cease."

After a while, the dog ceased barking and jumped around Ånun to find out what he was having inside the plastic bucket. There was a huge Chinese earthen pot decorated with a dragon in the garden. Bjarne filled it with water to make a small lake for the fish. Ånun capered around the pot seeing the fish gained strength and started swimming while Enka gamboled around in frolic to catch the fish and bring an end to its existence. Ånun who had healed the fish from its pain, clenched his fist to protest against this treachery of Enka. He tried to stop Enka's desire to annihilate this little creature of the lake and shouted as if Faust was shouting to Mephestopheles:" Strange, sterile son of Chaos, think anew, and find yourself some better things to do." To please his friend Enka consented to leave. But Enka seemed not to understand what made Ånun so angry. It was only a way for him to while away the time. Furthermore for him killing was nothing but obeying the laws of nature and why then so much anger and flame? Had not his friend understood that his love and affection for his fish was frivolous and doomed to end in vain?

After this little quarrel between Ånun and Enka, we got ready to go to Nyon, a small town founded by Julius Caesar at Lac Leman. It was about half an hour's drive from Geneva. There was a statue of Caesar, a museum of Roman history, Caesar Tower, and a few parts of the ruins of pillars of a Roman forum as the town's most interesting attractions. There was also a nice castle and a charming road along the lake for a delightful promenade. Ånun loved to visit Nyon because of its Roman history. His interest in Roman history was already a couple of years old and his knowledge of history came mostly from Grimdberg's volumes that he read now and then.

We found a place nearby the castle where two roman pillars were erected as memory from the past. Together with these pillars the blue lake with a few sailing boats leisurely plying in it and the white snowclad Mont Blanc decorating the background created a majestic scene. For us this scene symbolized the spirit that Ånun possessed. Therefore we asked Ånun to stand between those pillars in order to take a picture of him. He stood with his face looking downwards, eyes fixed to his right foot as if he was trying to feel the movement of the motion of the continents under his feet. He had correct information about how many centimetres or millimetres these continents moved in every century.

He was fascinated by the history of formation of the Alps. He had told us how Mont Blanc was formed by the collision of the African and European continents in the tertiary geological period about 60 millions of years ago, about the history of glaciation, how the valleys were formed, how rhinoceros and mammoths once roamed around the lake about millions of years ago. Now most of that old glacier had melted, the rhinoceroses and the mammoths had become extinct, the cinnamon trees and the subtropical forests and flowers had also vanished from the region. Instead of that there were a few white sailing boats, a few castles with well trimmed parks of the rich Homo sapiens. Scintillating in the sunlight of this noon, the shadows of death and annihilation were still roaming over the valleys and the mountains. Here Ånun was standing as the symbol of love and peace amidst the forces of terror and cruelty of time …

Death chanted a magical spell again in the Museum of Natural History two days later.

Ånun did not want to go out of the house in Genthod except for another fishing trip because he wanted to fully utilize the holidays for writing his fourth symphony. As Synnøve and Bjarne's eldest daughter was supposed to arrive in the afternoon with two children, I could convince Ånun that he would not have much opportunity to write music if he stayed at home. Realizing this unfortunate possibility he agreed to go out and decided to visit his favourite Natural History Museum.

We had to take a bus from the station in Geneva to go to the museum. Although we had visited this museum many times before, somehow we made a mistake and took a wrong bus and Death followed us. I thought he came again to fetch my life and became restless like a man on a scaffold going to be hanged soon. Feeling breathless, as I stood up from my seat the sun dazzled outside over the roman pillars in front of the entrance of the big museum buildings in Place Neuve and the golden coloured gate leading to the Promenade des Bastions. This gate opened my memory and I understood that we were travelling in a wrong direction. A lady instructed us to get down at the end of the Boulvard des Philosophes and walk from there to the Natural History Museum. Ånun and I hurried to get off. Although Death let me breathe after we descended from the bus the shadow of Death held me close to him at every step. Ånun seemed to be outside his grip. He was so happy! He was hurrying to go to the museum. He wanted me to speed up a little more since I was lagging behind him. This walk along Boulvard des Tranchees was for me a walk through the city of Hell where I saw the flame of death burning in front of each building I crossed. Ånun was like an angel who was moving through this Boulvard of flame without being touched by any fear as if he carried a secret spiritual power

43

with which he could wither all forces of evil. He was walking in his usual dancing manner - a plastic bag containing an umbrella and a few pieces of fruits was swinging constantly in his hand to express the absentminded nature of his character and his separation from the time and space where I belonged. In my space and time I was praying to Death to let me remain alive. I felt I had a great responsibility in taking care of a spiritual treasure and cried to Death, "Leave me free, I must live for Ånun."

As soon as we entered  the museum, instead of freeing me, Death gripped me even more severely. As Ånun took my hand and tried to haul me asking me to follow him upstairs, I stood motionless in front of the stairs feeling chocked. I told him that I was feeling very sick and we must return home, we should come another day. Ånun felt puzzled with my strange behaviour: I had insisted him to visit the museum, now when he came to study something he wanted very much to study, I insisted that we must return  before seeing a single exhibit. Exclaiming, "Pap..pa..", he glanced at me rolling his eyes full of surprise and confusion to express his unhappiness about such irrational and paradoxical behaviour. But I was so severely attacked by the fear of death that I wanted him to understand that I was really feeling ill. However, when hiding his sad feelings under the eyelids from where joy and happiness had streamed so many times to fill my heart he despaired, "Pappa, I looked forward so much to seeing something here. Are you going to spoil this for me?", I decided to stay in the museum hoping that this anxiety will soon pass.

Ånun knew exactly why he came to the museum. Before following him to see what he wanted to show me, I asked him to allow me some time in the cafeteria first. I felt restless and thirsty like an animal struck by a spear, struggling only with Death with its will to live. This anxiety of death had started appearing only a few days before leaving for Geneva and every time it came with such intensity that I started carrying the tranquillizer with me in case I might need it. The anxiety was so intense now that I took a tranquillizer with a hope of being able to cope with the situation. But it did not help much. I was afraid that Ånun would be able to discover my nervous condition and get anxious. Therefore leaving Ånun alone in the cafeteria I went inside a hall of exhibits of stuffed bison and deer on the same floor as if trying to hide from the eyes of Death preying on me. But soon anxiety developed for Ånun. It was like leaving him in a jungle where ferocious Death was roving around in order to fulfil a pleasure of killing. Seeing me Ånun was relieved from his sense of insecurity, "Pappa, I was searching for you. I was so anxious. You did not tell me where you went." I apologized for my behaviour and tried to smile with a hope to make him feel secure and safe. He interpreted my smile as an indication that I was feeling well and therefore took my hand and asked me to follow him in the museum. I looked at his eyes burning with curiosity and said to myself, "I must not spoil the day for him" and followed him like a shadow to fulfil a magical rite of Death.

Ånun dragged me through a hall where primitive forms of life from Cambrium era were exhibited. Only a few weeks before we left for Geneva Ånun had read about the forms of life that existed in the sea bottom about 500 millions of years ago. I remembered, he had shown me the monster like appearances of Opabinias and hallucigenias in his book to express his wonder about the mysterious creatures that once existed in nature. He also wanted to know from me the exact size of the trilobites. Since I could not give him a reply that day, I thought Ånun had entered this hall to find his answer. But only after crossing the hall, I realized why Ånun had come to the museum - to study his beloved Alps again!

He knew exactly where to find the model of the Alps. Here not only one could study the different layers of rocks and how they were folded creating the mountains, but also there was a light-and-sound programme explaining the history of the formation of the Alps. He had seen this programme before and therefore I wondered why he came to study it once again. Ånun never did anything without having a specific reason behind it. Some time ago he read about a new theory of the continental shelf and the mantel. It differed from the old theory that thin continental plates were moving over melted hot mantel. He once explained to me how rocks extended like roots of trees through the molten mantel under the mountain regions according to this new theory. I believed that it was probably the reason why he came to study the Alps once again.

While he was following the programme, I was sipping orange juice from a paper box in order to meet my intense nervous thirst and fate was moving over the Alps in a chariot, the winged horses drawing the chariot were stalking nearby in a labyrinth behind my conscious world of understanding. In "soul's rapacious cellar where human drinks knowledge as wines of grapes", I could not guess about the existence of the magical world that existed beyond the causal world of time.

After coming out of the museum, now, first he wanted to go to the music bookstore again. Death vanished as suddenly as it had appeared. First he enquired about the scores of Mozart's piano concerto numbers 17 and 19. As they were not available in the bookstore, Ånun mumbled a little and then said it did not matter, he was not interested to buy Mozart's piano concertos ,anyway. He preferred Beethoven's piano concertos instead. He explained why but I was not always knowledgeable enough to follow him. However, it was not difficult to understand that he very much wanted to buy the complete scores of all five piano concertos of Beethoven as he asked if he could borrow some money from me. As I knew his money left was not enough to fulfil any of his wishes, as a father full of admiration for the talent of his son, I happily accepted his proposal.

He jumped with joy while Death swished its blood-stained net to entangle this moment of happiness in a singular darkness beyond time inside a labyrinth. At that moment there was no way for me to know that he was buying those scores to take them with him in the grave. The sun dazzled, the clouds hummed the melodies, angels flew through the wind, light grew more and more intense as in a crescendo to engulf the human spirit in ecstasy and sky leapt in joy in the darkness of the universe as if conducting the orchestra of Heaven and the pages of the musical score of Beethoven's fifth concerto was moved on his lap in between his fingers like wings of unearthly butterflies intervening the measures, beats, rhythms and cadences passing through his mind. These rectangular white wings decorated with hundreds of dark spots of notes were fluttering a sense of joy of a fulfilled day. Ånun was totally absorbed. He sat in the train to Genthod beside the window listening to the fifth concerto while these butterflies were fluttering their wings without taking any heed of the external world or human sense of time. I got little anxious seeing that nearby passengers in the train were throwing glances at him. I was afraid that Ånun might feel uncomfortable with the reactions of the grown-ups who surely won't be able to understand that this little boy seriously understood the meaning of all those black spots printed on the pages and that he in fact was hearing the music in his mind. Therefore, I suggested to him that he better read the scores when he came home. But my words could not penetrate the music. The train moved, the time span, lights wove music in vision's deepest depth and Beethoven's fifth concerto wafted through the air in a silence. I understood he had separated himself from the world. Only the lights falling through the window glittered on his eyes to confirm that he was still in my world although his mind was far, far away where he was hearing Beethoven answering with the same virility of human spirit the cruelty of fate in his fifth concerto, too, as in his fifth symphony.

After coming home, greeting Synnøve's eldest daughter and her two children, Ånun went straight down to the room in the basement where he had found a record of the fifth concerto in Synnøve's youngest daughter's music collection. Since he came to Genthod he had spent much of his time in this room where he found peace for writing music. He wanted that I should also share his world and therefore asked me to come down to the basement to listen to the fifth concerto. While we listened, he followed the score. After exposing the part of music he was listening in the train, he wanted to unveil his own music to me. In order to do that he spread all the pages of his fourth symphony that he had written so far, side by side in rows and columns on the floor. He loved to exhibit his music this way so that we could appreciate the whole piece of music in its entirety. As usual these scribbling did not create any sound in my mind. To help me hear what he was hearing in his mind, Ånun started humming the melodies aloud.

Hearing this musical activity in the basement, the spirit of chaos entered wagging its tail. It was our Mephistopheles in the disguise of Enka again. The dog entered in the basement room as Mephistopheles entered in Auer bach's cellar hearing someone singing there. Instead of Faust, Enka had the two children with her. To show her interest in musical matters Enka started walking over the note papers spread on the floor. Ånun was highly fastidious as concern music and therefore rushed to save his music from such ugly appreciation manifested through twitching treatment under the paws of the panting dog. The children contributed to the animation with their games and ultimately it ended up in flame as in Auer bach's cellar demonstrating devil's interest in hocus-pocus and bestial humor to spoil human's interest in spiritual affairs....

Our original plan was that Ånun and I would go to Bern this morning. I intended to visit the university in Bern where I had been attached for some time some years ago. Ragne was supposed to meet us in Bern next day. But as anxiety of death lurked in my mind I became afraid of going to Bern alone with Ånun. As I thought this anxiety must be psychological I did not dare to tell anybody about the problem I was struggling with. I had suffered from pneumonia before we came to Geneva and therefore I found an excuse to change our previous plans saying that I was not feeling physically well. Ånun was not still able to finish the second movement and therefore any suggestion of going out was not welcomed at all. Ragne was unhappy to see that Ånun and I both had a tendency of not going outside the house. She wondered what was the point of our coming to Geneva if we were only sitting at home and insisted that we must at least visit museums.

I knew Ånun studied the history of the development of computer technology from the time of Pascal only a few weeks ago. He wished he could once see Pascal's machine or Leibniz's calculator or Babbage's analytical engine in some museum. I thought a proposal to go to the Museum of History of Science would excite his interest to pull him out of his music world. I suggested the possibility that we might find one of those old computers in the museum. But since I could not confirm that any of those machines were in the museum Ånun did not want to go there on such vague assumption. Instead he decided to go to the

Museum for Old Musical Instruments as mamma had suggested.

The museum was in an old building. When we came, it was closed. However, we met the curator who asked us to come back after four hours when the museum would open again and a guide would demonstrate the different instruments then. Before departing the museum we took a little chat with the old lady (the curator), reserved our tickets for a concert in the museum for Friday evening and I made a "mistake" in telling her that Ånun composed music.

Ånun never liked that we told anyone that he composed music. As I made this "mistake" he wore a strict tone like a kind teacher who loved his student but did not know how to discipline his student's failure to obey the rules they had agreed upon long time ago. "Pappa I have told you so many times before that you must not say that to anybody. They won't understand. Why do you do that again?" He failed to understand why I did not keep my promise. I felt small and had to beg excuse for the "mistake" as I had done so many times before. He told me that the principal, the inspector and several teachers at school and several parents of his classmates often asked him about his compositions. He was satisfied with this appreciation he received in his local milieu and it was enough. He did not want that we spread it to others because he was afraid that most adults would laugh if they heard that a ten years old boy was composing symphonies.

After this uncontrolled exuberance of a father's pride in his son's talent that resulted in a "mistake", this state of love and disappointment ended when we came to the Museum of History and Art lying close by. Ånun came here to see the mummies and the sarcophagi in the hall of the Egyptian civilization. He pointed out to one mummy and said, "Pappa this guy is about six thousand years old. It is much more than what I am going to live." He finished this statement adding a short laugh at the end conveying his usual humour. I laughed with him sharing the sense of mystery about life and death that his laugh tried to convey. I wished that Ånun should come and see the Sun god Re, the god of life in another corner of the room. But he got more fascinated by the small figures of the underworld and pulled me into that direction.

49

And Death sat there spreading the shadows of his hands around us. He was sitting in front of a balance measuring the activities of human life against the truth, in the throne of Osiris, the god of death and I was attacked by the anxiety of death again.

I felt thirsty and went to buy something to drink before following him further. Ånun had a great fascination for the Egyptian hieroglyphs. A couple of years ago he bought a book on hieroglyphs from this museum. Leaving Osiris and the underworld, he went to study how the hieroglyphs had evolved during different phases of the Egyptian culture and then carefully looked through the funeral inscriptions - those magical formulas from the Book of the Dead - written on the tablets. Only Osiris sitting on his throne knew their meanings.

Leaving this world of death and magic, the rest of Ånun's interest in the museum became concentrated in the Hall of the Greeks and the Romans. His interests in Greece spanned from Greek mythology, archeology, architecture, history - from Minnoan palaces, Ionic and Doric architecture to the legends of Minnotaur devouring Greek youth during the period of conflict between Greece and Crete. Nearly two years ago he had even given a lecture on Greek mythology in his school from the birth of Uranus to all the gods and goddesses of the Olympus. He also visited Greece more than one and half years ago. In the museum this time he got interested in studying Greek coins. A few of the coins were so tiny that one needed to use magnifying glass to study them properly. As he was not tall enough to reach the magnifying glasses I had to lift him up so that he could study the coins. "Pappa, you must also have a look" he asked me to study the coins as he found out that I was not particularly concentrating on them. He was like our extra eyes, extra ears, extra mind that helped us to explore in the deeper depth of history, culture, and different fields of knowledge constantly enriching our lives. He showed us things we did not see before, he told us about things we did not know about, he made us interested in things that escaped our mind. It was always so stimulating to visit any place with him.

We ended our visit in the hall of the Roman civilization, another culture he was acquainted with. Ånun loved to talk and when he talked one could feel the zeal and intensity of his interests. He talked till he could empty his jar of knowledge - which often took a long time. The amount of knowledge he scattered in a short time and the luminosity with which they glittered around could hardly escape notice of anyone present nearby him. The usual reaction of the adults was to laugh or smile hearing this little boy talking about things above their own knowledge. The security guard (a lady) attending the hall did the same while Ånun was telling me the story of treachery of Brutus against Caesar.

And a laugh of death echoed from the Mont Blanc when after finishing our lunch in an Italian restaurant in Pl. Bourg-de-Four we came to Jardin Anglais ,a park facing Quai du Mont Blanc. Sitting on a bench I was studying the map of the area around the museum and thinking if this area could be a suitable place to live in Geneva since the International School in the town where Ånun could go was nearby. Suddenly like Calpurnia's dream before Caesar's death "Graves yawned and yielded up their dead; Fierce fiery warriors fought upon the clouds which drizzled blood upon the Capitol...Like a fountain with a hundred sprouts did run pure blood...And ghosts did shriek and squeal about the streets". In this dream Caesar was standing in front of the Roman forum and was speaking moments before the conspirators stabbed him to death "The skies are painted with hundred sparks, they are all fire, and everyone doth shine; But there's but one in all doth hold his place;...Unshaken of motion: and that I am he". As Nyon was within the area my vision could reach, I remembered Ånun standing beside the Caesar statue in Nyon and gazing at Mont Blanc. He loved to visit this statue every time he went to Nyon. To Ragne and me Ånun was the one who held the unassailable rank among all whom we knew in flesh and blood. He was the special star in our mind the "one in all doth hold his place." He was unshaken of motion in front of me: He was silent; his head was hanging downwards; the weight of his body was balanced under his arms on the railing protecting the visitors from falling in the water; his hands were dangling in relaxed mood above the surface of the water; he was watching the movement of the water in Lac Leman in a meditative manner. It seemed he was trying to catch the tones of light dancing and passing away with the motion of water. The omen of death frightened me and I wanted to leave the park immediately. I broke Ånun's silence and suggested him that we must choose a different location to wait. He suggested his favourite place the Rousseau island.

His love for Rousseau had become more pronounced after following the television programmes on the French revolution. Only two months ago the two hundredth centenary year had passed leaving a vivid impression of the history of the French revolution in his mind. Ånun discussed with us all aspects of this revolution - from the life of the queen Marie Antoinette with whom once Mozart played as a child in Austria to the life of the revolutionary heroes like Danton and Robespiere and from the failure of the French revolution to the rise of Napoleon. Napoleon always brought in his mind a particular association Beethoven's Eroica symphony. First Beethoven dedicated this symphony to Napoleon. But when Napoleon crowned himself as emperor, Beethoven tore that dedication page in protest. Last summer when Ragne went to attend the CSSE Conference while the French were celebrating the French revolution, Ånun asked her to buy this symphony from Paris for him. Getting this record from Paris probably gave him stronger association of Beethoven's feelings of protest against Napoleon for his trampling of the rule of democracy.

In the Rousseau island he walked leisurly around the statute of Rousseau, watched the birds and the lights moving over the lake while silently composing music in his mind. Death was still haunting, the sun was dazzling, time was moving as silvery dazzle over the ripples on the surface of the lake, the sky was reflecting blue and green shades while the swans were swimming lifting their white feathers as symbols of joy over the silvery ripples greeting the wonderful day. And amidst this the laugh of death was still echoing from the surrounding mountains of the Alps and ghosts were shrieking and squealing in the shadows caste by the buildings around the lake. I shouted in my mind in fear, "Help ho! He comes for me!" Now breaking his silence Ånun came jumping in order to discuss with me the civil engineering problem of how the artificial island was constructed. As he held my hand the fear of death vanished and a will to live and fight against Death rose like a fountain gushing out of love.

The same fountain spouted from my heart when I heard Ånun playing Bach's minuette in G minor in the Museum of Old Musical Instruments in virginal only a few minutes later. We arrived to the museum on time -the demonstration of the instruments had just started. The instruments varied from a several thousand years old Mexican flute to a virginal, a predecessor of the modern piano. As the guide was speaking French I wanted to translate for Ånun. But Ånun did not like the extra noise pappa was creating . He felt embarrassed in being a source of this extra attention and asked me to stop. He said he could guess everything. However, when the guide asked if anyone would like to play the virginal instrument Ånun failed to guess what the guide was proposing. When I told him that he was allowed to play the virginal he first could not believe. But soon he realized that what I said was true and walked graciously to the instrument and surprised everybody by playing a Bach's minuet like a little master. In this unexpected surprise the adults started smiling and the guide hailed him " Bravo! Bravo! Bravo!..." One of the greatest strength of Ånun's personality was his modesty. He knew the art of handling such situations of pride with a beautiful countenance full of smile and shyness. There was no one else we knew who could teach us this art better than him. I felt proud of his beautiful manner. Soon the old lady (the curator) appeared and the guide conveyed to her the talent Ånun showed. She asked Ånun to play for her once again. Getting another opportunity was the best Ånun could dream about. His long fingers moved with equal mastery as before to impress the curator too. She wanted that Ånun must write back to her and opened a drawer and asked him to choose a picture postcard from the museum. Ånun searched in the drawer for a while as if looking for a particular one. Then chose a card with pictures of two contrabass from the sixteenth century that were hanging on the wall above the virginal. When I got curious to know, "Why did you choose those contrabass?" he answered, "Pappa you won't understand." And I agreed. As the curator spoke English Ånun felt at ease with her and started explaining Bach's music to her in his usual charming manner. The adults could not control their laughs hearing his unusual vocabulary of music and we found it wise to hurry out of the museum before the pleasant experience fulfilling the main purpose of staying in the town for so many hours could be stained by unhappiness again.

As we came out Ånun remembered that before he left the house he did not find the pen with which he was writing music. As he could not accept to write the music piece with any other kind of pen, before returning home he wanted to buy another pen of exactly the same type in case he did not find the old one. He bought the same pen with the same colour from the same shop. However it was still not the same pen. The old one had a scratch on it. He made the same scratch on the new one to make it look identical to the previous one. Ånun's world had many more dimensions than ours. In that world all objects he used seemed to carry feelings and emotions and he handled them with affections and care as if they possessed life and soul.

As we got down in the station in Genthod my mind got entangled in a strange world with different dimensions. Death reappeared once again. The sun was trying to illuminate his face with its golden soft and mysterious light before sinking in the horizon as if to expose his sinister intention before it became dark. In this light an intense fear of death overwhelmed my thoughts and took control of my mind. I felt giddy, my legs trembled, throat dried up, and a chocking feeling moved through the chest. I started walking hurriedly in order to escape from Death moving as a shadow over the Alps under the robe of the evening light in another dimension than the dimension of space and time. It was about fifteen minutes walk from the station to the house. The road passed close to the shore of the lake providing a nice view to the Alps. Death was moving graciously in front of my eyes over the Alps hiding behind the shadows covering the vale surrounding my mind. Ånun was tired after being in the town for so many hours. He was walking slowly in a meditative manner, possibly thinking of the bars of music he was going to write after coming home. I felt anxious about leaving him behind in that lonely road and decided to stop in order to win over my psychosomatic symptoms shouting inside, "I must live for him". I was caught between him and Death. Ånun was happy to see that I was waiting for him. He wanted to walk together with me holding my hand. As he took my hand a vivacious music of life rose in my mind and shattered all fears of death and a joy of life glittered as particles of light dancing as foams over a voluptuous wave drowning the mountains and the sky under the golden light of the evening sun.

As we entered the house Enka came wagging her tail to welcome back his friend and the children came running to tell him that they had caught as many as eighty small fishes. This great success in fishing particularly when Ånun was not with them destroyed his peace of mind. All the musical bars of his symphony that were ready for making their appearances on note paper had to wait till the excitement around the fishes swimming in the big pot in the garden was fully digested. Although Bjarne's promise that he would take him out fishing the next day helped to restore some peace, Enka's success in getting hold of some fishes created a hue and cry shattering the existing peace of mind. In this state of spiritual anarchy Ånun gave up his endeavour in writing music and joined the adult's world full of mundane interests    eating raclette and watching lotto drawing in TV. After finishing the meal he joined the adults gathered in the cellar room to watch the result of day's lotto drawing because Bjarne had bought a few lotto tickets for him too. The balls of the roulette rolled and then fell one after another through a hole announcing numbers that shattered all his hopes of winning. After this failure in the world of gambling , the evening ended in the kitchen discussing hypothetical question: What one would do if one own 33 million francs in lotto? When it came to Ragne's turn to answer, before she answered, Ånun sweetly jabbed mamma with his elbow as if to make her fall to catch his suggestion "What about to the 'democracy fund', mamma?" This became more enjoyable when he added a witty laugh with it which possibly was meant to be a satire to the hypocritical world of the adults. He knew Ragne was working on the questions of support to democracy that Norway was about to establish in order to strengthen the basis of democratic rule in the world and she had an intense interest in the issues of human rights. When it came to his turn, he refused to answer saying that he would not answer such a hypothetical question. When we all pressed him to answer, as usual he gave his characteristic Ånun like answer: He would first travel in the world to find out the best cause for which that money could be used. No one else made us think more about higher values and morals to live for and higher dimensions to aspire after than him….

The next morning too when I got up I saw Enka loitering under the table to win attention of her friend absorbed in spiritual matter. Ånun had got up much earlier together with mamma in order to write the symphony as Bjarne had promised to take him out for fishing before lunch. The way Ånun's fingers were putting notes on the papers without hesitation could give one an impression that he was guided by some higher spirit. I often saw a higher spirit enthroned in the bosom of this child who sttired the spirit of creation in him from some deep depth lying in another dimension than we knew. From this depth joys sprang, music rose, and reasons spoke. However, Enka seemed to be around him to accomplish the will of the Devil to prove nothing was worth, all spiritual deeds were doomed to vain and all struggles of the human will to aspire after the orbs of the Heaven were bound to end in loneliness, melancholy, pain and tragic disaster.

The task of booking a hotel room for the weekend appeared to be a demonic complot. The day Ånun and I went to the Museum of Natural History we collected brochures of Les Diablerets and Leysin from the tourist office in the station with the possibility in mind that Ånun and I could make an excursion to the Alps during the weekdays. Due to Ånun's symphony writing and my fear of death this was not materialized. I got the idea of going to Les Diablerets during the weekend. Les Diablerets was a popular place. There was a glacier and it was within two hours journey from Geneva. I asked Ånun for his opinion. He thought, too, that Les Diablerets would be a fine place. Making this decision I went to book a hotel room .

Since the weather was good and there were holidays for many school children, no room was available in Les Diablerets. Instead the lady helping me in the tourist office suggested to try Les Mosses, a village close by Les Diablerets. The tourist office in Les Mosses was close at that time and I was asked to come back after lunch time. When I returned without succeeding to get in touch with the tourist office in Les Mosses the lady proposed to try Leysin. Les Diablerets was only a short distance from Leysin and therefore I had nothing against that she tried Leysin. It was difficult to get a room there too. But, anyway, a room was finally available for us in Hotel Orchide and I was asked to pay for it immediately. Unfortunately I had not taken any money with me. The whole thing appeared to be like a roulette luck or misfortune on which one had absolutely no control. All plans were being shattered in this random movement of events and I had to accept the situations as they developed. In this uncertain world, the lady understood my situation and asked me to come back to pay before the tourist office closed at six o'clock otherwise, she warned, we could not get the room.

Things appeared messy. Ragne had the money. She said she would be busy at lunch and meetings, but there was a possibility that she would call me around 4 o'clock. I hurried to come back to Genthod in case she called. This hurry resulted in my forgetting to get down from the train in Genthod. I had to walk back from the next station in Versoix. This caused irritation. Everything seemed to be a roulette a kind of gambling.

As I came in the house, Ånun was sparkling with joy. He was eagerly waiting for my return. He had exciting news to convey: They altogether had caught sixty five fishes and he alone had succeeded in catching ten of them and most important of all, the biggest among the lot went to his honour. After showing me this particular fish which was probably a couple of centimeters bigger than the average size, he came to show me the progress he had made with his fourth symphony in the morning before he went out fishing. He was on the last page of the second movement. He spread all the pages on the floor in rows and columns to show me how far he had come with this music piece. He said the second movement was a short one. It would be followed by a long third movement "Allegro Vivace" which was going to be the most vivacious and important movement of the whole symphony. He also told me in which form the symphony was going to end in the fourth movement. My mind was struggling with time and those Rondo or Scherzo or whatever form he talked about whirled in my mind and came out of my mind without being able to leave any imprint on the memory. After presenting the first two movements of his symphony in written form and the last two movements in oral form he was curious to know how I liked his fourth symphony as a whole. Inside me I was feeling a state of chaos. I was irritated that I did not have money with me, Ragne did not call and the whole situation seemed to be complicatedly entangled with a series of uncertainties! While everything seemed like a devil's complot, Ånun started humming the melodies of the movements to help me appreciate his symphony and asked again "Pappa, what do you think?". My mind was trying to find a way out of this hell. More time passed, more the uncertainties increased, more intense became my will to fight against this state of uncertainty. I wanted to win. Ånun was waiting in front of me expecting an answer. I said "It is nice" without remembering what I heard or saw. The music seemed to have got lost in the devil's net. Ånun could read my mind more easily than anybody else . He immediately understood the emptiness of this word "nice". He felt hurt that I did not care to listen. He knew how to take revenge. He wanted to take this revenge by tearing off in front of my eyes the pages of the fourth symphony he had written. As he tore the first page half way, I felt a whip swishing through my mind and shouted in shock to stop him, "Ånun you must not do that. I really find it nice." I managed to stop him. This punishment by tearing off the music was equally painful to him as to me. Ånun managed to hurt us by hurting himself. He did things that we knew hurt him. He did it with a presumption that others would feel the same pain by understanding how much they hurt him by what they did or said to him. One needed to know him very well to understand what he really meant when he took this sort of negative action against himself. Ragne and I knew his subtle emotional way of reacting to others. We tried to tell Ånun that his subtle language would not be understood by others and he must learn to tell in simple and  straight language when he felt hurt to escape more trouble. Many times his friends said that they hit him because Ånun asked them to do so. They did not sense his delicate way of protesting against violence and trying to win over it by his mental strength. We were often anxious thinking how this delicate human soul would be able to adjust with the world!

After succeeding to make me take his music seriously, he went back to the cellar room repeating with intensity "I must work, I must work, I must work.." . While he was struggling with time I was struggling with uncertainty. As Ragne had not called I accompanied Bjarne when he drove to the delegation to fetch Synnøve. It was already more than half past five and Ragne was not there. It seemed hopeless and I decided to give up my struggle. But Synnøve wanted to help me with the monetary problem and the office secretary came with the moncy I needed just at the moment I was leaving. After that the desire to take up the struggle with time became aflame again. I threw myself in a taxi and anxiously watched every minute that passed. Ho! I won at last. The taxi dropped me in front of the tourist office one minute before six. As I entered the door of the office closed.

After returning to Genthod, I called our friends to inform them that our plans had changed and we were not coming to visit them. Ånun and Bjarne were in the cellar anxiously waiting for the result of day's roulette while Ragne was packing. Ånun had just started writing the third movement "Allegro Vivace". She packed this unfinished fourth symphony in the suitcase since we were leaving for the mountains next morning...

The next morning a witch came to hand over to us a key with number seven. It was the key of our room in the hotel in Leysin, " Orchide"-seven letters! She was the manager of the hotel. As soon as I looked at her face I got frightened. She had two teeth protruding out of her upper jaw. Her mind seemed to be crammed with thoughts. She talked fast in a harsh voice and her eyes seemed to be rolling distantly in a world of the evil. I never had such a fearful feeling looking at a human face before.

The room was poorly furnished. It was on the shadowy side of the building and therefore although it was a bright sunny day we had no sunlight in the room. While the rooms on the other side provided panoramic view of the Alps, only the shadows cast by other hotel buildings around were peeping through the window. From this side we only saw a curving road and cars plying across the shadows.

Before coming in the room Ånun was satisfied with the trip to Leysin.

The train journey from Geneva to Aigle was exciting as there was a wonderful view of the Alp and the Jura all along the way. The sun outside was so bright that Ragne had to pull the curtain on the window when the train passed Montreux and approached Chateau de Chillon. With this, a thought of death descended in her mind. She started talking about Dadu (my father) and a similar sunny day when my parents visited Chateau de Chillon about nine years ago. The panorama of the Alps was as beautiful as that day. In Chateau de Chillon a poet was once imprisoned. Byron wrote "Prisoner of Chillon" based on that story. After Byron many poets and writers had visited Chillon and it was no wonder that Dadu who was also a poet visited the place. "How strange!", she reflected, "Dadu does not live any longer!" He only existed as a poet imprisoned in the castle of our memories in the sunlight flooding the Alpine landscape decorated with the silvery glitter of the lake.

The poem was moving like Dadu's "Poem in Search of Itself" over the grayish violet vineyards awaiting for the spring and the white carpet of the wild flowers decorating the ground around the feet of the pine trees carrying the first clusters of words as hymns of life on the earth before coming of the spring. A castle, a church and a few mountain chalets were gliding away underneath in the warmth of the sunlight floating in the passions and delights of the human mind as a trolley train carrying us from Aigle ascended higher and higher on its way to Leysin.

In this poetic world, Ånun's mind was busy with technical problems: How did people manage to construct the terraces to grow grapevines along such a steep mountain landscape, how did one water the plants in this sloppy terrain and how could the grapevines grow in such an arid soil? Thus as long as the journey to Leysin lasted Ånun had forgotten his music.

But entering the room his mood changed as he remembered that mamma had packed his fourth symphony in the suitcase which we had left in the luggage box in the train station in Geneva. As he wished to write music he felt frustrated and whined: Why did we plan this trip to the mountains? He did not want to go anywhere. We tried to convince

60

him that this beautiful nature around would help him to get inspiration for his music. "I do not need any inspiration from the mountains. I do not intend to write any Tyrol music, anyway", he retorted and tried to make us understand that his fourth symphony was already composed. He only needed time to write it down on note papers. He loved intellectual challenges and was bright enough to accept an argument if it carried weight and therefore we thought the best way of helping him out of this frustration was to make him appreciate our point. We had to agree with him that visiting mountains was not any absolute necessity for getting inspiration for creative acts. However, he could not reject our point that one could not know exactly how an experience of a beautiful nature might affect one's creative spirit and broke in despair, "Yes..y..e..s,pa..ppa..." He seemed to agree without willing to agree. Anyway, he did not need any inspiration right then. We failed to understand why could not he finish the music when he came home and what made him so intense. Showing irritation we went out and he had to follow.

The lady (the "witch") advised us to go to Profondaz for a walk. She said there was a nice restaurant there providing a beautiful panoramic view of the Alps from its terrace. We could also take our lunch there. Before going to Profondaz we went through the tourist office for general information and to ask for advice where to eat in the evening. Since the moment we arrived in Leysin, I was obsessed with the thoughts of possessing/or renting a chalet there speculating that when we would come to Geneva to live, this place would be our weekend resort. Therefore I took this opportunity of enquiring about renting chalets in Leysin. Now Ånun felt irritated, "Again you are speculating pappa! Please stop it. Enough of it."

After this flip-flop of irritation and counter irritation we left for Profondaz. While Ånun was dragging himself behind us grudging: "I must work, I must work. I do not need inspiration. I am not going to write Tyrol music", Death appeared on the way. Again I felt the same psychological state- numbness, breathlessness and intense fear. I saw his dark robe moving as shadow over the Alps extended all around in my view. I got nervous and did not want to go to Profondaz anymore. But realizing that any negative suggestion on my side will spoil the trip for Ragne who badly needed a holiday to enjoy, like Ånun I also felt forced to follow her against my will.

There was a lot of animation in the terrace of the restaurant as people were taking lunch outside. It seemed Death wanted to follow me only up to this point. Then he vanished in the thin mist covering Aigle lying underneath as suddenly as he had appeared. I found this surroundings to be a beautiful setting to take pictures of Ånun. I brought with me the camera and lenses needed for better photography with a view of taking shots of Alpine motives I planned to paint when we returned home. Strangely, this idea of taking photographs of motives had come to my mind for the first time only just before going to Geneva. I had never done it before. Ånun became curious to know why I was taking so many pictures of him. When I told him that I wished to make a painting from Profondaz he requested, "Pappa, please do not superimpose different pictures when you paint." (He could read my thoughts as easily as I could read his.) Ånun disliked superimpositions of persons in different places and times distorting the reality for the sake of art. He did not want me to alter the time, the place and the surroundings. He seemed to have a deep attachment for each moment as it was. What we saw and felt only belonged to a particular moment of life in a particular place and he wanted that I respected this reality.

Ånun always tried to inject in me his love for the nature and reality and asked me to appreciate the aesthetic beauty in nature rather than the distorted world of the modern art. His most favourite artist was Renoir although he often watched the programmes on the livees and techniques of Titian, Turner, Van Gaugh, Gaugin, and Degas that we had in our video collection. He developed this love for art at very early age. His skill in drawing projective pictures often surprised us. We often wondered how he could do that without seeing the objects in front of him! He painted with my colours and brushes already before he became two years old. In Bern he often went up to the room in the attic to paint. His vocabulary at this age exceeded any normal vocabulary of a child: He painted with oxide red, Prussian blue, olive green, cadmium yellow instead of red, blue, green or yellow. In fact, the results of some of his paintings were so interesting that we exhibited a few of them at the art exhibition of the Diplomatic Corps in Bern when he was around two.

His love for the Alps was often reflected in his drawings. The last drawing he made before going to Geneva was from Villar - an Alpine village only about five kilometres away from where I was taking his pictures in Profondaz.

During the last year or so his talent for drawing and painting suffered in order to make time for his music composition. In Profandaz too, no talk of art could manage to distract his mind from music. After enjoying his favourite meal "Spaghetti Bolonaise", Ånun went for a walk on the little snow scattered around the restaurant in order to listen to his symphony in his mind. In the sunrays reflected from the snow crystals he seemed to be totally merged with "Allegro Vivace" playing inside. His face was glittering in lights of joy as a living snow crystal.

I remembered the carnival in the Trollåsen kindergarten four years ago. Ånun wished to be a snow crystal in the carnival. Not only he had beautiful imaginations but also for every idea he had ingenuity to find a practical solution to realize the idea. As he knew how to cut the shapes of snow crystals from papers he had no problem of realizing this wish. I only had to find a white pajama and a shirt for him . He glued large number of white paper crystals to fully cover these clothes he was going to wear. The problem of covering the face of "Ånun snow crystal" was also solved with equal ingenuity by making a snow crystal mask with cardboards.

Like a snow crystal Ånun always wanted to be one with all the mysteries and beauties of nature. He was fascinated by everything. His curiosity knew no bound. It spanned from birds, flowers, insects to shells, fossils, stones, pebbles and crystals. His knowledge of nature spanned from causes of lightening, storm and earthquakes to sensory perception and intelligence of animals, language of communication of the insects and the human endeavours in bio-engineering. To meet his insatiable thirst for knowledge we had built a small library of video tapes that covered wide aspects of life on Earth, from DNAs and bacteria to dinosaurs and history of this living planet from the formation of the Earth to the formation of the mountains and valleys of the Alps. With unbelievable fastness he stored all knowledge in his ever expanding memory without forgetting anything once heard or seen.

On our way back from Profandaz, this living encyclopedia collected a pine cone since it was unusually big and bought a little heart shaped pencil cutter from a shop to take back home. He loved this pencil cutter because it had black and white piano keys printed on it. After making these collections he seemed happy and found a shorter route to return to the hotel. He came dancing down the slope gracefully balancing the problems of equilibrium on the bumpy ground. He seemed to be dancing in an inner ecstasy of joy of being alive amidst the mystery of life around. The mountains were watching this dance like the young beautiful witches in Faust's Walpurgis Night ....

Again this dance of joy turned into sorrow when we returned to the hotel room. Ånun started weeping as he did not have opportunity to write music. Ånun was intense by nature. Everything he did, he did it with ardent passion and zeal. He often cried in exhaustion but seldom gave up before he mastered a thing he wanted to master or finished a project he wanted to finish. We were often afraid that he carried unrealistic high ambitions and anxious that he would be physically and mentally overworked. However, we had never seen him as intense as this before. He was weeping clenching the fingers of his hands and teeth. He was struggling with himself to control the intense outbreak of frustration. As no argument seemed to bring peace in his mind Ragne threatened that if he could not relax we would have to think whether it would be right to buy note paper for him in the future, believing that this threat would work to calm him down. But, instead of calming down he broke into more intense cry, saying: "Ma..mma, Ma..mma, you seem not to understand that I am struggling with time." We became worried to see him so desperate and tried to make him understand that such intensity was not good for one's mental health and he must be able to relax. We wondered why couldn't he finish the symphony when he came home? "When I come home I have to go to school, I have to do my homework, my friends would want to play with me. I never get time. The only time I get is during the weekends, but that is not enough for me", he tried to make us understand his situation. He felt that the holidays like this provided him the best opportunity to compose. We very well understood his frustration about the lack of time which had newly caused conflicts with his friends. We felt unhappy realizing that what he was saying was quite right and therefore without finding a solution to the problem we decided to leave the matter to Ånun himself. We only told him to be realistic about his ambition and he should be able to relax. I advised Ragne to let him cry believing that cry would work as a therapy. After this emotional exchange fear of death started lingering in my mind. I felt I had to have a nap and soon I fell asleep.

When I woke up I found Ånun in a state of joy enjoying the company of his mother sitting beside him in the bed. He was so dear a child! They were enjoying a wonderful time together full of love on both sides. Ragne was measuring his palm against her own. Finding that he had nearly as long fingers as hers she was surprised and asked "Why do you have so long fingers?" "Because it would be easy for me to play the chords on the piano", he laughed so that we did not misunderstand that he tried to crack a big joke.

It seemed the struggle was over. He wanted to go to the restaurant "Le Leysin" as suggested by the tourist office to eat his favourite Swiss dish, cheese fondue. The restaurant was down in the village just adjacent to the church about fifteen minutes' walk from our hotel. Already by then a thick darkness had descended on this Alpine village. The streets were dimly lighted by the rays streaming out of the window panes of the nearby houses and the showcases of the small shops. Occasionally cars were wending their ways like stray cats with shadowy shapes and glowing eyes as if chasing rats in the streets at night. We seemed to be those rats. We clung to each other to save ourselves from these mechanical creatures without hearts and feelings. All the time we had to protect Ånun as he was again absorbed in his world of music, talking about his symphony and was highly absent-minded. In this darkness Ånun was like a lamp trying to show us through his spiritual light a world of joy. Instead of listening to his music, in a clinging darkness I was obsessed with the thoughts of renting a chalet in Leysin .

As we passed by the church, I felt we were walking in a sacristy under the vault of Heaven where rats were running around, evil was pervading all directions, witches were breeding everywhere. Rats!..Rats!...rats! the earth seemed to be full of rats. There were thousands of rats, millions of rats, billions of rats multiplying in each corner shoving, bustling, crowding and clattering like a menace. Amidst this the stars were quivering like millions and billions of candles on an altar. Ånun once wrote: "In the desert there is a hole and in this hole there is an altar. As soon as you put the jewel box  there, ten of the most important wishes of your life will be fulfilled. But if you then touch the jewel box , the curse of fate will fall on you. In the end I desire to live really here." This was the last part of a story he wrote about where he wanted to live. I did not understand what he really meant. But now when I saw the sky, I saw the jewels on the altar. I saw the hole the black blue hole in an unending desert where the human soul wandered in thirst of meaning. There seemed to exist no meaning anywhere. Only fate was guarding the jewels. Once one touched the jewels, fate was ready to strike. And here, in this mysterious world he wanted to live. He wanted to open the desert he named "Shjarid", the twin brother of Sahara, by means of this jewel box. But fate was guarding the box placed on the altar.

Like in Walpurgis Night a higher spirit was flying around the altar through space under this starlit night over "giant valley's maze", over the majestic heights from where "torrent falls in ceaseless silvery flight". Through the vast space, the trees were scattered as pillars of an ancient dark city in ruins, mountains and rocks were mourning under frost and snow in the moonlight as in a huge ancient graveyard and Mephistopheles was flying over this landscape in a height …

Ånun refused to enter the restaurant " Le Leysin" when he saw a poster hanging in front of the entrance door announcing" dancing tonight". It seemed as if someone spoke in his mind, "The soul of evil dominates the folk." Ragne went inside to reserve a table while I waited outside with Ånun. He wanted to return to the hotel. We insisted that he should first come in and see for himself. Ragne tried to convince him that there was no sign of dancing - furthermore, it was very cozy inside and he was definitely going to like it.

After a long harangue when Ragne succeeded in bringing him inside, his ears immediately detected the music floating in the air. "Mamma, listen to the first movement of Mozart's minuet in G major", he became excited. As the visit to the restaurant started with such a happy experience he felt vivified. The interior was decorated with antique Swiss tools and utensils used in the mountain farms in the old days- some even from the time before Mozart including a clock from 1750 i.e. six years before Mozart's birth....

Before leaving this interesting restaurant Ånun discovered the dancing room where a man was playing Mozart's minuet in a synthesizer programmed to simulate the musical instruments. Fortunately, except the musician from Mauritius there was no one there. Ånun carried a charm that attracted people easily. The musician waved to Ånun inviting him to come. Ånun was very happy in receiving this opportunity to talk to the man. He seldom had any inhibition in talking to strangers. He talked to them as if they were his good friends or whom he knew well, making people feel comfortable with his friendly manner and talkative gestures. No one needed more than a few minutes to discover that there was something unique with this child. As expected, this musician also became his friend equally quickly and gave him a candy. The man was not able to express himself well in English. But it did not matter for Ånun. He seemed to understand everything and also made the musician understand what he was saying. He wished very much that the man played the second movement of the minuet instead of playing the first movement again and again. The musician told him, "It is a dancing place and therefore I cannot play any music I want." Ånun pretended to understand this rather odd logic and left the dancing place as if hurrying before the witches arrived there to dance.

The music of Mozart worked like a healing medicine to cheer him up…

Ånun was excited. He was talking scattering feelings of happiness. It made us feel happy to see that in the end he loved this trip to Leysin.

Suddenly I woke up in fear as I looked up towards the sky. I saw myself being surrounded by the stellar constellations -Ursa Major, Ursa Minor, Aquarius, Gemini, Cancer, Sagittarius, Cygnus, Cassiopeia, Perseus, Taurus, Orion, Cancer, Hydra, Virgo.... The dark sky was hanging like a dagger decorated with the most precious jewels of the universe over my head. Before Ånun started composing his biggest passion was the universe. The constellations that I saw in the sky, he saw every night when he went to bed under the upper deck of his bunk bed. He slept on the lower deck and these constellations glowed above his eyes. He travelled in the universe every night before he fell asleep. This interest in the universe started before he was two years old. Ånun lying on the floor opening my books on cosmology and gravitation was a common scene in our study room in Bern. If someone asked what he was doing the answer was, "Ånun is reading cosmology, theory of gravitation and mathematics." If someone asked what he was going to be when he grew up the answer was prompt,"I shall study cosmology and explore the universe." We had a film on the Saturn five rocket and NASA's shuttle programme and we had to show him this film nearly every night around this age. During his painting hours too in the attic in Bern he did not forget the universe. The solar system with the sun and the planets around was a theme he liked to paint. After coming to New York, this interest in cosmos and space science increased in an accelerating rate. Now his room was full of models of shuttles, rockets, satellites , lunar modules, command modules etc. and the book shelf was full of books on astronomy and space science from "Space, Time and Infinity" to "America's Voyage to the Stars". His thirst for knowledge was so deep that he started studying about each star in the constellations he created in his bunk bed. He wanted to know how many light years away they were, which one of them was in fact a star and which one was a white dwarf, a pulsar or a globular cluster or a nebula or a galaxy or a quasar. We subscribed to a astronomical magazine for him and made him a member of the Planetary Society around the age of five. His interest in all kinds of technology was enormous as well. Particularly, the rocket technology  from the principles of propulsion, construction of the ignition chambers and fuel tanks to robot arms and retrieval of satellites from space- ignited his passion most. This interest in rockets spanned from the time of Robert Goddard to the future project of constructing the Heavy Lift Launch Vehicles. His vocabulary far exceeded ours. He followed the coming of Halley's Comet with great excitement making Giotto, Vega, Solar Max a part of his daily normal vocabulary. His knowledge of Mariner, Pioneer, Viking and Voyager missions brought the planets and their satellites closer to us. He imagined one day he will live inside an asteroid building an artificial climate in which life could sustain. And already a few years ago he invited guests to his confirmation ceremony to be held in a space station. Before his interest in music started stealing his time, he wanted to join in an international contest for young people called "Together to Mars" announced by the Planetary Society. This contest offered challenges to develop proposals on topics relating to life support for humans for flights to, from, and while exploring Mars. Once he was asked to talk about the universe in his school too. In return for the world of knowledge he opened to us, he received a telescope as a gift on his sixth birthday, we took him to space museums and planetariums and bought books and models on space science .

His interest in space and cosmos, however, was not concentrated on scientific and technological aspects only. He was highly philosophical by nature. He often discussed metaphysical questions with me varying from the irreversibility of time to how matter could transform into energy or energy could transform into matter and how three quarks in a proton could form a structure and what constituted the surface of the particles. Including the basic ideas of the theory of Relativity he discussed such philosophical questions as the necessity of existence of something in the universe. "Why not everything is not nothing pappa?" he wondered. Around this age of six this philosophical discussion with me for about half an hour lying in the bed was the last ritual of the day before he fell asleep every night.

I was shuddering standing under the starlit night .I had rarely experienced such an unusual intense fear that rose out of metaphysical thoughts about the meaning of human existence in this cosmos. In the centre of the village   the place where I thought the labyrinth ended, I saw a bigger labyrinth. The constellations were guarding the exits of the labyrinth. Galaxies, quasars were flying in that dark night together with the higher spirit over a maze of the valleys of the dark, where torrents of lights were gushing through the cores of the spirals igniting the universe in a dim light. I was in another time many millions of years back from now. The lights that reached my eyes started their journeys hundreds of millions of years ago and, maybe, even more. By some magical power I found myself existing in the earlier age of the universe. Ragne urged me, "Look at the beautiful sky". When I refused to look at the sky she found my behaviour peculiar. I gave her my excuse, "I cannot see well. I am not wearing the right glasses." Instead in my mind I saw that the houses, the shops, the hotel buildings around were standing under the starlit sky like jesters of a strange world where constellations were awaiting the end of their existences like warriors in the cosmic vastness.

The power of the shadow seemed to have taken control of my mind. On our way from the centre of the village to the hotel I was still struggling with the intense fear of death. The witches seemed to be flying all around in the darkness. They were singing and dancing under the stars in my mind as if rejoicing the success in reaching a magical height over the Alps in the Walpurgis Night:

Ånun's mind was flying over the heights of music. He was telling us about the music of the second Viennaise school led by Schonberg, Anton Webern and Alban Berg   the Avant-guard composers who broke out of the traditional music dominating the cultural life of Vienna. He did not particularly like the music of Webern who was shot to death by a soldier during the war. Like modern painting, this new school was also a product of the world war. It grew between the first two world wars giving birth to atonal and serial music. Although Ånun was fond of tonal music, he also listened to twelve tone music with serious interest. He particularly liked to listen to Stravinsky and Schostakowitsch among the modern composers. As my knowledge of the modern music was poor, Ånun was explaining to me the rules of the serial composition trying to correct my misconception that atonal music was just random music. But anyway, we agreed that tonal music was best and he should stick to it. In spite of his open attitude to serial music, he seemed not to appreciate music of many modern composers. I remembered the last words of this discussion ended in front of the entrance door of the hotel, "Pappa can you understand why Olav Berg and Nordheim are so famous in Norway!" The death and witches left reaching the door and now I could smile to give him my response. The door flung open and he entered the hotel with us to spend the last night of his life.

After the evening's shock of fear, my brain activities gradually passed from alpha waves to delta waves bringing me down to sleep. All my knowledge about the brain came from my encounter with Ånun. His education about human anatomy started with a plastic model of a human body where all organs could be taken apart for reassembling around the age of four. Soon he got interested in the human brain and we had to buy him a model of the brain and the books explaining its functioning. As we had to read these books for him we learnt together with him about the cerebral cortex, the functions of the neurons and axions, the ways memories were stored, processed and accessed, the brain waves, the different phases of sleep, REM state, dream etc. From cerebrum, cerebellum, thalamus to even names of different nerve cells found place in the living encyclopedia i.e. his brain. A human brain contains about a hundred billion cells with a capacity to hold information equivalent to about a hundred thousand copies of Encyclopedia Britannica. No wonder, Ånun had enough space left in his brain. In later years this interest in brain led him to be curious about artificial intelligence simulating the functions of the human brain by a computer. In fact one of the reading materials he took with him to Geneva was a popular article on the artificial neural network.

This article was only one of so many other reading materials - from Bhagavat Gita (the core of Hindu philosophic thoughts), "Ninety Degree South" (book on expedition to the South Pole), Contra-point in Bach style, score book for Beethoven's Eroica symphony, two last issues of" Planetary Reports from Planetary Society", last issue of "Regnbuen" (a magazine of Save the Children Organization) to "Caesar's Laurel Leaf" (Astrix) and "The Forgotten Coffin" (Donald) - for this one week holiday trip. He planned to do all these readings while his main project was to arrange "Drummer Boy" for his music school during the holidays in Geneva. The music school had planned to stage this musical piece together with the local children's choir in the spring and he had got this task from his music teacher. His brain seemed to work much faster than ours.

Around three o'clock in the state of deep sleep, messages arrived to our brains  something unusual was happening. Ragne woke up detecting that Ånun was moving in his bed and making a groaning sound as if he was having a discomfort. It wakes me up too. Could it be that he was listening to Beethoven's ninth symphony in sleep when Beethoven was struggling with death before rising to the Heaven singing "Ode to Joy"? Ragne woke him up and noticing that he was warm she took his temperature and found slight fever (around 38 degrees). This made us a little anxious as we were going to return to Norway within twelve hours from that time. Ragne believed the fever could be due to the pollen or maybe the sunlight had been too strong at Profondaz. Since he was feeling so uncomfortable Ånun slept the rest few hours of the night next to mamma in our bed.

In the morning, the witch reappeared. She was roaming around in the dining room of the hotel in front of an Alpine landscape bathing in dazzling sunlight while we were enjoying a marvellous view of the Alps from our breakfast table adjacent to a big glass window pane. She was talking to the guests of the hotel. In turn, she came to talk to us too and smiled. The date was 25th - two plus five made seven! I felt scared looking at her face. Ragne told her that Ånun had fever at night but he seemed to have no fever right now. The lady said it must be due to change of air and suggested that since it was such a nice weather we should go to Berneux. After this conversation we took a few pictures of Ånun at the breakfast table with the gorgeous Alpine view in the background. In the very last picture the sunlight entering through the window came to symmetrically divide his face into two parts  the right side was brightly illuminated while the left side was completely sunk in the shadow. It was so symbolic! His face appeared to be absorbed in a music of light and darkness in pair of melancholy lingering in the mind. We had never seen his face so sad before.

He was thinking about the life of Mozart. The sunlight falling on the right lobe of the brain where the talents of music were stored probably stimulated these thoughts. While taking breakfast Ånun started telling the story of the life of Wolfgang Amadeus Mozart . He first told us about Mozart's childhood when he played with one year older Marie Antoinette, the daughter of the Emperor of Austria, who later became the Queen of France and ended her life in the guillotine during the French revolution. Ånun's love for Mozart dates back from the age of three/four. He loved to listen to someone reading the book on life of child Amadeus to him. It was often difficult to make him sit and listen - he giggled and jumped in excitements hearing about Mozart's "Kingdom of Rucken". It was so similar to his own kingdom! It was funny to know that Mozart also loved to create and play with long strange words like himself and had a dog like his own Snoopy. For Ånun Snoopy was as living a creature as Mozart's Pimperle - he ran around with Snoopy, played and talked with him, told stories to him. At the breakfast table Ånun particularly enjoyed telling the story how child Amadeus could say a lot of things to the Emperor and Empress of Austria without feeling afraid. He himself felt proud for the power that Mozart possessed as a child musician. With excitement in his voice and a pleasant smile in his face  he wanted to convey the spiritual power of music which was higher than the power of emperors and empresses. I understood that was the reason why he told us this part of the story. Ånun had a good knowledge about the lives of many composers as he had read biographies of Hayden, Mozart, Beethoven and Grieg and followed several programmes in the television about the lives of Mahler, Schubert, Tchaikovsky, Sibelius etc. Therefore I wanted to know from him when Mozart had been so famous in the royal courts all over Europe, why he had had to lead such hardships at the end of his thirty-five years of life. Ånun told us about the conflict between Mozart and the Archbishop of Salzburg which made Mozart's life so difficult. And he continued to tell us about the death requiem that a count assigned Mozart to write. He received this assignment through a mysterious person wearing a dark robe and whose face was disguised under a scarf. He carried an unsigned letter from a count who wanted to buy Mozart's requiem and publish it in his own name. The letter brought in Mozart's mind the thoughts about his own death. Mozart could not finish the requiem and it became his own death requiem as he had thought a few months ago. When Ånun told the story we did not know that at the same time he was telling us that his unfinished fourth symphony was going to be his own death requiem, I could not cognize in my mind that the man I had seen in Place du Molard turned up from the same world as the man who came to deliver the letter to Mozart. Ånun finished the story with a deep tone of melancholy - he was unhappy that no one knew where Mozart was buried. Ragne was writing a card (which Ånun had selected) telling mormor and morfar that we were just going to one of the mountain tops by telecabin before returning home. As soon as she finished this line a fear of accident flashed through her mind. Being impressed by his knowledge I told Ånun, "Ånun you seem to know everything". Without answering me he signed the card mamma had just finished and we left for the telecabin.

In Profondaz when we were resting after the lunch, Ånun had studied the map thoroughly including all the surrounding mountain tops and their heights the day before. He remembered everything in detail. He did not make a mistake of a meter when telling us how high Berneux was. From the same telecabin station we had a choice of going to Berneux or Mayen, another mountain area where there was a lake. Mayen was better for those who were interested in walking while Berneux was higher up and was meant for the ski enthusiasts. Ragne and I preferred Mayen while Ånun wished to go to Berneux.

We left this choice open till we came to the telecabin station believing that by then Ånun might change his mind. We packed our luggage and left it ready for picking up from the reception room after we returned from the trip. We planned to take a train leaving Leysin around 2 P.M. and then fetch our suitcases from the station in Geneva and take the plane back to Oslo. Just as we opened the exit door to go out, the "witch" reappeared again . She uttered her magic spell: "Go to Berneux." B e r n e u x!!! Seven fulfilling the fate!!!

Since we were going to a mountain top, Ånun was in a good mood. To go high up was the best Ånun loved in any place we visited from climbing up the stairs of the sun and moon pyramids in Teotihuacan

74

in Mexico or the Kukulkan pyramid in Chichen-Itza to the stairs of the Acropolis in Athen or steep road leading up to the Apollo temple in Delphi, for example. If in a place there was no such monuments or mountains or buildings, he found at least a big stone on which he could stand and satisfy his urge for height. One of his biggest dreams was to stand one day on the highest top of Himalaya without oxygen like Peter Havler and Reinhold Messner . He had only flown over Himalaya couple of times while visiting my family in Calcutta. Apart from an intense attraction to mountain expeditions (he watched the video programme on Havler and Messner's Everest expedition innumerable times) this love for Himalaya was also compounded with his deep interests in mythology. Goddess Ganges was born here from the head of Siva like Athena was born from the head of Zeus (Jupiter) in mount Olympus. He had once talked about the Indian gods and goddess living in Himalaya to the children in his school too. He failed to understand the fuss we were making because Berneux was only 2048 meters high while his mind was fixed much higher in the Himalaya upto a height of 8849.12 meters (Ånun always liked exact number).

Along the same way we had returned last night from the centre of the village, now we walked back towards the telecabin station. It was about a fifteen minutes' walk. This morning Ånun's mind moved back to the tonal music from the atonal world we discussed last evening. He was humming melodies of his last symphony as he was hearing the last piece of music he had composed in his mind. We often wondered: how could he write music without hearing it ? He had an answer," You can read, but do you have to read aloud to understand it?" He heard his music in a similar way and often joked with us, "If you want to hear my music, call the Oslo Philharmonic." To make it simpler, last year when he started writing his first symphony we had made an agreement with Ånun that after he finished his third symphony we would buy a computer software that would simulate his orchestral music. Of course, we made the agreement believing that it would be some years before he finished his third symphony. But who knew he could produce them even before one year amidst such immense scarcity of time! However as agreed, we planned to buy the necessary hardware and software as a Christmas gift for him. But fate did not want that to happen. The things we ordered from abroad had not yet arrived. Now, only a few minutes before he departed from the world Ånun hummed the melodies of the four movements of his last symphony for us all along the way to the telecabin station to help us share the joy of his life.

He said he especially liked the third movement "Allegro Vivace", it was the most beautiful movement of his fourth symphony. He asked me how many points I would give for this music in a scale ranging from one to ten. Right at that moment I was thinking about practical matters - like how long we should stay in the mountain, when and where we would take our lunch, the coins we had put in the left-luggage-box in Geneva station was not enough for so many hours, and why we did not take this opportunity to enquire more about renting a chalet in Leysin etc. Ånun was wearing his white collared red shirt with blue and turquoise strips looking like a beautiful bird decorated with a bright plumage. He seemed to be flying in the wings of music on his way. Although I was not concentrating to listen to what he was singing I needed to give an answer. I did not want to give him high points because I was afraid he would think pappa was not objective. I did not want to give low points either - then I knew I could hurt him. To strike a balance I gave him seven. Ånun was highly critical about himself and hardly whatever he did seemed to be good enough to fulfil his expectations. But when he himself liked the third movement he felt displeased with my judgement. To deal with the unhappy situation I added, I was using a logarithmic scale in which even Beethoven would not get more than eight and half. He found my logarithmic scale strange and turned to mamma for her reaction instead. Mamma gave him eight and half making him happy again.

The music stopped as we entered a shop near the telecabin station to buy picture post cards that he wanted to write to his friends in Trollåsen from the mountain top. The sun was very strong. Ånun chose a red cap with a heart-shaped Swiss flag with a cow in front in order to protect his head from the sun. This Swiss flag was one of the very first interesting objects in the world that fascinated Ånun most when he was only a few months old. In the last minutes of his life he chose a cap with the Swiss flag - a flag of the country from where he took his first steps in his journeys in the world of human culture. From here he had visited many cities and cultures -from Florence to Paris, from Dante, Da Vinci to Renoir.

Not only we loved him so much, he was loved by everyone because he himself loved everybody. His talkative gentle manner, humorous wit, curiosity and deep respect for all and, the smiling eyes, the movements of arms always trying to sling joys around, easily won everyone's heart. When he was born, the nurses in the hospital joked that he was so good looking that he would win every girl's heart . As Ånun won the heart of these girls in the first day of his life, so he won the heart of the lady in the counter of the shop in the last moments of his life too. She gave him a lollipop free of charge as a token of her liking.

There was a bustling and jostling crowd in the telecabin station waiting to go up in the mountains. Ragne and Ånun went to buy tickets valid for both Berneux and Mayen. As we were climbing the stairs towards the hall from where telecabins for both the places were leaving, I found it the right moment to make an attempt to change Ånun's mind from Berneux to Mayen. Till the last step I tried to convince him that we would possibly enjoy more going to Mayen instead of Berneux. But he seemed inflexible,"No, no, pappa it is much better up in Berneux. It is higher up. We would have much better view of the Alps from there. Please, let us go to Berneux." On the way from Athen to Delphi I had once shown Ånun the mountain pass where Oedipus killed his father. After hearing the oracle in Delphi, Oedipus walked in the opposite direction for not returning home in order to defy the power of the oracle that declaimed that he would kill his father. And exactly it was the path he needed to follow to meet on the way his father whom he did not know from before. No human will could surpass the fate.

Before we had made any final decision, Ånun queued up in the line for Berneux and we followed. However, there seemed to exist another power that was struggling against fate. Standing in the queue Ånun became hesitant to go to Berneux because he discovered that we were the only ones who did not carry skis with us. He did not want to do something which was very different from others because of his fear of being considered as an "eccentric". But as another "eccentric" like him going to Berneux without skis appeared nearby in his sight, Ånun found no problem any longer.

Each telecabin carried four persons. We three went inside one. The rise was quite steep making all of us a little nervous. As we rose higher and higher, while Ragne and I were trying our best to hide our nervousness, Ånun was relishing the lollipop and the panorama of the Alps that was being unfolded. With an intense excitement in his voice he urged us to look outside, "Mamma, pappa, look at d'Ai, Mayen, Famelon, le Fer...". He had studied by heart the names of these mountain tops and their heights in Profondaz. In the climax of this excitement as he started talking about the history of the formation of the Alps, the thoughts of death struck his mind. Looking at the crevasses underneath he became afraid that the telecabin might fall. Only adding, "I hope I would survive this trip", he became silent a minute before we arrived in Berneux. I tried to give him courage saying that such cabin never falls. Rightly, we arrived in Berneux safely without a fall and heaved sighs of relief. After this adventure was over, Ånun came out of the cabin jumping in joy. Lifting his left arm in the air he cheered in his usual dancing manner, "Pappa, pappa, we are 2048 meters high up. I am going to write to my friends" . He seemed to have fallen into the dance of joy again. Like the chariot of Oedipus the chariot of fate stopped in the mountain pass wending its way through the blue sky and stalked nearby hiding behind the blazing sun. Ånun's face was glowing in a smile of victory as if after a trenous struggle against the forces of the dark he had at last reached the summit he wished to explore in this light flooding over the Alps. As if, like Messner who went to explore the Everest without oxygen in order to discover himself, Ånun came here to explore his own being , "Who was he?". Here on the Alps he felt nearer his heavenly home in "ice and snow" from where he had embarked on his journey in time.

He wanted to run out immediately in the world of snow and ice lying outside the hall where we disembarked. We called him back and asked him to put on his snow boots before he went out while Ragne and I stood close to him as two body guards on both sides. As soon as we were on our toes to go out and Ånun was set to run, the next cabin started moving to stop his journey in this world. Only two out of four persons in the cabin had managed to get out while the "roulette" started turning confusing everybody. Third person fell as she attempted to get out of the moving cabin . The fourth one - the "eccentric" man without ski-remained imprisoned inside. Hearing a violent noise when I turned my head to the left I saw that the roulette that rolled through the rail carrying the telecabin had derailed in a state of motion at the 180 degree turning point and it was tumbling down towards us. In panic I threw my hand to save Ånun from the accident. But the calculation of fate seemed to be precise within a thousandth of a second. Our own movements, the speed of the telecabin, the time of derailment, our positions and the position of the telecabin so precisely coincided in space and time that although I was standing just beside Ånun only the tip of the mid finger of my right hand could reach near him before the roulette struck him on the right lobe of the brain. It was exactly 11.05 A.M. (1+1+0+5 made seven). I broke my finger tip, Ragne fell down and Ånun sank in a pool of blood. Without giving any one any chance to react against his cruel power fate came in the speed of light to slay a vivacious spirit full of joy. Within a fraction of a second Ragne stood up like an alert body guard to fight against the power trying to steal Ånun's life. But by then the cruelest force of death had already left completing the worst terror any Devil or God could possibly inflict on any human being.

# Chapter 3
# JOURNEY THROUGH THE INNER UNIVERSE

**(Contains excerpts from the book "Tathagata - A Divine Comedy for Our Time")**

So it was the end of a life! A new life started. It started with more vigor, force and intensity. I rose from the despair that had overwhelmed me and wanted to create the best my mind could create. In this devastated world the spirit reappeared once again and offered his help as the spiritual guide and asked me to pursue the task of writing the epic I was destined to write.

The epic, relating the journey of the universal man, who comes and goes life after life, that I had been trying to compose for about a decade, resumed. While standing by the grave, where Ånun was buried, I saw the islands between the realms of the sun and the moon where the mortal wanderers were sailing in search of home. It was an evening in the early spring. The sun was setting behind the graveyard, while the moon was rising on the other side. With it the characters of myths and epics of the world appeared in the vision and the central themes of religions, epics, philosophies and mythologies of the world descended in my mind.

All living creatures are caught in Heaven's way where the sun and the moon play the roles of the hands of destiny. According to this Heaven's way all must die in order to resurrect again. Mortals with lack of wisdom and knowledge of Heaven's way try to escape the wheel of life, death and resurrection as Gilgamesh of the Babylonian epic and Odysseus of Homer's epic tried to do. Odysseus caught between the islands of the sun and the moon searched a route of escape from the tumults of the sea without any success.

Thus with the death of Ånun I embarked on writing "Tathagata's Journey" where gods, goddesses, muses, nymphs, Devil and Angel appeared from different layers of consciousness in which the existence was enmeshed in a cosmic backdrop. The reality of existence in flesh and blood was enwombed in several levels of mental spheres where existence was also immersed in myths and dreams that did not have boundaries in time and space. The journey of Tathagata, who comes and goes riding the wheel of life, death and resurrection life after life, spanned different levels of consciousness: On one level he appeared as a mortal associated with the material existence and the sensory experiences where logic and reason spin the web of thoughts and actions; in the other level he existed at a higher plane where mind shared the level of the "Buddha-consciousness" that sees every existence as one with the entire cosmos. From this level of higher consciousness the journey, at the level of the logic and reason and sensory perceptions, appeared illusory, where images of the reality change and fluctuate constantly like the reflections of a moving world in a Hall made of walls of mirror all around.

While I embarked on this journey I discovered again the nature of the higher consciousness and saw myself as a part of the Buddha mind that penetrated through all existing beings. Buddha mind radiated from a realm that existed beyond the material sphere where molecules and cells functioned according to the laws of nature forming the aspect of existence that one call "born in life". In this world, which is "born", the matter competes following laws of nature, and seeks to settle into order and tranquillity, which they may never receive. It is driven by the "burning fire", or energy of the earthly existence that animates all.

Like the universal energy of the healers, the Buddha mind, sitting at the centres of everything, radiates in the cosmos and penetrates the chakras controlling the flow of the life energy in all. By connecting oneself to this level of consciousness one may bring order in a chaotic movement of the physical world and arrange things to fall in harmony with heaven's way.

In this journey the individual identities disappeared and merged with the protagonist of the journey, Tathagata. As parts of Him all human beings, who had lived, are living and will appear in life in the future, were wandering in search of the paths through different realms of the mind. As many in one, fragmented through different urges of the mind, Tathagata was moving through different layers of the "reality" that existed at different levels of human consciousness.

These layers of the "reality" exist like different auras around the physical body. By using the power of the mind one can expand the realm of the "reality" to higher spheres and move into vaster and vaster arenas of consciousness – in the end, arriving at the cosmic consciousness and becoming one with the cosmos. This "reality" starts at the biological level that rises from the need of the physical survival and reproduction at the level where life is mostly governed by instincts. Here the will-to-live dominates. In the next level the will-to-power, that may secure advantage over the competitors and implant one's hegemony over other human beings appears. In the next higher level, consciousness expands beyond the bondage of the senses. In this sphere the reality becomes entangled in dreams and myths. It generates the power to create a "reality" of one's own imagination independent of the mechanical motions of the things driving the instinctual mind as a dark force of the nature. Beyond this creative sphere of the poets, the musicians and the artists, where the power of the unconscious may still lurk, lies the sphere of the contemplative mind of Tathagata. In this level knowledge, reason and emotional urges of the creative minds are synthesized into a super-mind that can elevate the experience of the "reality" to a higher sphere of consciousness. Beyond it lays the realm where one may connect to the cosmic mind that penetrates through all existing in the living and the nonliving worlds.

In this multilayered "reality" the journey began as a poet accompanied by the Guide of the Soul. It opened with the vision of the journey of the mythical Odysseus who was thrown in wandering over a tumultuous sea stirred by violent storms and lightening passing over the graveyard. It was the journey where all life was caught between life and death:

"*In the universe where there seems to exist no light far out in the depth of the sight,*
*Where in the infinite the sensual world the finite forms describe,*
*In an Eldorado of vision, where the inner light a journey of the soul*
*in search of beauty inscribes,*
*While the fabulous voyagers in thoughts and dream,*
*Depart the senses' streams,*
*I see a boat carrying the treasures of jewels and wealth moving towards*
*a distant land,*
*With vast glowing shores of golden sand.*
*With hearts aloft in passion filling them with ecstasies of dream,*
*The soul sails across the sea towards an island unseen.*
*As the riches of the shores the mind allures,*
*Like shifting clouds while amidst desires the heart feels insecure,*
*Feeling the fierce intensity of the burning sun,*
*The mind plunges as oars in an unknown sea as plunderers in search of*
*a nocturnal land,*
*Where no sailors have ever gone.*
*Under the blue sky, where the space infinitely extends,*
*Forest, caverns, rocks, and ridges breaking waves in foams the adventur-*
*ous mind's thrilling joy maintain,*
*Passing by huts, villages, and towns,*
*Where people live, suffer, and mourn,*
*In the impulse of nature the wandering mind feels passion torn;*
*Like pirates, sailing from their Aegean home,*
*In the ever-changing sound and light churning the foams,*
*The bellowing mind feels captivated under an endless dome.*
*While beyond the ethereal-bound,*
*Where a starry sphere dissolves in a mystery unbound,*
*Where all boundaries merge,*
*In the depth of the sky the sun, as a ship of passion carry the plunderer's*
*urge,*

The water, as awakened mind's vivid dream,
Like gold flowing out of emerald green,
Turns yellow on the white foam that spread silken skin,
Sprinkles fine sprays of bubbles that try to reach the beauty that emanates from the sun,
And in the blind eyes follow the motions of the churning mind behind the stern.
Behind the waves, where the mind in wonder sleeps,
Behind the mountains and caves, where light merges with eternity,
Where, in an imagined shore,
The steps of the beauty shine as steps of a goddess in a golden shrine,
While waves in the wind breathe out mystery's whispering brine,
In vision's wandering, intoxicating the world,
I see drunken Bacchus with his jar of wine.
Steering the ship of the sun towards the world below,
While the setting sun spreads in the heart a dreaming glow,
Over the blazing hill pierced with rays,
Where soul, and will enjoy with nature wanton light's revel and play;
Granting glory to the drunken world joyous and gay,
While beating drums, and rattling cymbals Maenads lift the world from the burden of flesh,
In a magic of frenzy,
Throwing arms upwards in search of deliverance in a world bound to flesh,
Bacchus pours from his jar the wine,
While the frenzied women undress.
Like a boat, steered by the pirates of the heart,
When human grief, suffering and cries to the shore arrive,
Where the power of love the beauteous world revives,
The sun, carrying the pirates of the soul,
Sails across the sky,
Descends towards the ocean behind the hill;
Where cypress trees standing as green lanterns around the temple of the goddess of Dawn seduce the mortal will,
In the slopes leaning towards the archipelago,
Where the sun a luminous spectacle hauls,
The frenzied dancers in madness respond to Bacchus' call.

*As I contemplate on this drunken world,*
*Bedecked with vineyards growing along the slopes,*
*Where the sailors fall in delirium without any hope,*
*That hampers movements and brings the conscious mind's journey to a halt,*
*In an ocean of salt,*
*The ferment of ivy, leaves and grapes,*
*Carry the fragrance of Bacchus' wine around masts and sails,*
*Slowing the rhythms of the muscles bring the conscious mind's journey that ends in a wreck.*
*As the green water penetrates the hull,*
*The rudder and the anchor are devoured by a sea over which the mind floats as an azure gull,*
*Where the pirates on sea,*
*Sink before they are able to extort from life the desired ransom at the port of call,*
*In a dark-blue world the waves dance and scroll.*
*As the sea spews foams towards the horizon bending towards the dawn,*
*In the mind creatures of unseen shapes leap out from a depth from where all life are born;*
*Dazzled by the vibrancy of the light of the stars,*
*In which cosmos appears very far,*
*Curving and bending,*
*Rising and descending,*
*Creating clouds of fog,*
*In ecstasy they dance appearing and disappearing from crags and rocks.*
*In this delirious world, they constantly form and deform in many colours and shapes;*
*While the evening light tries to define the contours of the inner world in curled up fire that burns the flesh,*
*As Bacchus lands on the shore of Naxos to marry the goddess,*
*Radiating inner rays,*
*I see Ariande in his gaze.*
*As the stars appear as jewels studded on the sky with golden threads,*
*I see the bridal crown of Ariadne being lifted to the heaven over an ocean, where vision wanders on the waves;*
*In a boat, that from shores to shores,*

*Life to life,*
*Many dimensions of existence steers...*"

The journey breaks after shipwrecks, which bring him to take shelter in different unknown islands where love, happiness and beauty give temporary reliefs from the wretched destiny of life, which continues again. The Guide of the soul draws the mythical Odysseus to new journeys over the sea again and agian. With the hope of finding a way to home, which he has lost, Odyssey time and again submits his life to the treacherous destiny.

Every human being, who is a part of the universal journeyman, bears similar destiny of Odysseus. The protagonist, who makes the journey, is not any particular man from any culture, place or history. He is the universal being, of whom all human beings are parts. The concept of this man is very similar to the concept of the "whole man" as in the Hegelian philosophy. He is perpetually repeating the wanderings of Odysseus, who is reincarnated in the living man. He is the mythical archetype, who internally reincarnates within each person, and bears the spirit of eternal wanderer beyond the boundaries of any individual culture. Each living person is a copy of the one in many, who has already lived as others and repeats the journey of the previous characters, who have lived before in history. Beneath the superficialities of the individual personalities, each person is a part of the mythical man rather than an individual. As Nietzsche's Zarathustra exclaimed, every existence is entangled in an eternal recurrence of the one that has existed before as a part of the eternal wanderer. Like Odysseus every person is striving to escape the wheel turning between the shore of the islands where life burgeon in opulence driven by the power of the sun and the world of the death and destruction appearing as night. In this eternal recurrence there are storms and winds bringing ceaseless turmoil of history where the universal wanderer appears and disappears wearing the masks of innumerable individual characters.

*"Like actors with masks in a theater, that is the world,*
*Who is nowhere more visible than in the depths of their inner light,*
*In the Time Hall, faceless men and women play roles wearing faces,*

*And enter the arena of life as ritual players, who live and die, and with
whom all living goes to sacrifice.*
*With changing of light and darkness, as they enter in and exit from the
rotating stage,*
*In the Time Hall, drama of myths of gods and demons perpetually re-
peats again and again.*
*Wearing faces,*
*Inside masks,*
*While dancers swing as whirling wind swirling in time,*
*They come and go as parts of a nameless fugitive, who is trying to escape
from life's turbulent fate.*
*In bursts of frenzies as butterflies opening their wings,*
*In a strange rendezvous,*
*Where moments fly from cocoons of light,*
*In light of the moon,*
*Or of day swimming in endless waves of rays,*
*Or floating in starry maze from the poles to the highest mountains' crests,*
*Swimming in joy of life and love,*
*They come and go as nameless fugitives caught in the hands of fate.*
*There is no specific direction of their life,*
*One does not know where to go,*
*Only in hearts' echoes one knows that there exists no passage wherever
one may go;*
*There is only wants to live and love without being released from the sens-
es' play,*
*Responding to desires without dallying away,*
*It is a theatre, where there will be always something that will remain
understood and unknown.*
*It is a tryst to freedom,*
*A joyful frenzy of floating on colorful wings,*
*Without any direction and no place to go..."*

Like universal personalities reappearing in time and place, while bringing always irreversible changes in history, these characters are similar
but never the same. These changes give the journey a meaning and a
purpose.

This archetypal Odysseus -one in many - is also Babylonian Gilgamesh, who is made of three parts. In one part he carries a body made of matter that is subjected to the material laws and bound to the phenomenal world revealed to the senses. In himself he embodies all matter that constitutes the individual bodies and forms. In this aspect he is conditioned by the external world governed by the material dynamics throwing human beings to the struggle for survival. In another aspect he carries the spirit that is universal and lies outside the sphere of the sense-bound world. In this domain man dreams, imagines, projects new realities, seeks freedom from the sense-bound world and aspires for the realm of the Divine.

The man, who is made of these three parts, makes a journey through a complex reality made of different layers of experiences that interpenetrate each other. In one layer he moves through the experiences of the awakened state of the mind. In another he journeys through the unconscious realm that surfaces in dreams. A mythological world, which surges through symbols of different religions, penetrates these layers and emerges as the dimension of the reality which bridges the conscious and unconscious worlds.

Then there exists the historic dimension in which the life passing is rooted in the history that has passed. The man living in the present is the same man who has lived in history before, though the elements conditioning and shaping the human life may have changed. The historic man regenerates and relives in the present wearing different costumes and masks.

Tathagata, who had fragmented and disappeared in many layers of realities, and become indistinct and diffused, as the wanderer moving through different spheres of consciousness, appeared wearing a mask of a poet. Accompanied by his Divine Guide I saw myself as the one who had entered in the stage of life as "two-in-one" - as a mortal of flesh and blood and a divine being who existed beyond the realm of human comprehension.

Thus the universal drama of life, in search of love, beauty and meaning of life and death unfolded on the stage, where I was rotating inside the Time Hall.

The writing of "Tathagata`s Journey" began soon after we moved to Geneva. The centre of the Time Hall became the apartment where we lived in Quai du Sujet by the river Rhone. The river after passing by the Rousseau Island, fell in Lac Leman (Lake of Geneva). We had moved there a few months after Ånun`s death. This luxury apartment in the centre of city of Geneva lay on the top floor of a big building complex. The aprtment was attached to a terrace roof as big as a small garden. In this Time Hall of Illusion as a part of Tathagata, I was composing the universal journey of mankind. The removable glass walls, which separated the garden and the living room and my office, once taken down, made the interior of the apartment one with the outer garden. From these rooms we had a nearly 360 degree view of the Alps and the Jura Mountain, which engirdled the city of Geneva. The "Jet de Eau" on Lac Leman belonged to the same open view that extended from the terrace garden towards the lake. Berneux, where Ånun died, loomed at the distance. It was a marvellous place to live! The old city, lying on a small hill with St. Peters Cathedral at its top, where Ånun and I had walked for the last time, hang in front of us as a huge canvas spread across the glass walls. Through this "canvas" where reality was revealed through senses in its details, other realms of the consciousness penetrated this Time Hall.

When I started composing the epic I had little idea about what would be its content. It evolved as I got in the process of writing I watched like an outsider how the journey gradually unfolded without my intellectual intervention in organizing and structuring the content. At no stage of the writing it was clear to me how the content and the form of the book might look like in the end. The writing was driven by a mental process which appeared to be controlled by the inner guide. He was taking the man bound to the world and ego to a journey trough different realms of consciousness, that constituted the higher nature of existence.

During this process I understood that the so-called reality was multidimensional. The experience of journey of life depends on how one engages with the world and which capacity of the mind one utilizes in exploring the content of the reality. Different realms of consciousness reveal different aspects of beauty and meaning of life and create very different concepts of joy, pleasure or suffering.

The journey first went through the instinct-bound world where wealth, power, seduction and frivolity ruled human life.

"It was a lonely wandering where man was separate from all. Like dreadful monsters where man wandered alone in treacherous paths. From precipices man had thrown themselves in the raging sea, in solitary search of beauty and love had jumped in the abyss of happiness full of sensual lusts. Forgetting wisdom they had taken chances, and in foolishness plunged in the crevices that were deep, in hurry moved forward in the fire of the will, and as voluntary acts embraced the beauty weaving the sorcerer's webs that plunder heart's passions in devilish meticulosity and skill. The demonic hunger that devours was called freedom, wantonness and the power to endure the consequences of the folly and lowliness of the spirit were the definitions of life's courage, to sink deeper in disgrace and like cunning and lurking creature despising the noble souls were the way of emancipation from the unworldliness.

Except desires there was nothing that was worthwhile. Anything but merry-making made them weary. There were no higher goal but a valiant rejection of everything that demands from man sacrifice and urges to seek path outside physical comforts. After marriage, bearing child, then slipping away, fluttering and creeping from bed to bed from mistress to mistress, in blindness being awake, inventing in lasciviousness a hell, seeking happiness in dragging oneself in intoxicated states, oppressed and weighed down by the emptiness, melancholy and self-contempt, in this village there were surging clouds over the sea and the dangers of going across.

All around there were supple snakes and slippery witches. In seafarer's delight there was the tantalizing wickedness of freedom like fetterless hunting hounds and bitches. It was a tortuous abyss of the animal instincts. In this shore of the human sea, in a human abyss, riches squandered in filthy passion of squandering the wealth in the desire's bottomless brothels and gambled against themselves by merrymaking and night-long danc-

*ing and bets. There as the ultimate man I had entered the festivity of life by wearing a mask and trodden the path of suffering in order to awaken the man from the sensual slumber that was abysmally deep. When he was awake I had gone my way across the gulf through the forest towards the mountain path. Sea bore me. From shores to shores I saw myself rising with the sun and going down with the darkness of the night. This sea was supernatural. Here I sailed as the ultimate man. It was a journey to overcome the tumults of passions that create waves and try to wreck the wanderer's boat apart. Once born in flesh and blood here man falls in contradictions with himself. The instincts intoxicate; the passions bewilder; the contradictions between the body bound in causal chains in the needs and necessities of life and the spirit seeking unbound freedom beyond matter create tumults of conflicts. Illusions creep. In war and peace with oneself one feels torn and riven. Once man fails to hold courage and follow the guidance of the inner light, one is wrecked apart and is washed away.*

*During this journey I had seen many lands and seen myself among many people. There were many subterranean caves, many vortices and eddies of whirling disturbances rising from these caves, and always a constant fear of death. There were many surges of exalted moments, many wing-bits of thoughts desiring to fly away from this dangerous wandering on the waves of life to the home from where I had come. There were many islands and archipelagoes, inexhaustible number of hidden beaches where one could feel refreshed and renewed as a new seafarer, find oneself anew as parts of the ultimate man. Here between earth and eternity I had felt bound together between man and God. Drawn from below and lifted from above, I had sailed from shore to shore carrying away with myself the trembling joy of awareness of myself as always a new man and always the same one, to whom all wanderers on the sea belong."*

After passing through the world bound to instincts, the Guide gives advise to the journeyman to leave the ego-bound will, and instead act following the higher will that resides in human mind:

*"Here in the village those who dwell,*
*Live in a delusion that is dismal and wild,*
*As flames of a furnace in Hell,*
*Here in hearts' tempestuous fire desires will swell.*

92

*In an infernal world, where possessions human beings possess,*
*In an abyss of the mind, that is precarious and dark,*
*Like a hellish bird with mighty wings outstretched,*
*In stench and smoke,*
*In a subterranean path where evil soars,*
*A penal fire spreads like a burning gulf.*
*As it steers its flight,*
*Chaos rises towards a higher height,*
*And obfuscates sky's celestial light.*

*In such an ardent night,*
*Move away from the path, where desires and passions dwell,*
*And follow the enlightened path, that can free man from the will-to-power,*
*Which makes man abominable and cruel.*
*Do not pursue mind's rebellious thrills,*
*Follow the Creator's will,*
*Although free will life's purposes may fulfil,*
*Know that there exists a higher will,*
*Which is above reason, which is tied to the senses' swirl.*
*Know that what may appear as darkness of God,*
*Carries a light that can illumine the hidden corners in the heart,*
*And what senses may perceive as light may be a realm of the blind,*
*Where sense-bound man wanders in the dark.*
*Do not act against the divine will,*
*In the world, where your sense-bound experiences are immersed,*
*Let the human will and the divine will merge.*
*Leave the world that is chaotic and dark,*
*And move towards the shore,*
*Where a boat awaits for a spiritual journey-*
*Go and embark.*

*The beauty, and love whom you search,*
*You won't meet her in flesh and blood.*
*However, as you will move along your destined path,*
*You will meet her as the muses of music and arts.*
*In streaming wind,*

*In light's lustrous blaze,*
*You will see her unveiled.*
*In the bosom of the nature, where feelings of tranquillity in wonder will*
*shine,*
*You will see her as a bejewelled goddess bathing in sunshine.*
*Along branches of trees, where nature love's mystery entwines,*
*You will discover her as a celestial maiden,*
*Scattering beauty's glittering signs.*
*As a goddess of arts you will see her knitting in your mind light's loftiest*
*designs.*
*While her beauty will ascend in the glade,*
*Raise your head,*
*Walk towards the light that will beckon you with its blaze.*
*In murmuring joy, when wind will play with leaves and blades,*
*Stand aright to see her transcendental face.*
*Where rays swimming from dawn to dusk,*
*Will ascend and descend with hues of colours leaving golden sparks,*
*In mortal's eyes,*
*The beauty will never be shut,*
*Open the window through which light will penetrate and wash away*
*the darkness of the senses' nocturnal lust."*

After the search for beauty and love the instinct-bound lfe ends in bondage and suffering, Orpheus appears as other character from the mythological world. He is the Greek musician of Heaven, whose music makes dead world come into life again. He represents the Divine power that brings back life in the spring from the death of winter. In the psychological plane he is the guide who leads the mortal towards the transcendental domain. He is the beloved of the muses of music, poetry, and art who accompany the Greek god Apollo. The beauty, who enchanted the suffering man in the village festival, now appears as the beloved of Orpheus.

In search of a transcendental love Tathagtha, as the poet, enters with the Guide of the Soul in the next realm of the journey called "Forest Path": Here muses sing, dance, play music and recite lyrics. In this realm he can not distinguish among reality, myth and dream.

"In this island there was a forest. It was the forest of life and death where trees drew nourishments from the soil and energy from the sky. It was the forest bound in a serpentine fate of life, death and resurrection. It was the path through which one could discover how the whole creation was sustained. At dawn when I had entered the forest I had seen myself split as two but strangely united as one. On one side there was a shadow of myself and on the other side the light that was casting the shadow. I was divided between darkness and light. Though there was no darkness and light. The objects around created this illusion of darkness and light. As light accompanies darkness and darkness accompanies light I was my own companion. All around I saw the life in the forest moving through such contradictions. The body was contradicting the spirit, the passion was contradicting with the desire to renounce, will was contradicting with itself. Truly it was a maze of the real and the unreal. I was seeing myself and then disappearing from myself and becoming someone else. I was never sure when I was awake and when I had fallen in a dream. I knew not when I was within myself or outside myself, when I was one or the another, when I was shadow or the light, when I was separate and not-separate from the rest, whether fingers of some unknown destiny was regulating my wandering, or I was causing the happenings by my own choices and actions. I was not sure if I was betraying myself or I was being betrayed by someone else. I only knew that I was searching myself, moving towards home through a riddle of existence that was difficult to comprehend.

Here love and beauty seemed to be riddle. The male and the female were often the same who were reversing the roles as myself in pursuit of the other and the other in pursuit of me. When I desired she appeared in the higher path and when I sought her in the higher path she appeared as desire. There was a thirst for love for the other half and at the same time a love for the self. One enraptured the feelings from the senses, the other entrapped the soul in the senses ropes. One was the sun and the other was the moon engaged in an eternal battle of the mythical serpent and the eagle.

In this forest there was a lake- a lake that was also me. Beside a secluded stream it was the lake of Eros where Narcissus had seen himself in multiple images scattered in reality, myth and dream and Psyche had thrown herself in the longing for love that only death could redeem. This *lake was also a part of the sea that had penetrated through the rocks and stones and reached this forest in the realm of myth, reality and dream. Here images formed according to the will that surged with Eros - the incomprehensible irrationality that drew man to deeper and deeper domains of the consciousness that merged with the unconscious world of archetypal symbols and dream. Every step brought me to many paths in many domains in different psychic states. Gradually the whole forest turned out to be a kind of tarantula's web, spinning in different threads different patterns of images that entangled the existence deeper and deeper in ad-infinitum layers in a sea lying in the psychic depth. Every path was knitted with many other paths. It was difficult to know which path to choose. They all seemed different and ultimately seemed to come back to the same. Groping for a path I had wandered in this multiple reality as the ultimate man.*

*There were incredible beauties, the hunters, the stags, the hounds, many colourful vegetating, and monstrous shrieks of the birds and animals sending adverse signs, and fugitive trying to escape. It was a veritable labyrinth of the blind paths entangling the wanderer in the complex maze of the existence that spanned from time and space to domains outside time and space. There were melodies, ecstasies, notes, that diverted the vision in different ways. The huntsmen were struggling with the beasts. The will to exist was struggling with the will to perish; the will to life was seeking the will to death. It was a forest of veritable contradictions that created a labyrinthine maze. In this labyrinth I had wandered as the man with multiple awareness of the life that varied with the depth of the journey of the soul through the domains, what man calls the domains of the "conscious" and "unconscious" in and outside the boundaries of time and space.*

*You may ask what I had been seeking? What is the meaning of this labyrinthine journey where everything exist in a non-temporality with present, past and future as indistinguishable and the reality as an illusion of the will that gradually disappears with the knowledge of the existence that is an emptiness infinitely vast? What is the meaning of this journey where most journeymen will go astray and perish in the blindness of the heart?*

*Hear about the way through this labyrinth and the blind alleys of the mind where man may get entrapped unless man makes use of the higher* power of the mid that illumines the world and the different layers of the inner darkness and light. With this power it is possible to see the greater depth of the sea from where I have risen and arrived. In trying to escape from the world where there exists no physical means to escape, in willing to free oneself from the symbolic world where many different worlds are enmeshed, in confronting the monstrous existence that is the invisible aspect of oneself, in trying to move beyond the domain where all movements return again to the labyrinthine maze, there lies the process of self-knowledge, the awareness of the multiplicity of the whole in many different folds. One can know oneself as submerged in a multifold reality of existence, whose experience and knowledge can never be exhausted by any one. One can be aware of oneself as the part of the whole infinitely spread in worlds after worlds, in different levels of consciousness as a part of the ultimate man, who is beyond all knowing and understanding by the individual minds, who possesses restricted awareness and experience of life. By making this journey one will know one's infinite possibilities as the free will moving with the whole in infinite numbers of paths and understanding that in wandering, dreaming and confronting the monster like forces in the labyrinth there lies the possibility of being illumined and enlightened as the great rising star. Those wanderers who do not succumb to this fear are drawn closer to the height of the ultimate man to be illumined by a light from where I have risen to bring man the knowledge of enlightenment of the great mind.

Do not wander in the darkness. In this forest I had found the river to where many rivers meet – always flowing aloft and flowing alone. It is the river of the spirit all souls are beckoned. It is the river of the will that branches in innumerable paths and penetrates different domains and heights of the mind creating the sensations of reality and forming illusions of dreams. Innumerable are its tributaries. One never exactly knows where they go. As you, I, and he the tributaries of the mind run from dendrites to dendrites, bifurcate in innumerable branches, penetrate the grounds, rocks, mountains and evaporate in nothingness before one is able to know where they are going and what there is to know. They move through thousands and thousands of trodden and untrodden paths, willing to return and willing to go away, without really knowing what is the best way. But the man of true knowledge knows the slopes through which one may pass and meet the sea from where I come and in which will may *be freed from the tumults of the confusions on the way.*

*It is the river of becoming, the mind's mirror reflecting in innumerable spangles of rays the will that breaks as foams and churns with the opposing forces of the nature and mind creating emotions and thoughts. In innumerable fold of mirrors it commands the rays and reflects the beauty of the mind of the ultimate mind. The living creatures, nonliving too, see in this river the sacrifice. Like trembling leaves in the sunlight, the images of the birds or the beasts or the human kind tremble, break, revolve and rotate, creating unfamiliar shapes in the waves disperse never truly knowing where they go. In this stream of the will I had gazed at the multifold images of myself, always uncertain in shapes, always breaking away to join with the spangles that float in the sunshine over the currents dancing with the rays. I had thus seen beauty and love flowing through the forest as part of myself divided and separate in the other half of the mirror where in perishing man understands love and loving man perishes in the stream moving towards the ultimate way. It is a love that creates no desire.*

*It rises in the breast as the light that warms up the body and illumines the whole mind. With it man turns into a river that originates in the sea and flows to the sea carrying the fragments of the body as amorphous dust floating in a golden light moves in the mind. There is no suffering in this willing; there is no pain and joy. Eternally recurring it is the will that redeems man from the suffering of existence that you have already heard. You may ask who is He? How shall you know Him? In this multifold mirror which image of Him you will grasp as the true image of Him? In this streaming will how shall you still your thoughts and contemplate on the love that stills every movements? How in this multitudinous movements will you be able to grasp Him as the One, who remains unmoved? These questions are not easy to answer and even more difficult to comprehend with answers that are based on the experience of man. Although I am the enlightened man I do not know my own nature through the process of human thoughts. I exist domains and domains beyond where human thoughts, as willed and known by man, are non existent and there is no willing, in the sense man wills, at all. I have already spoken of the multiplicities of the images and the worlds where my existence extends that are not finite, countable in numbers and not possible to fathom within a framework of knowledge based on the concepts of separation in time and space. I am the shadow of myself as well as the light of the rays from where the shadows spring. I am the innumerable spangles of rays and the waves dancing with the rays - streaming from a stillness deep within that can never be approached with the knowledge or thoughts. Down the surface of the sea where you see me and hear me speak I am a movement towards stillness passing through the infinite stages of the will that in the depth of the psychic domains gradually ceases to will. There is no form that is more real or false than any form in which you may my image contemplate. As I have said before, He is infinite, unknowable and beyond comprehension of even the sages.."*

This forest existed around the Time Hall i.e. the apartment in Geneva, where the journey that unfolded in my mind as streams of ideas, visions and words revealed by the guide of the Soul. Behind my writing desk there was the terrace garden engirdled by mountainous view. The "Forest" existed between the snow-clad mountain tops looming at the distance and the physical body that was experiencing the world through the senses. The garden was my gate to this dreamy realm of artists, musicians and poets.

This forest did not exist in a particular place and at a particular moment of time. It was "the forest" with which all forests were one. It was a part of the psychic existence where things could exist without existing in time and space. It was partly one with the garden, partly one with the verdant world decorating the slopes of the surrounding mountains. It was a projection of the reality through imagination and dream. Here the so-called reality was a pandemonium of worlds where many worlds penetrated. Different projections of the sense bound experiences floated as streams of illusion. Inside this illusion I was a part of a psychic continuum, where I was not separable from other existences, which I could not comprehend as an individual being, who existed at a particular time and place. Coming in contact with the material world, in this illusory realm my mind was becoming conscious of itself as ego and will bound to an individual, whom I called me.

*"It is a story where I have crossed a sea, journeyed over a river, gone beyond the reality in the past, wandered through domains where the*

time has no definite meaning, gone both ways - towards the past as well as the future. Like in images in the mirror I have walked both in the real world, that is virtual, and virtual world, that is real. This river plunges into the sea after passing through the forest, crossing the cities, and then winding backward.

I have already fled from many forests, many cities, many wars and battles. I have wandered alone from many shores to shores. Now I have taken refuge here to gaze at life,that I have left behind. Amidst the diversity of life, that creates a chaos and disorder as results of the competitions for life, I see the naked world, that is frighteningly real. While things battle with things, life wars against life, the beauty breaks forth carrying colours and warmth of the sunlight, like an irreducible absurdity, I see in the nudity of life the beauty of the world.

While fleeing I gaze. Like a person enthralled by the beauty of the colourful maze, I look at the world in strange somnolence - as if, neither dreaming nor being awake. I wish to separate my one half from the other half, enter as other into another world, that is inside another... thus I travel ...deeper .. deeper ...pass through history, time, myth ...stalk in hell, or fly in paradise... in order to find out who am I? In front of this beauty I see the hairy leaves, that hang around her naked flesh. I contemplate on the jungle between her thighs where passion creeps and rises from abdomen to the breast, and a desire of love points towards her organ of sex. This sight makes me forget the fear of death. I stop as a bewildered stag in a strange illusion, and follow the passion's drags, that bring me to the lake, where the beauty bathes as a woman of blood and flesh. Like a lovely woman I discover her mysterious flesh. With eyes wide open I stare at her nudity that seems absurd but true. Like a goddess she sprinkles rays in the eyes, scatters feelings in the body, and generates the sensations of the serpentine power in the lower part. I see the world revealed as wonder of the senses, absurdly knitted with another world that is outside the sphere of time. She overwhelms reason and I enter into darker and darker world to seek unnatural relations with her body and flesh.

I do not understand this play of destiny. I stand, gaze and look at the stream, where I see her bathing. It is on the other side of the mirror, on the opposite bank of the river. Since the time, when I have left the shore on the other side, the reality floats as nothingness in my consciousness inside the mirror. The river has become time; the forest has transformed; the *beauty has become one with the women of flesh and blood, in whose sex I have felt trapped in a darkness of the mind. In a jungle, where venous serpents have writhed and hissed, huntsmen have pursued their preys, in front of her nudity I have felt drawn deeper and deeper in a darkness. Then feeling a sudden fright I have tried to run away. In trying to flee I have made false judgments and fallen in the danger that I have wished to avoid.."*

In the multi-dimensional "reality", where human existence was entangled in the sense impressions moving as ever changing mirrors all around, one's life was reflections of the life of other individuals moving around. In this "reality" Tathagata was watching the multiple images of himself moving in different directions. In one direction he was still entrapped in the sense-bound world of passion and desire; in another direction he was seeking the transcendental love of the Muse. In one mirror he was watching himself as a hunter in the forest, while in another he was moving as a romantic poet in search of a transcendental love.

It was a realm of contradictions and confusions where the Guide appeared both as Angel and Devil:

*" Though my power both the earth and heaven spans,*
*I am not what you may believe I am.*
*I am neither light nor night,*
*Some call me Devil, and some call me the highest Angel of light,*
*Some believe I am a power that comes from the celestial height.*
*Some conceive me as Satan, who is the source of earthly evil and all miserable plights.*
*Some invoke me as the prince of the night,*
*Who in death and destruction takes immeasurable delight,*
*While some worship me as an Angel lifted in a splendid light in a heavenly flight.*

*In the human fantasy, that knows no bound,*
*I am imagined as a father of lie, a deceiver, a leader of disobedience,*
*a great dragon for whom a fire in hell rises to create an everlasting suf-*

fering profound.
Some also imagine me as a prince of darkness fighting against the principle of light,
They see me as power-loving, lustful, covetous, conceited fellow flying in the height,
Or as a luciferous, sinister creature obsessed with vile,
Whose character, temperament and idiosyncrasies are only meant to corrupt and defile.
To some I am insanely libidinous and malignant, whose body is spotted with unusual marks,
And they believe that I dwell in a bottomless pit of the hellish dark.
On the other hand some see my godlike birth,
Who soars as a messenger of light as the sun on the earth.

They see me as holy, infinite and co-eternal with God,
While good and evil are creation of the mind, that is unable to understand the will of the Lord.
Some see me as the divine knowledge that helps man to understand the meaning of the temporal acts,
The dynamic unity of reason that ties human experiences with facts;
Some see me as the creative reason, who no form and fantasy can describe,
Though hidden they think I manifest through the laws that God to the world prescribes.
Some see me as the power of the mind, which sets norms and rules to the human will,
They beseech my help so that the will of God in their life may fulfil.

Some conceive me as the power of discursive thinking in a contemplative mind,
Which is a great source of knowledge of the ultimate reality to whom all human will should resign.
Some imagine me as the mediator between the earth and heaven through whom the cosmic principles can be known,
Like the light of the eternal crystal - God's shining stone,
They see me as the power through which the cosmic mind has eternally shone.

*Some see me as the bearer of judgment, idea, notions of ethics that bind*
*the earthly dwellings of man with the eternal home;*
*Though I am not made of any substance they consider me as the guide*
*of reason of the mortal made of flesh and bone.*
*Some conceive me as the divine nothing revealed and related to the*
*world by thoughts,*
*And perceive me as the luminous idea that emanates from Thoth.*
*However, my image varies with varying interests of the nations and*
*tribes,*
*They see me as evil or good depending on benefit or sacrifice.*
*With changing history I am one's God and other's demon,*
*One's devil and other's Simon,*
*One's Michael and other's Mammon,*
*One's Satan and other's Angel,*
*One's dragon and other's Gabrielle, Uriel or Archangel.*
*You may call me by any name that you may like,*
*Whether one calls me Angel or Satan I am always alike.*
*In this world, where often truth is lie,*
*If you wish I can be your guide,*
*Where using reason and knowledge man rises from hell and falls from*
*the paradise,*
*I can bring man out of this world to a world where heaven and hell ex-*
*ist side by side."*

The drama in the forest ended in cry and yell of the blind man. After the sufferings, that lurked in the realm of dream and imagination,
where the mortal may wish to take refuge by fleeing from the world of
the senses, the consciousness was lifted to a higher realm. Here unconscious urges, dreams, myths and reasoning and contemplating reflections fused together creating a new consciousness of "reality". The
Guide brought the poet out of the forest and took him along the path
of the philosophers.

*"Thus I search myself, my freedom, my own world where at the end*
*everything turns as illusion. Sitting in this place, where no one sees me,*
*I think back of the life that I have left behind. I can see the contours of*
*the sea, the forest, the lake, the castle, the gates, the garden, the dark*

*black world, from where I have fled. I see the mirror, the reflections on the river, the rippling light over the stream scattering the moments as the time passes by. As I consciously contemplate, my mind dissolves in the stream, my face becomes one with the masks of the others. The shadows and lights, carrying away the images deep within ... somewhere... in the depth of the vacuum...without any spatial beginning or end, become one with the void. I watch my flesh dispersing through nothing as someone who is not the same as I was. It flows, moves, oscillates and swings. With the reflections on the waves time penetrates. I no longer exist as someone who had lived, walked, wandered as me. In the mirror I see me in the nothingness, in which I am totally absorbed. It is my way of crossing the island of solitude. While the fear rises with the waves, as the glittering flickers of thoughts, I move away and try to escape from the river.*

*I try to understand: Is time mind? Is this river mind? Is this conscious reflection only myself strewn on the surface as innumerable spangles dancing on the ripples, that in reality do not exist? There seems no way to know. All knowing seem to be dissolved in the nothingness. What I know remains confined in my thoughts that no longer can express what this knowing would mean. I remain invisible to myself and indecipherable by knowledge. In the mirror I have turned into a collection of spangles that has no definite meaning, no particular form, no identity, or any movement except the flow that is one with motion on the other side beyond time and space. In this mirror each time I look at myself, the images disappear. I cannot recognize the rests that remain. The eyes, the noses, the mouths, the limbs, the chests, the bellies, whatever parts that had once defined my body, become so unfamiliar. It seems, with me on the other side of the mirror, I carry another existence, a new state, a new life. There also I flee, move, wander and search the part of myself that is left on this side, where I am "now" and where my consciousness floats!*

*I have become transparent to the gaze of that other one. He is also transparent to mine. Thus as I stare at the mirror in the river, I see my own annihilation and emergence on both sides. The form, that defines me in a spatial boundary, disappears in a nothingness. I pass into another form, another domain, another existence, that is not yet connected with time. From here, where I am, I emerge in a state with no time, no past, no future - only a present, an unchanging void!*

*I exist in order to look at myself as object on one side and conscious-*

*ness on the other! The both states negate each other. And by negating and fleeing from each other they create the illusion of time and the existence that I call "me". In this irreducible nothing where all are absorbed in a consciousness, that is never able to define itself, or know itself as it is, negating is the very foundation on which the consciousness arises. This side of the mirror, where I see the sea, the void, the island, the beach, the forest... constitute the side of the contemplative consciousness. I am absorbed in a nothingness on the other side."*

Arriving in this realm, the consciousness was elevated to the cosmic sphere. A music rose and moved as waves in a sea of nothingness made of strange vibrations that oscillated in the mind without oscillating in the physical space and time. They moved in a realm of pure subjectivity where the notes expressed the vibrations correlated by mathematical relations defining the harmony of the musical structure. In sequences of concepts that could exist simultaneously in mind, it held the notes in a mental space which turned into music to the ears once the notes were represented in the material world through the vibrations of the material instruments following the events in time. This music was pure, unstirred by the temporal oscillations, unpolluted by the ear, and untouched by violins, violas, flutes, drums etc.... those material instruments that created ripples in the senses.

From the time of Pythagoras and Plato the universe had been conceived as a material manifestation of a music existing in a supremely intelligent mind. Music was number, and the cosmos was music to the Pythagoreans. They saw in the relationships between the harmonic intervals, the predicament of the perceptible and the imperceptible universe. For Plato the universe was made of nested rings related to the musical octaves. The cosmos was described as a set of nested whorls which created a series of rings - like the rings of the fixed stars, the sun and the moon, and the planets. On each such ring a Siren stood and sang a different note. The eight whorls thus brought forth a scale. Such ideas related to the musical harmony behind creation of the universe remained dominating views in the western culture till the days of Kepler. The ideas related to the vibrations of strings again had gained ascendance in the theories of physics during the last decades of the twentieth century.

*"As the transcendent light from a supreme mind,*
*Like Plato's Timaeus where in the nested spheres - cut away in sections*
*and rings,*
*The universe plays the harmony on the celestial strings,*
*Where Demiurge has composed the music assigning to the planets and*
*the stars their motions,*
*The principles of harmony are above all equations.*
*I hear the music of the stars, the planets, the cosmos*
*Neither at rest nor in movement,*
*Neither in ascends nor in descends,*
*Moving always following transcendental curves and bends.*
*As the music rises to higher pitch,*
*I hear the deepest tone from the lunar sphere.*
*The stars, with the swiftest speed, play the keys of the highest tones.*
*What Pythagoras, Plato, Cicero had called the spheres of celestial bliss,*
*Vibrating between man and eternity,*
*Though octave sounds do not comply with the scientific reality,*
*I hear in them the rhythms, that universe's perfection reflect,*
*And feel the coexistence of violin, viola, contrabass, flutes, horns, drums*
*in the pattern of waves,*
*My mind being engulfed in an eternal blaze.*
*The time that is past and the time that is future,*
*That in turn the eternal present contains,*
*When compounded with the motions in chains,*
*Create the harmony that is perfect in shape,*
*Transmit vibrations that are mathematically perfect and tuned to the*
*light moving on the hyper-surfaces in higher space.*
*From the crystal sphere, that has many more dimensions than what man*
*perceives in the earth-bound state,*
*I hear the melodies of eternity, the polyphonic chants, the tones*
*in unison with the whirling world in flames.*

*In the interstellar space*
*Where the vibrations and the rhythms fill the darkness,*
*The strings in tension break into different components:*

The movements in the mind carry harmony in the consciousness,
The musician of the souls tune the ennachords beyond the rules of science.
From the cosmic mystery where the proper motions are attuned to the music of time and space,
Reflecting the reason - the Mysterium Cosmographicum- in numbers, magnitudes and shapes,
The amazing order of the universe rises in the mind without sounds and waves.
Thus the mind hears music without any pressure in the air,
Listen to the polyphony of the past, the present and the future – far and near.
Vibrating at points in space and moments in time,
As proportions, order, symmetry, geometry, connectivity, continuity, dimensionality, and topology,
As music of astronomy, astrophysics, and cosmology,
The harmony of the spheres as mathematically ideal,
But not expressible by intervals of harmonic scheme of chromatic order,
Reverberate through the cosmos as a symphony of the eternal accorder.
The perihelia and the aphelia of the planetary revolutions,
The complex motions of the trajectories in evolution,
The arcs traversed in time, the surfaces spanned, and the work done,
Draw in thrilling precision the perfection of the music emanating from the sun.
Geometry of non-Riemannian kind,
Or pre-geometry without differential forms,
Non-descriptive, undefined with coordinate and measure,
Non-physical in relation to the possibility of visual openness and closure,
Discovered as pure subjectivity,
Formed through logical compatibility,
Hypnotize the mind with rhythms emerging from eternity.

The consonance and dissonance of the Pythagorian kind,
In the octave scheme, that the Greeks have defined,
Are the expressions of the pure thoughts reconciled
in the domain of space and time.
Though according to the Euclidean scheme, the planets do not revolve,

*The orbits do not attune with the Pythagorian forms,*
*The music of the ratios, the notes of velocities fall in harmony and sym-*
*metry*
*Where time is entwined on the surfaces of the topological forms;*
*Keeping time in association with space,*
*While space is time and time is enwrapped in space,*
*In wrinkles, rolls, and waves,*
*The music of heaven rises as mind's cosmic blaze.*

*In the music that I hear,*
*I recognize the vibrations from stars,*
*In the forms of the moving spheres, which contain the orbits moving*
*around the globe,*
*I can distinguish the different notes from the strings producing the har-*
*mony of the whole.*
*O Guide!*
*I wish to rise to the domain from where Apollo creates such beauty of the*
*mind from his golden robe.*
*Bring me to the path where the cosmos unfolds...".*

The Guide appeared as a winged Angel and lifted him in the sky in a
journey through the cosmos.

*"In the silently shining, motionless path where all radiance are remain-*
*ing,*
*Where there is no end of the time without beginning,*
*The flowers of fire, the distant lilies, and lotuses of colourful radiance -*
*forming the ethereal petals - have emerged in starry splendour from the*
*points at height,*
*Past and future seem to be woven in the threads of astral light.*
*Undeniable but still unattached to human emotions,*
*Where the rays are renouncing the senses and breaking apart from the*
*carnal world that binds mind in time and causal motion,*
*Like crystals of the heaven emerging from an immense fire emanating*
*forth,*
*The stars form arcs and gates of light in east, west, south and north.*
*In this nothingness - the empty eye, that emulate the world that is beyond*

the world of the living - the sense's tomb,
There are celestial doorways decorated with drapery,
In the curtains embroidered with brightening glimmer of the gem-like
radiant star there are celestial embroidery.
Their zigzag harmony,
Astral polyphony,
Bring to the mind a supernal world's fervent songs.

As the harmonies glide over pulsating light,
Through cracks, that asunder the masks of the hidden mystery  and open
the shore flooded by  the flaming tides,
In fleeting shadows, where the things are happenings without  seeming to
be happening,
Tornadoes, typhoons, cyclones, tempest are summoning the smokes to
erupt, and create tides,
Where the new born stars pulsate,
Beyond the triumphal gates,
Bathing in stupendous light,
The nebulous clouds drawn under and below left and right,
Steer the eyes where the mystery the marvel of the beauty radiates,
And in the mirror of time the innumerable stars the colours of rainbow
reflect.
In the void, where the stars flicker as lifeless gems in communion with a
world that is beyond,
In the domain, where there seems to exist no sorrow or pain,
In a wordless world, that mesmerizes the mortal eyes,
A twinkling festivity rises, lightens, lifts the eddies and halos  and fills the
landscape in a glow from the bottom to the height.

In this unchanging harmony nothing is futile, ephemeral  or frightening,
Though merely an atom in the infinite,
There is no crushing storm, no cloudy torments, no tempest in the mind
that brings suffering, and tear.
In the open eyes, the shining stars reaching to the depth of heaven,
The boundary of the mind seems ineffable and vast.
Where Atlas, the titan, holds heaven on the shoulder beside the garden
of the gods,

*The moments seem not to die,*
*In silence of the starry world, as a petrified figure, he stands in the sky.*
*In this garden trees, flowers, insects, that I know, and those I have never seen,*
*All await to die and be reborn..*
*Bound and finite, carrying forms,*
*They breathe in the fire illumining the celestial garden of the gods.*
*In this cosmic sphere I see Apollo moving in the chariot drawn by the swans,*
*The illusion of purity and beauty of starry maidens wreathed with radiating jewels,*
*Who were not visible to my eyes before.*
*Over illumined clouds rising in the forms of pillars and columns,*
*Above the thunder bearing power of a burning urn,*
*I also see demons, beasts, and birds,*
*That pervade the world,*
*I see smoke and dust that reflect images of innumerable forms.*

*In an inner harmony,*
*In flashes of light I behold the inner union of darkness and light.*
*Here, there are shadows that divide the delusion between that are accessible to light, and which are beyond,*
*Through the webs, where like self-illumined gems, the stars shine in uncountable forms,*
*There seem to exist paths that may lead to an everlasting immortal Home-*
*The land of never-returning,*
*The domain where things, that appear moving, move not,*
*Unperturbed by the motions of the sun and the moon,*
*The luminous chariots of appear ascending, or descending-*
*Though there is no ascending or descending of the gods..."*

While flying through the cosmos the Guide explains the mystery that lies behind the creation of the universe.

*"The universe is not a sphere that expands and contracts like in a stable oscillating state,*
*It has much more complex destiny allotted by fate.*

*Carrying clusters and super-clusters each universe coils and moves away
from its previous space-time state.*
*It dances away from a central attractor in order to return to it as spiral-
ling coil,*
*And falling towards the attractor matter dissipates into void.*
*Thus the universe enfolds towards the attractor,*
*And in turn unfolds as it dances away.*
*As the new universe picks up the spiralling motion,*
*The space-time emerges in opposite direction,*
*And moves in a new space-time different than the old,*
*That has connection with other domains through topological loops I
have already told.*

*It is like a nonlinear dynamics where the space-time are generated anew,*
*In this eternity that never changes, everything constantly renews.*
*There exists nothing that can be called truly fundamental,*
*In the magical dance - universes' eternal hula-hoop,*
*All constants change through the coiling space-time loops.*
*It is a labyrinth so complex that by using the logical process of the math-
ematical kind,*
*It can never be comprehended by the human mind;*
*To formulate it as a set of equations may even be beyond the power of
God,*
*Those who believe that it can be done are ignorant and stubborn arro-
gant lot.*
*You should know that everything that move and change in all universes
are connected and bound in an eternity -*
*The attractor, towards which and away from which the universes fall and
rise,*
*Cannot be understood in its entirety.*
*Each point of space and moment of time exists in eternal past and future
beyond the visible sight,*
*In darkness they are bound in domains of light.*
*Once matter comes into being from the void,*
*The light creates the illusion of space.*
*Mass can be seen as a phenomenon of order and pattern illumined by
rays.*

Once matter moves in the speed of light,
Everything sinks in the infinite void and night:
The space dilates,
Time becomes timeless.
The structure of time appears in consciousness because the senses that
perceive the world are related to the world's material content,
Which are caught in the flux of motions flowing through space-time
curved and bend.
Only when in the consciousness, order and patter, creating the phenom-
enal world dissolve,
The mind is able to see the whole - but it may never this mystery math-
ematically resolve.

What you see as the universe, is the part of the whole connected to your
sight by the rays of light,
More we speed in this height,
The physical time dilates more and the space contracts.
If we move in the speed of light,
You will see the eternal as void and night,
Where there exists no beginning or end, past or future - but only the eyes
staring at the universe kindling the mystics' sights.
Hindus have called the cosmic rhythm of the creation and dissolution-
The dance of Shiva creating the ring of fire inside which
he remains at eternal rest.
Like a dynamic whole without beginning or end,
He is immanent and at the same time everything he transcends.
Like what you see in galaxies,
He rests in earth, air, water and fire as spiralling eddies in streams, vor-
tices and flames,
As the whole and the same.
Turning through himself as the energy that wakes everything to con-
sciousness,
He reverberates from the highest structures to microscopic domain creat-
ing repeated patterns of order in time and space,
In winding paths he forms the world out of chaos as the god who is the
source of all dynamics at rest.
All universes, all manifestations converge on him and diverge from him,

He breathes the world out as the rays from the diamond beam,
And receives in himself all - seen or unseen.
It is possible to attain the consciousness of this still point free from turmoil,
Hindus called it the Diamond Body,
Chinese named it as the pearl of perfection,
That connects to the human consciousness through highest mystic reflections.


Through the expanding spirals through which universes emerge,
And the contracting spirals through which the universes in the void immerse,
A labyrinth penetrates,
That is depicted in all cultures and religions in different forms and shapes.
This labyrinth creates and dissolves, expands and contracts, reveals as well as conceals,
In it consciousness appears as spirit and will.
Often the mystics have represented the spiral as a labyrinth of intricate form,
That curves, bends, as if, depicting the spirit residing in fire, tumults and storms.
This labyrinth you will often find in the ancient world depicted on the tombs,
Invoking the spirit, from which the dead are reborn.
Such labyrinth represents the spiralling windings through space and time
The ordering and the guiding power, which brings all to growth, and returns all to the cosmic brine.
On the heads of many sculptures of Buddha you will see this spiral and labyrinth engraved,
It is the symbol of order and inner tranquillity -
Eternity in ephemerality -The sign of the creative energy, that with its radiant unfolding has brought order from chaos.
It represents the synthesis of Eros and logos.
Through acts of spiritual growth and evolution,
That brings matter's dissolution,
Through this labyrinth passes the path of journey towards enlightenment
The pilgrim's progress to the peak of the labyrinthine hill - life's highest

*attainment.*

*In the Megalithic and the Neolithic world you will find stone  structures
with carved spirals guiding the holy-spirit along the labyrinthine path,
Which lead all creations from the relative and transient state to the tran-
quil sanctuary deep in the heart.*
*In India on talks about the eight-fold stages of the mind winding through
the labyrinthine path,*
*In Babylon it represented the entrails of the demon in the great forest
guarding the labyrinth of death and birth.*
*This spiral labyrinth, where as the divine and the mortal two parts of
Gilgamesh met,*
*Is the symbol of a union between time and eternity,*
*The finite and the infinity,*
*The male and the female,*
*Yang and Yin -*
*Storm and tranquillity.*
*From the tiniest ephemeral matter to the highest forms this labyrinth
passes,*
*Here, all beings are engaged in a battle with their other halves,*
*And strive for union with the Divine source of compassion and love...".*

Tathagata being enlightened about the creation of the universe felt
compassion and love for life on Earth:

*"O Guide! There seems nothing to seek beyond,*
*All that outstretch in time and space, that is nothing and still moving for
aeons,*
*Which have enwrapped the world beyond which there is nothing greater
to find,*
*Are nothing else than the illusion of the mind.*
*In this labyrinthine path, where in the shinning corner of the heart,*
*Love and beauty never departs,*
*Beyond the moon, the sun and the stars the unknown and the unfathom-
able as a luminous ball revolves,*
*In a divine loneliness I see the whole cosmos evolves.*

*O Guide!*

*Everything feels strange, appears hidden,*
*Everything seems chance ridden,*
*Not determinable but still determined by reason.*
*All that once appeared straight and true,*
*Seem complex, imaginary, unreal, illusory and untrue.*
*O Guide! Riding upon your luminous wing,*
*I have seen this cosmic world in dance and swing;*
*Like sitting upon a floating island I have gone far*
*To discover that I am one with stars.*
*This stillness around that never speaks,*
*Whispers in words that enter this world like lightening blitz.*

*O Guide! This silence and solitude seem to be charged with words,*
*That no speech can grasp,*
*The words that I have heard on the earth,*
*Express stillness of silence where everything remains unheard.*
*You have brought me aloft from the forest path,*
*To listen to the music of the stars,*
*Now my heart wants to hear no more,*
*All I want is to merge with the silence of this cosmic dark.*
*My thirst and hunger for knowledge, had brought me to the watery brim,*
*Where, like Tantalus, I once stood as the eternal victim.*

*O Guide! I do not wish to attain any further height,*
*I do not want to know any more- I have seen enough during this flight.*
*As a half- mortal and half- god I have risen above the mortal land,*
*Towards the shore where stars appear as sand;*
*Where darkness like Harpies sing the immortal songs,*
*I fly on and on...*

*O Guide! You have taken away the illusions from my eyes with the celes-*
*tial flame,*
*And shown me the beauty of the supernatural dame.*
*You have brought me beyond the sense's grasp,*
*Where Isthar holds her golden cup;*
*Amidst the clouds of flames,*
*In the winding streams of the fiery fuming lanes,*

*You have shown celestial scene amidst starry crags, creeks, dunes and planes.*
*I desire no glory on earth,*
*No sorrow lingers any more in my heart;*
*With the strength of wisdom you have filled my mind's emptiness,*
*And elevated me above sorrow and happiness;*
*Here there is nothing to learn except the teachings of love,*
*More I have grasped, more I have become one with the stellar dust,*
*More I have felt my hunger and thirst,*
*More you have made me one with the void where galaxies fly from the centre where the universes end and start.*

*O Guide! The radiant light!*
*Who brings the knowledge of heaven to man from cosmic height,*
*I hail thee!*
*O glorious Angel!*
*You are the power of the inner sight.*
*Bring me down to the world, where man wanders bewildered in the forest path,*
*Where the summer light ripens the fruits,*
*The earthly love merrily sails in breeze through forest and wood,*
*Let me descend to the world that shines as a blue sphere of love,*
*Through the blazing clouds and azure waves,*
*Let me go down to bring to mankind the Divine rays.*
*Bring me down on the land washed by water and breeze,*
*Where beauty of life springs from seeds,*
*Where birds sing and songs overwhelm all speech,*
*Where tongues tremble as sounds of magic,*
*Where rugged rocks, wind torn reefs sink deep,*
*Like the dragon, the storm clouds gather on the mountain tops before they take abysmal leaps,*
*Bring me in the world "there" beneath.*

*O Guide! In purest love for all that exist,*
*Let me descend through the labyrinth without entrance or exit.*
*O winged soul! Where man is destined to suffer in the mortal world's eternal story,*

*In selfless love let me plunge in the earth's fire without seeking joy or glory.*
*In love for life let us leave this lonely sphere,*
*And come down among mankind by swinging around the spiralling stairs.*
*Where amidst poverty, dirt, misery and happiness,*
*Man is bound in punishment in a world where thunders and storms rage in lightening madness,*
*The suffers in the village encounter the danger of going-across,*
*Let us start our down-going where man is crucified on the cross as the Son of God.*

*Let us return the way Zarathustra had gone,*
*And trace by the incandescent path above the sun.*
*In the eternally imperfect world that is driven by contradictions,*
*Let me seek in human beings my own perfection;*
*Let me descend to rise above myself as a brighter flame,*
*Let me go below the sky in order to rise above, and remain one with the transcendental flame.*
*Lower me down from this emptiness,*
*From this sphere above joy and happiness;*
*Bring me back to the corporal state where life is bound in joy and pain;*
*Where the power of gravity imparts strain;*
*Accompany me through earthly heaven and hell as my guide and a friend…".*

This journey had transformed me into a new man bringing an end to my scientific career. The description of the mystery behind the creation of the universe given by the Angel brought my research activities to a full stop. Though the creation story had no empirical basis, the way my mind was besieged by the supernatural presence convinced me that the theory of the Big-bang must be wrong. I believed in the revelation by the Angel than the scientific theories being discussed by the researchers at the European Centre for Nuclear Research (CERN), which was only a short drive from this apartment where I was writing about Heaven. A power unconceivable and unknowable to human mind was breaking through the rational barriers and lifting me to a consciousness that pervaded the entire cosmos.

People around me wondered why I, who was so obsessed about the great mystery of the cosmos, did not make use of the opportunity to live in Geneva in interacting with the scientists at CERN? Though I had been at CERN several times earlier as a young scientist, in all those four years, when we lived in Geneva after Ånun's death, I did not visit CERN even once. I was completely possessed by the phenomena of the other world from where, I believed, I was receiving knowledge, wisdom and vision of the universe without using the formulas and equations and crunching data in sophisticated super computers at the research centre.

When people asked what I was doing, I could not tell them about the strange world that had possessed my mind. So they never understood why I was isolating myself and not interacting with any scientific community anymore. No one had any clue about the existence of the Time Hall where I was wandering with my Guide who was lifting my consciousness through different spheres to connect it to the Great Cosmic consciousness.

Truly there was no other character in this journey, except myself. It was a story of a man of flesh and blood who had lost his identity as a man of flesh and blood and searching an identity in the other world. I was writing about the hidden world from where passions, desires, feeling and emotions of all human beings had risen to create the universal destiny of human life caught in the tumultuous journeys along the shores of sexuality, seduction, power, love, dream, illusion, hallucination on one side and desire to escape beyond the boundaries of all sufferings and seek peace in the company of God in the other world. I was not writing about any individual man, or woman imprisoned in their individual desire, suffering or joy, but about the universal man, who takes individual identities shaped by different social, cultural and historic contexts.

It was a story of the archetypal woman and man who lived and enacted the drama of life and death. Through me and my life's passions and desires driven by ambivalence, conflict, contradictions and confusion I was trying to gaze at the entire arena of human activities involving all dimensions of the mind. In this Time Hall I was watching the innumerable images of the same being emerging as different characters. These characters were reflections of Tathagata in innumerable mirrors swirling around in the perceptive world moving with time.

# Chapter 4
# CHRIST-MAN RETURNING ?

I n the Time Hall I was moving in an abstract, virtual, imaginary space penetrating the real world. The story was appearing in my consciousness as collections of thoughts and words from a world which is difficult to comprehend. Without any auditory or visual counterparts, the characters, events, scenes were appearing as a collection of abstract thoughts carried by associations with known images of the real world. These collections of symbols and words were not triggered by the senses connected to the external world. These were experiences outside the domain of the senses that cannot be measured with apparatuses and detected by electronic circuits that have a causal behaviuor very different from the "spiritual facts" that involve no physical signals but can interact with the material world forming the mental state that I was experiencing.

"This is purely subjective and not verifiable by anyone else but you. Why should anyone have any faith in the assertion you are making that they are spiritual facts", analytical philosophers and positivists, who embrace empiricist principles as the foundation of human knowledge, would immediately defy such experiences as nonsense. "If we cannot have any empirical basis for the understanding God and he is incomprehensible by human knowledge, then such being has no significance and meaning to us. God is only a complex idea framed by assembling several domains of ideas appearing in our own mind? Aren't divine attributes conceived in terms of human attributes magnified in an imaginary scale? " According to the renowned English empiricist philosopher David Hume all ideas are derived from sense impressions. It is not possible to think about anything which we have not perceived, or felt in the mind. Ideas which cannot leave impressions verifiable by sense perceptions and our mental abilities have no meaning. The idea of God, as an infinitely intelligent and wise Being, arises from reflecting on the operations of our own mind, augmenting, without limit, those qualities we aspire in us as human. "If God is so remote and incomprehensible that we cannot have any relevant impression that can serve to make an idea of him in the human mind, then he must be meaningless." He will argue.

*"Anyway what do you mean when you talk about Angel and God?*

*If you mean that they are no physical beings but mental experiences appearing in your mind creating awe and wonder of the mystery of the universe and life, it may make some sense.*

*However, are your experiences the same as the other mystics and religious people have experienced? How can one verify that they are similar when we see such a variety of religious ideas and experiences that are incompatible with each other? There must have a way to check if one is a religious fraud or not. What Bible says is very different from what Krishna or Buddha has said. So where should one find one's foundation of belief in God?*

*You make a claim that your experience has a profound impact in your life, which have disabled you to act as a normal human being. But why should it necessarily mean that it has any divine connection? Don't you believe that strange hallucinatory experiences resembling something like yours can be generated by the use of drugs?*

*So what would persuade a skeptic to believe in any supernatural existence?"*

*"Do you claim that we cannot describe religions or anything religious using scientific, rational language because such experience is not based in empirically verifiable facts, which is the basis of science? Will you subscribe to the idea that rational language is not only inadequate for*

*describing the religious experience, but also irrelevant to the entire discussion of spirituality as Rudolf Otto claims in his book "The Idea of the Holly"?*

*If the religious claims have to be accepted, it must be proven by science. Scientific methods have proven to be the best way of acquiring knowledge about the world, because by this way one can falsify assertions. If religious claims cannot be falsified what should be the standard of judging such knowledge?*

*Will you claim that God has nothing to do with the material world and heaven occupies a realm outside the realm of the human experiences? Do we live in two realities: One accessible to rational mind and the other to the irrational intuitions and feelings, which do not merely transcend reason, but rises above it? "*

The empiricists a la Locke, Berkley, Hume and the analytical philosophers a la Russell and Wittgenstein and the logical positivists a la Ayer and Popper would call such experience nonsense or meaningless. Their experiences seemed not to have crossed the boundary of the world perceived by the senses and logical framework of the mind that affirm and falsify in a structured mode conceived through a "useful" language. They would argue that the experience I refer to are not known entities like physical objects or mathematical relations that can be connected through logical propositions that are meaningful. By meaning they mean verifiable. By verifiable they would resort to instruments and senses and reduce the world to the experiences with which most human beings are easily acquainted and thus simplify the existence to the crudest material level once again. They are "honestly" concerned about finding out all that there is, on the hypothesis that there is nothing but matter and no method is true than the methods of the physical science and every other proposition are redundant and false beliefs except the materialistic beliefs that they adhere to. "For the sake of truth" they adopt logical constructions that can falsify everything else than what can be arrived by scientific method, and proof the truthfulness of the conclusions and inferences they wish to draw with their brilliant logical methods, that forever remain bound to the experiences of the material world and the instruments of the senses!

They would call these experiences of a greater mind driving the process of my writing non-demonstrable. They would also argue that it does not belong to any logical truth that will be able to produce some operational certainty by crunching out numbers as proof that can be subjected to falsification by other facts operational in other environments of the scientific world. According to these "sincere "minds among the modern philosophers, the language has to be purified and cleansed of the accidental accretions of the thoughts that lead the language into unwarranted metaphysical domains that make no sense in terms of verifiable experiences.

Wittgenstein will say that silence is the only proper response. Matter concerning religion, aesthetics and questions of the meaning of life cannot be formulated in languages. The attempts to say anything about such themes will not only be against logic of what language is capable of saying and turn into a futile babble of words. The attempt to say something about something that is beyond language is waste of time and will corrupt the very profundity of the subject that one wishes to speak about. The words are inadequate in describing the things that matter most for human beings i.e. to seek knowledge of the profound aspects of the human existence. The attempts to speak about them can only be fruitless.

For him language has this limitation because it represents totality of propositions that can determined to be either true or false. All that can convey an understandable meaning can be expressed through such propositions. If one expresses oneself in propositions that do not convey meaning one only conveys nonsense. He establishes the necessary and sufficient conditions in a linguistic expression by virtue of which the propositions can be meaningful. He establishes this meaning by investigating how propositions acquire meanings. For him there is only one way all languages are meaningful and this lies in the deep structure of the language that bears certain relation to the world. These essentials conditions in the meaningful language will display the essential nature of the reality in which the language is embedded. The logically minimal conditions for having a meaningful descriptive language reveal the "substance" of the world in which language exists. Thus there

124

exists correspondence between language and the world and language gets its meaning in virtue of its relation to the structure of the world. A language that does not bear this relational structure of the world is meaningless.

For Wittgenstein meaning of a word corresponds to the object for which it stands. The world is made of such objects and the relations among objects form facts of the world. Propositions describe facts by describing how the objects in the world relate to each other. And these propositions can be either true or false depending on if the relation expressed in the language correspond with the objects of the world they describe or not. And these facts of the world are independent of thoughts. The words at the deepest level should involve real names or simple signs referring to atomic parts that are logically irreducible into smaller parts in order that the expressions won't run the risk of being meaningless. These ultimate constituents must exist if the world exists at all. And these propositions involving the logically indestructible, permanent and unchanging objects must bear sense that will mirror the structure of the world. The truth of such most fundamental irreducible propositions is independent of other elementary propositions and these atomic objects enter into combination of the other atomic objects to form a state of affairs of facts. The possible ways they can enter into combinations fix the form of such objects. The sum of the possible ways describes the state of affairs. In this state of affair such an object entangled in the affair constitutes an element of the reality.

There exists a timeless order of the possible states of affairs in which the objects can enter. Thus it entangles all other objects and possibilities. The totality of the existent and the nonexistent possible states of affairs is the totality of the possible arrangements or the whole logical space. A meaningful proposition has a sense in virtue of the ability to describe the state of affairs of the whole logical space. But the names of the objects have no sense because they are mere labels and labels say nothing about the world. However propositions have sense because they describe the facts. The world is the totality of the states of affairs as described by elementary propositions. The arrangements of the names with the propositions, if true, reflect logical isomorphism between the language and the world and involves mapping of the world into words. It brings one to one correspondence between the linguistic picture of the world and the elements of the state of affairs that they represent. Thoughts, for Wittgenstein, are a proposition, constituted of psychical elements representing the facts of the world.

Since language reflects facts and gets its meaning from the names of objects that refer to something in the world, it does not have the capacity to say anything about matters outside the world of facts related to objects. Therefore although religion and the meaning of life may manifest in our mind we cannot say anything about them and make any sense of them in a language. For him the language has only the capacity to talk about the factual natural science and what this language can really do is to say things about the structure of all fact-stating which are devoid of any fact of the world. Unlike Russell, who associated with the names the bundle of the present content of the sense experiences, for Wittgenstein one can say nothing about the enduring, unchanging atomic objects. To say anything about them would make them describable and reducible to even simpler structures, that would be a contradiction with the most fundamental proposition of his philosophy.

In order to get rid of the metaphysics these are attempts to justify ones' believes by ad hoc conjectures about what the world is without any deeper justification than believing that world is what is described by the physical science. They seem to make this hypothesis their primary spring board to discover truth and argue that all meaningful propositions should be analytical or describe experiences that are empirically verifiable. Any proposition concerning the nature of the reality would be a factual scientific and common-sense proposition whose truth or falsity could be established only by the tests of experience that are meaningful to physical science, that in turn are formulated on the basis of a scientific theory.

After circling around the visionary Hell, as described in Dante's "Divine Comedy", Tathagata returned and entered in a city in modern time, where the philosophers argued that spiritual and religious statements or any statement expressing similar ideas are not factual synthetic statements but expressions of emotions and feelings depicting the irrational behaviour of man. For them, such statements even do not describe the fact that there is a subjective psychological state which constitutes these feelings that refers to the spiritual realms.

Its inhabitants had amassed weapons of immense destructive power. They have risen against Heaven and were trying to free the dwellers of the city from the fears of any Divine power. Here Tathagata saw women and men worshipping the Devil and his followers. A superman had risen to free mankind from the hallucinatory realms created by religious feelings and ideas.

*"Here the world was conceived as mechanical. The concept of the reality was derived from the inter-relationships of the things that appeared and were subjected to comprehension by the experimental methods of permitting concepts that fell within one's conceptual framework and the categories of logic that contradicted and repudiated the validity of truth unless they fitted with the causality of the things. The world was seen from outside, described and defined by experimental methods that recognized nothing but the relationships of matter in space and time. The will was hypothesized as the procreation of matter and a mechanical intelligence that is antecedent to the functioning of the will. It was called clarity of thoughts by which man wished to dethrone God.*

*They took world's command, played dangerous games of law of chance, made discoveries that removed the limitations of the perceptions, brought the remote parts to nearness, with prodigal cleverness liberated man from the boundaries of seeing and hearing. They freed man from feeling pity in accepting the higher order of things and brought an awareness of great independence. They extended the frontiers of freedom outward in the material world while the boundaries of the inner world shrank. The possibilities to explore beyond the realm of matter - the vast domain of experience of the human souls - were narrowed down with the progress that they called enlightenment. It was the freedom from the slavery to God and an awakening against religion, a voluntary submission to the Devil, who wished to make man more powerful than the angels of God.*

*All moralities were addressed with aversion to divinity. All behaviors were prescribed as brave and courageous that destroyed emotions*

*through analysis of science and vivisections of the mind. The spiritual-*
*ity, and symbolisms were discredited as the timidity of the mediocre and*
*the weakness of the hearts. They believed that the paths to seek truth and*
*freedom rested in all permissibility of glories that heighten man to cul-*
*tivate oneself. In painfully denying of everything except science and the*
*judgments of intellects, that beget no distrust in the reality of the world as*
*made of material dust, there was an attempt to triumph against heaven.*
*The man conceived himself as object - an object of himself, mirroring no*
*soul, but gazing at itself in the apparatuses. His existence was nothing*
*but an appearance produced by random accidents and chance. They af-*
*firmed the freedom of the human will that as a machine that can take self*
*command. As industrious scholars they wished to free humanity from*
*the naivety and stupidity of the people still seeking religious paths. They*
*were the bearers of the new will of man."*

It was a city drowned in technological innovations, where people wandered in virtual spheres. They had created this city which resembled
ore like the city of Maya (Illusion) where people communicated with
each other at vast distances and fulfilled their needs of love and pleasure by using technological means. They believed in a mechanical world
that an following natural laws and chance, where competitions and lib-
erty to act according to one's free will were higher than anything other
goal.

While wandering in this city he heard the sermon of the Chtrist-Man
describing the nature of the spiritual being who had returned to life
bringing messages from God:

*"In the time before the beginning or the beginning before the time I*
*knew not myself. There were no myriads of things, no beings, no heaven*
*and earth but only a sea that I shall talk about. There did not exist light,*
*gravity, directions or percepts. In that void and nothingness there existed*
*nothing that could be associated with right or wrong. Nothing was deep;*
*nothing was high. There were no sun or moon, no life and death, no*
*transformation of the shapes that bring association of time and space.*
*The life was not an illusion because the illusion is something that the ma-*
*terial world generates. It was not dream because dreams are governed by*

the intellects and percepts. It was a realm of the limitless.

I do not know how I shall describe. It is similar to the emptiness that penetrates the mind. It is an awareness of pure light that does not associate itself with the rooms or things or the time. It is boundless and massless, substanceless something that resides within itself. It is always there with ultimate fullness. Invariable, without end and beginning, containing the future in the past it is a world about which it is difficult to form clear understandings and concepts. Everywhere pervading but nowhere scattering the light or projecting itself on objects, it is the void preserving the structure of the universe in emptiness.

In complete harmony with itself, as a whole, without form, without any definition that can identify it with anything else but the being of the emptiness where rests all souls, it is the formless sea of the void that all relationships of the cosmos uphold. It is very difficult to comprehend because knowledge depends on something that it contradicts, opposes and annihilates before it becomes knowledge of things. Cause, causality, end, beginning, nothing, something, the attributes and essences of beings, man, God, nature's hidden marvels, the rivers and streams where the motions assimilate the myriads of ways, appearances and disappearances, eternity and ephemeral evidence of transformations and change that depend on each other and strive to go across, things seen with the clarity of the lights and things far beyond, all sorts of tranquillity and turmoil of the matter and mind exist as non-existence or existence in oneness in this whole.

I am a wanderer who has risen from this void beyond time and space. I am beyond and within the boundaries that define the qualities of matter and the domain of intelligence and awareness that extend within and outside the myriads of things. I have risen from the unaffected and motionless world as a stranger to myself. Assuming form in the world I am the incarnation of the being who has assumed consciousness though he is neither substance, consciousness or thought. I am the ultimate man who has sprung from the depth of the mystery that no one will ever understand.

Do not think of me as the man who is framed in flesh and blood. Though I stand in physical form I am a perplexing phenomena, a miracle that you need to understand. Though you see me in body I am empty, infinite and one with the great ocean. I have come here to reveal to you *the endlessness of the being, the ultimate knowledge about the emptiness from which I come and to which I shall return. Although I see, hear and breathe know me as the ultimate man, the mirror in which all human beings may see himself and herself in an incarnation that can never be fully known or seen. I know it will cause confusion when you see me . But do not draw any conclusion about me because I am beyond all conclusions and judgments of the human minds.*

*The man, whom you see, who speaks about the unspeakable, carrying humanness who disguises himself with all human characteristics, beyond his mask he is the deep ocean - all streams merge in him. You may ask why is he here? Why does he masquerade? Why his eyes and ears are no more different than mine? Why does he feel pain, grief, trembling in the heart as all others who are alive and bound in the senses' chains? Do not be confused. Know that as the man he realizes his sacrifice. He sacrifices himself in suffering and pain for the sake of the humanity. He is above all sages and all "superior men". All must sacrifice themselves as man life after life before they can be one with Him.*

*I know it is hard to understand what I am saying. I am the man whom you can never fully know. From the weakest to the strongest, from the tiniest to the highest I am present. I am identical to and different from all. I exist in all ages. I operate in errors, in free spirit, in impassive souls, in the myriads of will in turbid chaos. I am also in the minds of the sages who have their minds in full contemplative control. However I appear to be separate from myself when I reveal myself in form. I am the wanderer who has risen from the boundless ocean and beyond the characteristics of anything that will make me a character who can be understood and known.*

*You may wonder why am I wandering? Where had I been? Where from have I come to spread the teaching of the ultimate man? I have already told you about the ocean from where I come. It is not an ocean you can measure or fathom with the senses or the mind. It is the dwelling of the light, the being who is never born. But how am I manifest then? How do I preserve body and at the same time remain bodiless? How am I revealed in the world when my existence can never be truly revealed ? It is a mystery that is truly difficult to comprehend. First of all know that I am not what you think I am. Then realize that I am not one. I am infinitely many in harmony with the whole. In myriads of existence where things* manifest, I am not bound although through everything I penetrate. Once things form through appearances I am visible as something that appears by negating the knowledge of the existence that I am. There is no way of avoiding this contradiction in which all existence are bound with the great mind from which I come. I am not in the body where, you may believe, I reside. Beyond this body I have a different body in the realm of God. It is the body of the ultimate man. It is a mystery that is beyond the capacity of any language to explain. By the will of God this body is able to relate itself to the physical form floating amidst myriads of things moving by cause or chance. This relation is beyond comprehension of anyone. You may ask why do you see the ultimate man as a man speaking to you? If he is multiple and infinite how does he appear as bodily separate and distinct from others as an individual one? Know that I do not exist in one plane or in a particular level of existence or awareness. My existence is spread in many layers, many spheres, in realms after realms, in dimensions inside dimensions that are difficult to fathom with the limited awareness that man possess in the awaken state. This infinitely complex domain can be subjected to vision and awareness through a material body in the physical plane. However every awareness is qualified by the nature of the body to which it relates. Unless the ultimate man relates Himself to a body of an individual man, it will not be possible to bring forth concepts that may appear meaningful to man. The great mind, from which I arise, has therefore related Itself through a body to bring forth these messages to man.

The physical characteristic of this man is no different from you all. The mental realms that are related to the problems of the survival and needs are also the same like yours. But there exist innumerable realms of existence to which the body of the ultimate man is able to relate. He can move to the realm of the time and space in the domain of the inert matter as well as rise to the realm where he is the light of God. Know that I am the ultimate man. I have come to tell you about my wandering, my sacrifice, my suffering, my crucifixion in life.

Try to understand what I say and for the liberation of mankind come with me to sacrifice yourself in the life's pyre in fire and blaze. With your sacrifice you will rise to the great mind from where I come. Sacrifice the way I have done as a wanderer wanderings from the divine domain to the sense-bound life in sufferings and blaze. Understand the meaning of

*the crucifixion of the divine in the tree of life - the cross, with four sea-
sonal directions upholding the unsurpassable destiny of life and death
- and follow me to sacrifice to bring forward the awareness about the
path of salvation from the abyss bound in life and matter- bound human
fate. I am the ultimate man who shines upon all human beings as stars
and also follow them to the abysmal dark. Hear about my journey how
I have crossed the gulf, passed the hidden islands of passions of the heart
and reached the forest path, seen myself in the lake of Eros as Bodhisattva who is searching in himself the great mind in the mirror of the illusory world, and watching his life in the blindness of the manifold world,
through multiple of life striving to realize the freedom of the will and the
union with the great compassion and love. Hear about the path of reason, knowledge of the self- gained through the knowledge of the chaos,
and the dance and harmony of the cosmos strewn with the stars. Listen
about the Minotaur destroyed, the freedom from destiny, the light of the
illumined mind trying to rise to God. Hear about the will, the profound
contemplation of the mind and the self-command, the journey towards
the self, the man of flesh and blood gradually becoming one with the ultimate self. Listen how the ultimate man, as a stranger to himself, sprung
from the great ocean, have carried the ashes of the pyre in his wandering
towards the summit of the unmoved mountain, as a tormented man of
flesh and blood has striven to unite with the tranquil ocean from which
he has come. I have come to tell you about the vision of this ultimate
man: The songs of the mountain, the fountains of love, the music of
the divine drawing man towards the eternal path, the beauty rising, the
light above the great sea before the eyes, the trembling mirror of the sky
near the summit, and how I have felt seeing the abyss underneath full of
pain, suffering and darkness in the valley through which the wanderers
were still trying to pass. Hear from the ultimate man about the illumination before the summit, while the guiding spirit had disappeared, the
hail of light, and the voice rising from the sea had called me to repeat the
journey once again. I want to tell you about the cataclysms, volcanoes,
eruptions and the premonitions of the destructions to come after which
the valleys covered with ashes will turn into flowering valleys of great
beauty no one has seen before. This is a sacrifice for the new will, new life
springing from the sea from which I come. Hear about the sacrifice of the
ultimate man in down-going to the abysmal suffering of the life on Earth*

in love for mankind to guide the wanderers in the valley to the mountain path. Hear me and try to understand what I am saying and follow me to the down-going for the sake of the suffering man.

During this wandering once more I was awaken in the village beside the sea. It was a shore where the suffering man dwelt. In the poverty of knowledge, that they called happiness, they lived in miserable ease without caring for heaven and hell. I had returned in the village in search of the spirit whose company I had lost in the mountain path and who had told me to go to the graveyard in the abysmal valley where he would resurrect to show man the eternal path. It was not any dream or a fiction. There seemed to exist an eternal purpose in this suffering . In contradictions, confusions, willing, doubting, trying to free oneself from the misery of the life and the dismal illusion of the pain and joy of the unenlightened minds, there were wars, sorrows, contempt and despises. In follies man sought pleasure; in willing to perish in passions man hailed the flames and madness by willing to win freedom for oneself by destroying others and doing to others great harms. The life was a suffering where every one was a prey of another. There the teachings of virtues were foolishness. Everybody devoted maximum efforts to win advantage that they hoped will secure them maximum span of life. None wanted to die. They wished life could be eternal. With hatred, envy, falsification, lie, and always looking for enemies everywhere they wanted victory and triumph over everybody. The life revolved without values. Nothingness, emptiness and solitude flew as poisonous flies in the market place where the life was a trade of flesh and blood, a hellish cross-road of travellers who did not give a damn about who lived or died. They practiced revenge, preached inequality of different races and men, soured the souls with self-conceits, worshiped fearlessness, violence and hate, and like solitary seafarers in faithlessness sailed to fetch pleasures against warnings and adverse signs of fate.

In this island there was a forest. In this forest, in front of the multifold mirror I had fallen asleep. In images and flying bits of illusions, that make the world, I had seen myself awake as many human beings in search of paths outside the forest and beyond the river and the lake. Through this inner domain I had risen in the celestial world and in love of knowledge aroused the free spirit of reason. I had seen man struggling with himself in search of truth, in dangerous paths seeking answers that

*will eliminate the role of destiny and fate. Like philosophers and mar-*
*tyrs, who had sacrificed their lives for the sake of truth, I had seen man*
*questioning, doubting, in a protracted battle with themselves, in belief*
*and non-belief, searching a proof of something that can not be proved.*
*They were trying to overcome themselves by throwing away beliefs and*
*faiths in predestination. By cruel ventures, which bind man in concepts*
*that are falsely conceived, distrusting everything and screening every-*
*thing that could not be related to the causal links, and the logic sprung*
*thereof, in tortuous ways they were turned against the existence of the*
*Self. For them there were nothing beyond the domain of matter and the*
*laws of science defined in time and space. With suppositions, hypothesis,*
*axioms, introspections, vacillations, and constant refinements of the logi-*
*cal methods of interpretation, inversions, introversions and narrowing*
*the erroneous consequences of the conditioned reflections, they blinded*
*themselves deliberately in their ventures of finding the right conclusions.*
*Everything were judged with suspicion. Precisely where they understood*
*nothing they reduced the understanding as the science of things - to get*
*rid of the divinity and heighten the man as the courageous Godless being.*

*You may wonder why did I wander lonely through the streets in this*
*world of the irreligious men? When they shouted God is dead, what did*
*I think? When the city slept in the darkness, the souls felt comforted with*
*the polluted river, when man was tied with a rope in a dangerous path*
*with the superman crossing the gulf as an animal shuddering in fear and*
*at the same time feeling the excitement of the adventure, danger and*
*happiness of freedom of will, you may ask what did I say, what knowl-*
*edge and awareness had it brought, how did I talk about virtue to these*
*dangerous men? How did I myself go across?*

*Know that as the enlightened man I love all. I sacrifice myself for love*
*of mankind in order to lift them from the darkness and downfall. When*
*they play with dice, ask no one any favour but as free spirit seek no chas-*
*tity but pain, in downfall, losing and perishing seek freedom's reward and*
*gain, as the ultimate man I do not look at them with contempt or dis-*
*dain. All human beings are born with the chaos of the will that unless*
*illumined by the knowledge of the self may lead man astray. I had told*
*them about the dancing stars, the rhythms and music of the universe*
*and the chaos that brings everywhere the whirling disturbances trying to*
*shatter everything apart. I had talked about the love and the compassion*

*that flow in and from the sea where the unmoved moves and from which they bring forth the motions of matter and souls burning as stars and the ethereal bodies flying under the lights descending on the world. As you may understand they did not understand, could not always follow what I said. In the market place as faithless men they had listened and shouted again and again, "We do not believe what you say. We know long ago God is dead. Go away. There are many among us who feel hatred for you. We love this place where God is dead. We do not need to hear from any illumined man. For us there exists no ultimate man higher than us. With God he too is dead."*

*You may wonder why did not I abandon them and go away? Why my heart still felt a torrent of love in the valley of suffering and grief? Know that as the enlightened man rising from the sea I am a tumbling cascade of love that seeks to plunge through the impassable paths. I always will to come where there is darkness and the shadow. Where sorrow and sufferings clog all paths I come trilling as the sounds carrying the light of love. Great love does not seek revenge or feel pity and shame. Nothing can humiliate the love that does not look with pity to anyone, to whom all are equal and same. It knows only the path of forgiveness. When they tried to drive me away, I trembled in the mirror of the heart as the burning flame living for eternity touching the sunlight and the shadows of the abyss truly seeking suffering in sacrifice for the redemption of man. It is truly difficult to understand this love of the illumined man. Journeymen follow me to sacrifice. You may be able to understand it at the end. This love does not go weary, never goes blind, or never delights itself in punishment of the spirits, who seek freedom and strive to know themselves. Most paths of life are treacherous and difficult to go across as I have already said. In every step there are trials and tastes. Believing or not believing in God are not really so important. They are only different ways. As God can never be understood the belief in the divinity without comprehending reality and attaining the capacity of the mind to penetrate in the conscious way the multi-fold planes in which existence is entangled or, on the other way, trying to comprehend reality by reducing existence to the space-time domain without knowing that reality of the multifold way and infinite domain of the mind are equally dangerous and full of errors. However for man there is no other way of knowing but through erring in life. All knowledge must proceed through errors by eliminating relations that seem false and incompatible with conditions and concepts of life. Thus knowledge of the nature of life and things are essentially the knowledge of experiences and concepts that the life or things seem to be not. There is no way of knowing the so called things-in-themselves as they are. Likewise there is no one way to free oneself from the multidimensional web where every life is entangled and from where there is no one identity of man with which man can ever escape or enter the gate of heaven or hell. All human beings are in a journey together in this multifold world as one being searching to return home from where they have come. In erring one knows what one is not and thus becomes aware of one's own nature through negations and as someone who he might possibly be. There are infinite possibilities of this knowledge and inexhaustible paths of approaching the Self. Most paths are torn with contradictions and sufferings because this is the true way to know and become aware of oneself. Know yourself as the journey man and sacrifice your life for the liberation of man. Be aware of the wholeness and the innumerable paths in which all life are entangled and bound. There is nothing that can be called individual salvation. When true reality of the existence lies in the spirit, who is whole, you should know that individual salvation is only an illusion of the mind. Do not wander alone in the street in search of freedom that brings separation from the whole, creates deepest solitude and may result in self-destruction. Move forward and come home. I know it is not easy to understand. But follow me. You may comprehend this teaching at the end.*

*You may have heard from the madman shouting on the other end of the market place about the coming of God and the world's doom. But hear from the ultimate man the mystery that is much more complex and profound. God is dead and alive. He is both. He neither comes or goes, nor does He send the sinners to damnation or resurrects the chosen souls who have received His grace. He is the light and shadow, united in both. However, He is neither darkness or light, nor matter, spirit or ghost. This concept is very difficult. I do not know how shall I rightly explain. He does not appear as any particular person but is immanent in all. He sends His illuminations to the darkened minds through the ultimate man, who is neither a person, nor a spirit but a mysterious creation. This ultimate man is similar to and at the same time different from all. He receives energy from the profound source of knowledge where there is no concept of* moving further or crossing any realm or going beyond.

I know that you will not understand but believe what I have said about my nature before. You may know me better if you follow me and make the journey. You certainly wonder about the journey after I had fallen in sleep in the mirror, that was the river in me. By now, you probably understand that I talk in allegories and cryptic language in order to bypass the concepts that may distort the things that I wish to explain and which are very strange to be grasped by using the much used concepts. Languages distort the world and reflect the concepts and believes that man have constructed on the basis of the experiences that are simple to communicate by negating the world as they are. Therefore I distort the language in order to bypass the concepts that man are quick to define before I may have them defined. In this deliberation logic has its place when it self-contradicts and illumines through negations of what is said.

You may wonder after leaving the market place, which path did I choose? I cannot tell you exactly the way you may like to conceive. As said He neither is and is not. On one side of the river He is and other side He is not. On the banks of the river He is immanent as existent and non-existent as Bodhisattva, who is coming and going in the wheel. I went downward and went across the market place towards the path where I joined my companion, whom I had left in the forest. I am not the one as you may like to believe I am, as I have said before. I could move both ways at the same moment - one inside the realm of time and space and the other moving across the world towards the mountain way. If you follow me in this journey you may gradually understand what I am saying. Do not jump to the conclusion that I had left for the mountains leaving the wanderers in the market place. At the end they followed the man, who immerged from me, to the sacrifice in the village and I followed Him towards the illumined way.

You may be curious to know what did I see on the mountain? As I said I did not go alone. As I woke from the sleep I saw in front of me a glaring light on the mirror, whom I could easily recognize as the divine poet, who was the guiding light in the forest, where I was following Him as a shadow. I had followed Him as the dual united as one moving through the labyrinthine web. He had told me that I was the ultimate man born from the sea destined to move to the mountain way, I must climb higher to the mountain top to merge fully with Him and ascend the stairs of *rainbows before I would be able to visualize His full splendour as the light of illumination. On this height all dualities would dissolve and from the summit nothing would return except the energy that can communicate with the man moving in the ultimate way.*

*As I moved higher my heart trembled in love as the sparkling lights in the golden glitters of the rays descending on the valley underneath. " Thou shall choose my path. Thou shall be the holiest of man", I heard a "voice". The "voice" reverberated in the mountain landscape. " Thou spirit is myself. Thou journey is my journey. Thou fire and ashes are the fire and ashes from the flames that I ignite. Thou body is illusion. Thou soul is created for liberation. See thyself as myself and behold in this mountain landscape how lights are vibrating in love and trepidation. Purify yourself in this godly illumination", I heard the voice vibrating from mountains to mountains and echoing time and again. "You ultimate man! Climb. Ascend to the height where you will be one with the splendid light", there were immense cascades of light that dissolved the feelings in a light, that I can not describe.*

*It appeared as the heavenly "voice"- outside my body, somewhere unknown from where it was communicating with my soul. I felt exalted. It seemed to me that I was hearing the "voice" of God. Truly I felt as if I did not exist in time and space and I was not what I thought I was. Indeed, I was unable to grasp who I truly was! There seemed to exist someone else who was bearing me as body and flesh against the gravity and weight. I found contradictions within myself -always lost as someone else, and always knowing that I was the spirit of the ultimate man in journey within myself towards the heavenly home from where I have come. I know, it is not easy to understand. But listen carefully. The language is so accustomed to falling back to the experiences, that are superfluous, that it is difficult to explain with language the experiences that sink deeper than the experiences in time and space. Although this experience can not be described in language the language is the only way to communicate and fathom the relations between the worlds known or unknown. It is a veritable contradiction. Therefore it is not possible to know who was me and who was the light, who spoke and who heard, who gazed and who walked, who was in me and who was outside in Him, who was moving and who remained eternally unmoved.*

*I saw a hermit on the way. As I said I do not know who he really was!*

*He was wandering in the mountain in complete harmony with himself. He was out in the mountain landscape in quest of something. Hearing the mountains' voice he was moving along a path that was dangerously steep. Any moment's lack of concentration of the mind would have pulled Him down from the illumined precipice to a great dark abyss. Along this path living and dying seemed to hang in a thread. In reverence to the goal, the great sanctuary of light, towards which He was moving to, He had no fear. In His face there was no sense of anxiety that could disturb His concentration and deviate Him from his path even by the measure of a hair. With a god-like glance and lustre in His eyes and insatiable thirst for light He was climbing the precipice. Upward He was ascending. Like an exalted image of an illumined mind, glowing in the light, He was advancing. Like an elevated spirit He was surging as a river that was moving to meet the sea - far away, alone towards the summit from where He did not wish to return.*

*In this landscape from high rocks brooks were tumbling, the streams were plunging in impassable caves, and there were lakes that had risen from the river and taken rest in the tranquil mountain glade. There was a blissful freedom under the soft luminosity of the distant skyey arch bending down to earth feeling the giddiness of the soaring height of the illumined path. It seemed if one could rise to the top, all sufferings would cease, all desires of begetting or becoming will come to a halt, breaking the clear sky the great love will pour, in the trembling mirror of the heart the eternity will vibrate in the strings of feelings playing the unearthly notes. You may still want to know who was this hermit, who was the shadow, who was the guiding light, who was being illumined and who was He who was illumining the mind? Although I did not know through any language all the relations between them all, like you something unquenched and unquenchable in me also wished to know, "Who am I? Who is He? Who is the guide and who is that shadow being guided towards the light? " The glaciers twinkled in trillions of stars, scattering spangles in the heart the light leaped into the empty void, like dancing beats of flying stars a great love awakened the will, and the fountain of light again rose with the voice, "Trust me. Thou art me, one with the eternal Self. Through the process of thoughts, that flows in the river of the human will, and are conditioned by perceptions, it is not possible to know the relation between the guide and the guided, who are imperceptible and inconceivable by human thoughts. Relations between us can only be known through revelations as the ultimate mystery that will remain eternally unknown." "Who is the hermit then?", I repeated. As the music of a divine flute drew me upward to an eternal path, over the stones and pebbles where I stepped the fountain spoke, "O ultimate man! your vision and sight are still bound in the fallen state where human senses operate. You are looking through something strange and unknown, profoundly mysterious and eternal with a consciousness that are polluted by worldly visual images. The hermit, who is climbing towards the sanctuary carrying in the mind a strange mystic marvel, is truly a fugitive of your worldly state, who is contemplating on the eternal marvel. Strange to Himself, sprung from Himself, He is carrying the ashes of the world to the mountains. In the loneliest wandering, sleeping on stones, gazing at the stars, hearing the echoes of the tumbling streams from the mountains to the mountains, and listening to the whisper of the solitudes from glaciers to glaciers, gazing afar at the divine world, He is striving to know who is moving His soul as the great fountain of love. He is the man in the forest path moving on Bodhisattva's way. He is Buddha- to-be, who would again return. He is once the blind man who had gone across the river in search of the enlightened way. He is still striving to overcome the bondage of the ignorance, trying to see the true self beyond the mirror and reflections on the river becoming and begetting thoughts, that create the will and gazes at itself in the spangles of rays. He is incarnate and immanent projection of the Self among the living creatures, who has realized the bondage of the procreating life and is looking at the hundred fold mirror, and concentrating on one image, practicing self control to overcome the illusions of the mind trying to bring him astray. " You may wonder was He the ultimate man glittering, trembling and ascending towards the summit of love? Was He the unchanging man changing through all lives, with many masks, who was striving to overcome the bondage of illusions and ignorance resulting from images in the mirror entangling the will in the web?*

*Was He the journeyman still seeking the company of the divine poet? Was He living or nonliving, was He true or false, was He an image of the ultimate man still loaded with weight walking towards the weightless world hearing the muffled sounds breaking through the shadow under his steps? Was He me, was He you-to-be, was He him who is never known?*

*Like you I also had wished to know. Like you I was also entangled in the web of thoughts, that are conditioned by the human percepts and determined by concepts built on phenomenal transitory world, that begets no truth but is founded on the illusion itself. Maya had still enwrapped my soul. Therefore being the ultimate man Himself I also could not know.*

*In this state I learnt about the secrets of the world, heard the words flowing from the mystic light. I had to interpret these words to make them meaningful to understanding by the mind constrained to exist in the material body moving in space and time. One calls it the consciousness of the being that reflects upon itself - negating and positing itself through a multifold patterns of thoughts entangled in the will and matter as a web. Here everything were empty, everything existed in the eternal present without any future and past. What was becoming was, and is, truly what becomes. On the lonely mountain bearing the ashes in eternity I was the hermit and I was also no one. Wearing the body of a man I was in a journey through the will as the creator and created bound as One. It was a fable of eternal existence. Here I had awaken from the sea as twofold-existence - myself and He - that reflected each other, who were separated in time and space but united in other dimensions.*

*You may wonder am I the one who was supposed to return? Yes, I know, you won't understand, but jump to no conclusion. Even the ultimate man can not explain everything that can be grasped easily by sense-bound human beings - as I have said again and again. Something you can not know unless freed from the bondage of Maya that the whole universe pervade. Follow me to sacrifice. You may be released from this ignorance at the end.*

*As I was climbing and coming home to the Self, wandering lonely towards the summit from where the rays were descending to illumine the abyss beneath, I was returning to me, in the most difficult part of the highest mountain with steepest cliff under which there were the longest crevices abysmally deep, indeed I had felt the presence of the sea infinitely deep. It was spread before my eyes as nothing above or nothing below. Upward, downward, everywhere rocks and pebbles were asleep as the tranquil souls; in high and low there were down-pouring and rising of the boundless love; backward and forward there were eternal reflections of shadows moving upwards or going downwards; in a maze of happenings where things already happened or going to happen the ultimate man* was returning to and emerging from the same being sailing on the waves surging and sinking in the eternal man's vision of reality and dream. In this sky insurmountably steep, in this sea unfathomable deep, I saw the summit and the abyss united in the mirror where on one side there was the sky and on the other side the sea divided by the mountain ranges guarding the valleys underneath. On one side there was the hermit bringing the ashes to the mountains from the sacrifice in the pyre burning by the shore of the sea and on the other side the

suffering humanity was gazing at the mountain summit waiting for the ultimate man to return from the world beyond the sky sunk in the invisible sea, beyond the rainbow's gates.

Here I had wandered long, heard the unheard, spoken with the unspeakable, in the silence listened to the mountains' songs. Here in stillness the words had come and in stillness had roamed in the wilderness floating with the mountain songs. Here more I had climbed more I had felt one with the light and the pebbles and stones. More I had risen more I had seen myself as bright as the glaciers in deepest contemplation in the lighted soul and as unmoved as the mountain rising to heaven's home. You may wonder why did I return? What made me leave the path to the highest summit to go downwards again towards the suffering abyss from where the hermit was carrying the ashes of the pyre to the lighted sanctuary towards which He had gone? You certainly understand the allegory where the sea rises to the mountains, forms the glaciers and from the mountains it pours downwards again bringing the rocks and pebble of the summit to the sea from where it had once risen from the eternal nothing - the void, that is my home. To know more about this down going you need to follow me. After that you will grasp the reason what makes the ultimate man to return.

"O ultimate man! You must go down as a shadow of man from the light that I am. Go to the grave to redeem the dead and awaken the corpse", like a commandment the voice rose again: "Humanity is not free. In down going to the suffering world help the grieving and weeping man in the abyss seeking to be free. In love for man follow this commandment from the light to whom you belong."

You may wonder was it real or a premonition? As you may understand it was a premonition of the doom that will come. Before the destruction comes I have come to tell you about the ultimate man and His *teaching of the enlightened way.*

*Wanderers awaken! Sleep no more in the slumber of the heart. Dream no more in the illusory world. In eternity you are born, in eternity you will go. In love of eternity as recurrence of the ultimate man I come and go. Purified with the new will I am going downwards in love for man to the village to bring to the world the news of the down-going in love for man. This down going is a sacrifice of life for the sake of the renewal of the earth. Sacrifice your life in the altar of God, and follow me to the suffering and torment of life. Repeat the journey again without being moved by it."*

Being aware of the great scepticism that existed among the scientists and philosophers about the existence of God, before going down the poet asked the guide:

"Before I go down, tell me what path shall I choose and what mask shall I wear? How shall I prepare myself for the encounter with the women and men?"

*"Born of woman and man, your physical appearance will be indistinguishable from other human beings. Entering the world you should make yourself indistinguishable from the women and men while you encounter them. Both as Man and God, you must move as Man and work for the will that has created you as the messenger of Heaven. God will move with you. Prepare yourself for the matter-spirit world's destiny that may affect your physical condition. Working amidst women and men you will work for the matter-spirit world's meaning and the common man's way to find the spiritual way. You should know that the world is God's love and the world is saved by the existence of Man-God who is moving in the worldly arena of women and men. Knowing yourself as Man-God, know that God has willed your existence in order to show the women and men the enlightened path."*

"The paths, that move downwards, are full of danger and distress. How shall I go down knowing the sufferings on the way? In sin how shall I remain sinless? In living with men and women, who suffer from hunger and thirst, greed and lust, and exhilarate or feel distress over love and hate, how shall I remain aloof and at the same time remain engaged in the world, where men and women work and strive for fame, honour, power and fulfil the instinctual needs driving the activities of the days?"

"*Enter the world as if you are nothing but one of them. Knowing yourself as the one moving with God, who has come to the world to make man move to the enlightened way, work and move in the down-fallen state. Know the women and men as your parts. Knowing their desires and lusts work so that they can know the greater path. Go the way all human beings are going under the darkened vault and make yourself the world's meaning by moving as Man-God among them. Go the way the women and men are searching fame, honor and seeking to control the forces that dominate over the matter and exposed to the dangers of the matter-spirit bound fate. Free the women and men from the ignorance that have darkened their ways. Work for the freedom of the world that is bound. Assume yourself as world and will, and no-world and no-will, and move as the world and will and no-world and no-will. You are working and moving in order to make men and women move towards the world where nothing work or move. The world is awaiting your coming. Go and move along the darkened path. I shall move with you and guide you through the sufferings that cover the world. You are the Light of Heaven that will illumine Earth. Bound and free, go and move as My Light! Enter the suffering world and make the world know about the Light from where you have come.*"

"I wonder, without any scientific proof of Your existence in the world, how Your Words will be able to change the world, that is driven by the will and thoughts, that are bound to instincts and associations of the material world?"

"*Entering the world as a common man of flesh and blood you will bring to the world the understanding of what God is and is not. How the words will move is determined by God's Will and you should move as I instruct you to move. Though proof about God cannot be given through observable methods known to man, your existence will give proof of what I am. Knowing you as visible, tangible and human, though invisible, intangible in the realm of God, man and woman will know the dimensions in which God exists and exists-not. Knowing Me and the world united in Man-God, world will realize the concepts that are required to fathom the dimensions of the existence that are beyond the knowledge of the matter-bound world.*"

"They may ask for concrete proofs beyond what I say. How shall I talk about proof of someone and something that is beyond all proofs and how shall I convince myself that my existence itself is the proof of the existence God? "

*Meaning of proof is devoid of meaning once it is extended to explain a domain that is not matter-bound. Hear from Me the Soul's proof that will prevail over the proof that contracts with the matter-bound mind's obsession to see and observe. How your soul impinges in the world and creates thoughts is the Soul's proof of being in the world and the will and beyond proof by experimental methods that man uses. Hear from Me the proof that can be disproved by the experimental methods but will cause soul's turmoil once it impinges in the world and the will. After you go down and move among them, the world will experience this turmoil. You know this turmoil and therefore will it not be enough to convince you what God is? Knowing how it stirs and tears and moves, don't you feel convinced about the power of Heaven that has created you from Him? Convince the world by stirring the world in the way I have stirred your heart. Being torn, baffled and confused and helpless against the power of God - the way I have made you submit to the Divine Will - make the world feel convinced about the power that works as the power of God and make man submit to the Will that leads to the higher path. Go down! The doubts will stir the hearts and by such stirring of doubts God will remain unveiled. Knowing this go!"*

"When I shall encounter women and men they would like to know about me, where I come from, when am I born, what did I do in my life to live, what path I have pursued to achieve the knowledge that I have achieved. What shall I tell them? When they will ask me about my family, my profession, my social rank, my position with respect to other human beings, how shall I answer?"

*"Knowing you as Man-God, walk among them as a common man, who is no different from others and tell them that you are a man of common birth with abilities and disabilities of a common human being. Tell them that you are a common man of uncommon origin, who has appeared in the world in order to make the world know about the destiny of the common man and their salvation in Man-God who is walking with them. When they will try to build an image of you, tell them that you are not who they may think you are. Knowing you as someone ensuing from*

*me, walk among women and men and tell them that you are never born, never working as a worker of the world, never pursuing any knowledge and fame and any worldly power that make the ranks and positions of the people in the world among the working lot. Tell them that your home is the world and also outside the world, where you are moving in the matter-spirit state as one with the Divine. Knowing you as the part of the Divine tell women and men that your knowledge comes from Heaven and your method of knowing is not the same as the other women and men. Knowledge of Heaven is not knowable by man without God-Man who brings it to the world through His appearance as a man. Knowing the Divine know yourself as Me who is moving to make man understand the knowledge that cannot be known through the darkened mind's intellectual path.*

*As to your family and home, the worldly man and woman will not understand what you will be saying. Tell them that your home is moving with them and their families are your family. Your family is a part of them. Knowing your family as the worldly women and men they will think that you are a worldly man and thus make an association with the common human beings, who they know. Knowing you as the part of the same they will want to make you as one of them. Your life will not appear any different and thus by willing to be a man you will work to make them understand the way the Divine has appeared among them to make them know about God."*

"When they will ask the story of my life, how shall I talk about myself? When they will want to know about my childhood, my youth and the life that I have crossed, what shall I tell, when I know that the man they want to know about is the one who is just another like them?"

*"Knowing yourself as Man-God, walk and hear what they want to tell you and listen from you. Knowing your world as not one and the same as theirs, tell them that your story is more or less similar to the one, who is not you but one like them. Knowing yourself as all, tell them that the stories of all human life are parts of your story and the story they want to hear is not much different from the one they already know. But knowing this story, that has been told innumerable times, they will not know the story of the man, who you are. Your story can not be told because there cannot exist so vast a book that can contain it all. Knowing you as a man of common birth, is nothing more than to know a story of another one,*

*who is only one in the multitudes who are the same. Knowing one story is only another story told by many before: It is the story of man, who is not different than the man about whom they want to know. Tell them that the story they are asking to know is the story of themselves and not the story that will tell them who you are."*

"You ask me to go and become one of them. When they will ask me to come to their homes and participate in the festivity of life, that brings instinctual pleasures, how should I behave?"

*"God-Man has moved out of Godly realm in order to save mankind from the path of the instinctual life and the domination of the powerful over the less powerful ones. Knowing your Divine Home you should mingle with them and behave as if your life is matter-spirit-bound life. How can they make you life and death's movement when you are beyond life and death? How can they make you matter-spirit-bound when you are Divine? Your world is not the same as the women and men. Knowing this, make yourself a part of the instinctual life and move through the worldly women and men. Knowing your home is Heaven work and move with God in life who loves women and men. When they will ask you to move in the down-fallen state together with them, will not the movement - though you should remain in life that is instinct bound. Know what makes them seek the down-fallen world, what moves the souls to errors and sufferings of life. Know how do they will and act in the matter-spirit-world. Seek the way that will make them free. Assuming that they are moving in the path of the worldly destiny, which is making the instinctual life fulfill the movement of fate, work and move among them as someone who cannot be touched by the destiny of life and death. Knowing yourself as born of Heaven, move and live in the festivity of life and make your soul work in the matter-spirit path as Man-God moving with women and men."*

"When woman will fall in love in search of a love that invites the body of blood and flesh to participate in the process of procreation, knowing the down-fallen movement of the will, how shall I accept or refuse the love, that allures women and men?"

*"Knowing your home as Heaven, your life as the life of God-Man, know that woman will not be able to allure the mind that is bound to the Will of God. Knowing the woman of flesh and blood attracting with her love and working for the matter-spirit world's destiny bound to life and*

*death, remain attracted but not seek in her love the down-fallen state of the instinctual pleasure that creates and destroys. Born of woman and man your body too is bound to the instinctual world and the destiny bound life, but do not work for the instinctual pleasure though you may remain attracted to her love. Repel her when she will come as the destructive power of the instincts and move away from the matter-spirit-world. When she will seek in you the love of God, who does not exist in flesh and blood, move to make her a loving partner of yourself. Born of Heaven you are love for all. How do they love when they love not God? How do they make love without loving the movement of God, who is moving with them? How do they love in flesh and blood when love despises the instinctual world and seeks matter-bound world's liberation from the instinctual path? How do they make life instinct bound and love not what is not instinct bound? Knowing the answers, the woman will not seek from you the love that she seeks from a worldly man of common birth. God's love is bound to make her seek love from you but not as a woman who is pleasure bound."*

"While refusing her pleasure seeking love what advice shall I give? What shall I ask her to seek when she will seek in the flesh and blood the love that attracts the destiny-bound fate?"

*"Born of Heaven, your life is not the same as theirs and therefore the way the Divine life acts is not the same as the common human life. When you give advice to them about what they should seek from a common human life, give them not the same advice as you will do when they seek your love. When they will seek from you the instinctual love make them aware of the love that is beyond. Born of common woman and man, when they will seek love of common woman and man, make them aware of the down-fallen world that attracts man and woman to the instinctual love in order to fulfil the destiny of life and death. Assuming that they are working for the fateful down-fallen world, and making them aware of the matter-spirit-world's method, by which it maintains the cycle of life and death, advise them to move away from the instinctual path as the path of salvation from the suffering world. Knowing the way the destiny operates and the way to free oneself from the suffering world, advice the women and men to act and move to seek God's Love instead."*

"How will they seek God's Love among common women and men? If they all abandon instinctual life, what will uphold the cycles of life and death?"

"*God's Love is moving in the world as Man-God. He is working and moving in the world in order to attract all by God's Love to Him. Both as Man and God your love is moving in the sense-bound sphere as well outside the domain where life is instinct bound. Bound to these spheres, your life is the meaning of the world and the world is the arena where your Love is manifest. Worldly woman and man should know themselves as parts of you and seek through you the love that is manifest as the world and the will. How do they love when they love not flesh and blood? How do they reproduce without the instincts producing the desires and lusts? How do they make themselves above the desires when desires and instincts drive the reproductive needs? As double of yourself as Man and the world and the will and God without any movement and working of the world and the will, your existence is the common man's existence and the Divine God's movement in the world. Knowing the world, that is, and the world that is not, as parts of the unity, that upholds all in the process of life and death and moves them towards the domain of God, work and move and make the common woman and man move with you. The woman and the man should seek you as their guide and submit to the power that can make them relate their love with the movement of God-Man. Entering the world you will make them enter the domain where Love is working to free man from the instinctual domain. Knowing the world and will made of Love and loving the world - the way God-Man does - they will know how to make love that will make them beloved of God. God-Man is the way to make love manifest in the world. Knowing Him as one of them, working and moving with Him, men and women will realize the movement of Love of God that makes all manifest.*"

After receiving these replies Tathagata started his descent.

A hymn in praise of the cosmic man, with whom Tathagata was one, rose to arouse all existing beings :

*In the forest where spring blossoms and leaves fade in the fall,*
*Life and death return to all,*
*From dewdrops dripping on the grass at dawn,*
*To the emptiness reaching out beyond the silhouette of the mountains*

*slipping In the west,*
*In the sunrise and the sunset,*
*In the emergence and submergence of the night and day,*
*All things echo the ethereal shivers.*
*Here Tathagata- neither existent, nor non-existent,*
*From a vacuous sea appears in the forest in a boat,*
*In going beyond he comes,*
*In coming he goes;*
*Between heaven and the earth,*
*Between the sun and the moon,*
*He moves from the village to the mountain summit towards the emptiness where all things have their source,*
*And returns to the world from emptiness riding the dragon force.*

*He has an outward appearance that moves in a paradoxical path,*
*Neither searching nor meditating when he gazes quite at the earth,*
*Without words the highest state of the Bodhisattva's mind he grasps.*
*He clings to nothing, craves for nothing,*
*Nothing he discriminates;*
*With contemplation, introspection and intuition, his awakening mind fulminates;*
*He regards the world as unreal seen as a vision,*
*Where all things change as illusion;*
*Living life after life he guides man in the path of compassion,*
*And helps man to vanquish suffering that rises out of delusion,*
*And lifts man to the domain of inner illumination.*
*In the object he sees himself as subject,*
*As a subject he sees himself mirrored in the object;*
*In both he is neither subject or object;*
*He becomes aware of existence through negation;*
*Between the two sides of the mirror he is one;*
*In disturbances he remains undisturbed,*
*In quietude he meditates in the ceaseless commotion;*
*In the relativity of going and coming,*
*He rests tranquil in the wheel of motion.*
*Without walking he steps,*
*Without stepping he walks in the insubstantial world,*

*In the impermanence and emptiness he wanders as substantiality and
permanence;*
*All worlds exist as parts of His mind;*
*Awaken in the realization that all realms where causation have cause,
Consciousness form,*
*The being and the non-being of things flowing in the conscious stream
shape the world where the reality form, change and deform,*
*There is no reality but the habit of the conditioned perceptions that are
neither right or wrong.*

*As all characters of all generations,*
*Starting from the journey of the first,*
*All over again he journeys wearing innumerable different masks;*
*These characters have no name,*
*They participate in the eternal play as travelling, wandering,*
*Going to and coming from mountain hermitage,*
*Or the village homes;*
*As laymen or monks,*
*Searching immortality across the world,*
*They burn in the fire,*
*In search of the limitless light,*
*Leaving behind the untrue body fly with the angels in the celestial night.*

*The causes of suffering is the very dialectics of the body and spirit that
no one can escape,*
*Here everything is balanced in the opposing scale,*
*In accepting evil and pain one may cultivate good,*
*In renouncing happiness one may realize the true source of happiness
and attain ultimate Buddhahood.*
*It is a state universal and transcendent,*
*Unlimited in time and space,*
*And everywhere perfect and the same.*

*It is the great compassion - the highest summit that all must climb
alone;*
*It is Bodhisattva's way that passes through the sky through Earth's dust
and stones.*

*Wander along the river and dwell in the emptiness in the mind su-*
*preme,*
*Ascend to the darkness,*
*Stand under the pole,*
*Where beginning has no end attain understanding of yourself as a part*
*of the starry souls;*

*He is no being, no one, with no name,*
*But still He is One without form,*
*Unveiled in multitude of forms.*
*Where the physical forms vanish He rises as the spirit of light,*
*As harmony of the world rising as the celestial song,*
*Where He merges with darkness to restore the attributes and characters*
*of the world that constantly change and reform,*
*He remains hidden as emptiness, placidity, quietness, stillness retired*
*and withdrawn from the fire, air and storms,*
*He controls, unfolds, impels all things on their course,*
*Still dwells in tranquillity that generates no force.*

*Know this enlightened state,*
*And do not seek to escape when you face life's trials and tests.*
*Go the way Bodhisattva has gone;*
*Do not withdraw in pain;*
*Do not hide in disdain;*
*Go forth in the roads where dangers may daunt,*
*The fears may haunt,*
*Follow the destiny of man,*
*Where the dragon breathes,*
*The serpent writhes,*
*One moment rising, next moment descending the will wanders freely,*
*Knowing that inner being is preventing or encouraging one to halt or*
*go on,*
*Follow the one, who is going,*
*Return with the one who is coming,*
*Although wishing neither to go or come;*
*Above all cravings and desiring follow the movements of the enlightened*
*mind's inner supernal sun.*

Do not succumb to sorrow,
Enter deep caves without fear of death,
Walk over the fields filled with graves without losing the tranquillity of
the inner state;
In wretched circumstances remember you are the journey man destined
to move on the mountain way;
If you unify your inner visions where you see Bodhisattvas beckon from
many paths wearing many faces;
In multi-dimensional real- dream- mythical world where He wanders in
the human consciousness,
Harmonize your consciousness in the divine will,
Attain the spiritual intelligence that is immutable throughout all exist-
ence;
Amidst evolutions of things and life,
Attain the enlightened state beyond living and dying.

Everything is spirit's abode;
Everything dying is being reborn;
Seeing withered carcasses, pyres and ashes,
Do not err and believe that beauty resides where things have forms,
And wither away when the body is cast off;
The illumined mind can differentiate the forms from the conditions and
cause,
In thoughts can penetrate the mystery of beauty that no eyesight is able
to penetrate,
In darkness he sees luminosities,
In myriads of things sees nothing but conditioned causalities,
In formlessness discover the true beauty of things.

Do not let your mind be agitated by the conditioned pain,
Embrace in your mind the unity of the whole- the stillness in emptiness
that is serene;
Control the perversities of the will,
See outside the absurdities of the acts that every life fill;
Develop attitudes and intentions to merge with great unity,
That also has dimensions outside the layer of rationality and so called

*reality;*
*Lift yourself above the illusory state of human birth,*
*And meditate in the stillness of the heart.*


*There is no just one land and just one perfect way,*
*All existence flow through multiple of worlds that inside the perceptible*
*world dwell,*
*They penetrate each other in different dimensions of time and space;*
*The world in which man lives at present,*
*Is embedded in many other worlds spanned from future to the past;*
*Temporality is only a conception and man's mental construct;*
*Which govern the perceptions so that mind with the material reality of*
*motion and rest can adjust;*
*In a single life time of man many lives are spanned,*
*These dimensions penetrate various realms of consciousness that un-*
*folds as man more and more the mystery of existence understand.*
*All these worlds,*
*Like the one in which one feels, touches, sees and hears and calls his or*
*her own,*
*Are caught up in never ending process of formations and disintegration,*
*Ending in cycles to the beginnings as they return,*
*Through extinctions and regeneration they can only be known;*
*Rearranging the past existence as life that is present,*
*In a constant flux causing the conditions that are destined to pass,*
*In the world with cyclic death and birth,*
*They penetrate through emptiness and illumine the consciousness wak-*
*ing from the unconscious dark;*
*In these countless lands Bodhisattva appears as many Bodhisattvas in*
*different levels of awareness as guide of man.*


*To elucidate the meanings,*
*And make aware of the truth that no words can expound,*
*To avoid the shortcomings of the meanings that with the follies of*
*knowledge all knowledge afflict,*
*To undo the faults of the discursive reason that with causes and condi-*
*tions conflict,*
*He preaches in similes and parables,*

*In all levels of existence he teaches in a way that can not be understood*
*by reasons alone;*
*Go the way this Bodhisattva has gone,*
*Listen to him in all the different worlds where he appears as guide of*
*man;*
*Be aware that you are another journeyman destined to follow his*
*Enlightened path.*


*He is not any one man,*
*He is multiple in one,*
*Like a single intelligent being that manifests to knowing through inor-*
*ganic matter and organic life,*
*Although existing in every dimension,*
*He is not in direct contact in time and space;*
*Through waves he communicates with parts that remain separate in the*
*future, present and past between  the celestial spheres and the*
*Earth-bound base;*
*The intelligence of this whole,*
*Is greater than the parts that form the unity of the soul;*
*The place and time where and when he his teachings expound,*
*Are multiply interpenetrated from heaven to the Earth where man is*
*sense bound;*
*The light from his mind the countless shores illumine,*
*Beyond the limits of space and time in the mirror of things shine,*
*As someone never been seen and never known before,*
*He is everywhere, in all spheres, extending from the sky to the mortal*
*world where he is many fold. He is beyond the sun and the moon,*
*But still knowable through the lunar and solar lights;*
*He is beyond the laws of things but still in nature of things he is im-*
*measurably bright;*
*The lights that he emits form in the minds pure concepts,*
*Through numbers, principles and laws he emerges in the world of per-*
*cepts;*
*Take faith,*
*And believe him as the upholder of the events and causes;*
*Remove from your mind the sorrow and distress;*
*Be comforted and remain reassured of his compassion that upholds*

the existence of the innumerable species and races.

*I have seen him in myself;*
*Know thyself as manifestation of Himself,*
*And follow the path of Bodhisattva in the journey through the forest*
*in search of the Self.*
*Know that this suffering is the way to enlightenment;*
*It is an expedient means by which He shows man the greater way,*
*Come to know that those that seem inauspicious and portent,*
*Are the vehicles in the seekers' ways;*
*Concentrate your mind;*
*Be fearless and awaken in the journey on the boundless waves;*
*His doctrines are hard to understand;*
*But I have heard, practiced and achieved the goal beyond which there*
*is not much more to understand,*
*There is not much to comprehend beyond the knowledge that in all liv-*
*ing beings He is incarnate;*
*Through concentration of the mind you will be able to cross this forest*
*bound by destiny and fate;*
*You will be able to see yourself from a higher state.*
*There is no one in blood and flesh,*
*Who can fully understand His incarnation at different states in varied*
*times and places,*
*More one will exhaust the thoughts in trying to grasp Him as a living*
*being,*
*More he will multiply in the vision without any limit of seeing,*
*In ten directions through numerous groves,*
*Joining through multiple dimensions all inflows and outflows,*
*As appearance and influence - latent or manifest,*
*Inherent in the cause but not determined by the causal effects,*
*Embodied in forms from the smallest parts,*
*To the dimensions that is beyond the capacities of thoughts to hold,*
*Like a single mind beyond all pondering and seeking,*
*As Thus Come One he is manifest among the beings."*

Was this epic journey, which unfolded in my mind for many years, truly a divine intervention after the death of Ånun? Or, was the journey through the different spheres of consciousness, which had opened over the grave, a meaningless construct of a shocked and traumatized brain? Was this writing a paranormal phenomenon, or a babbling of a mind overwhelmed by a tragic accident on the Alps?

To confuse me more, the picture of Ånun, kept over the piano, had been behaving in a strange way since I had first noticed it couple of years ago. The picture faced the sofa that had become my place of meditation in the Time Hall of Illusion in a new apartment (from Quai du Sujet in Geneva it had now changed its place with the apartment in Bygdøy Allé in Oslo).

# Chapter 5
# SPIRITUALITY VERSUS SCI-ENTIFIC REASON

The picture frame over the piano has rotated towards the wall as usual. I have not been able to explain the mystery behind this phenomenon. A year ago, I made an attempt to understand what could be causing such bizarre rotation of the photo frame showing Ånun playing the piano. Once the rotation was put under experimental scrutiny it stopped moving, as if, to puzzle and fool me and create the impression that it was a hallucination. It cannot be any hallucination because whenever it has rotated against the wall I have physically turned the frame and placed it facing the right direction on the piano again and again. Apparently it seems to be paranormal. I doubt it. It must have a physical explanation. May be, the vibrations caused by the passing heavy vehicles, like the buses plying by Bygdøy Alle, could be causing this rotation. But why always in the same direction and why does it stop rotating after it has arrived at a fixed angle of rotation, and why the other picture frames kept over the piano do not move at all? I have stopped bothering about these questions and, by now, accepted this rotation as normal phenomenon that belongs to the "reality" of this room.

This library room is a place where I meditate, listen to music, and write.

Now and then I also transform it to my studio for paintings. It is the most used room in the apartment, which lies along Bygdøy Allé, well known for the chestnut trees that decorate it. There is a small balcony attached to the room. It hovers above an open air restaurant lying two floors underneath.

The apartment receives lot of sunlight from morning to late in the evening. Therefore there exist ample opportunities to grow flowers in the balcony. After the spring has arrived the chestnut trees along Bygdøy Allé are in bloom, the pansies are subtly following the draft in the air. When look closely with microscopes I find an unseen world animated by bacteria around the roots of these plants. They live in the soil in order to help in decomposing the dead material into the aminoacids and proteins needed for the growth of new life.

Everything is breathing in this world...the bacteria, the soil, the petals, leaves...including myself, watching this world of plants, which has healed itself from death to life by using the energy of the sunlight. They are absorbing nutrient and waters, carried by the vascular capillaries, and distributing this to different parts of the body! I am an integral part of this life that is being helped by the bacteria, water, air and nutrients.

In fact, I am not very much different from the microscopic organisms! The trillions and trillions of cells, that have composed my body, are like the bacteria, cycling and recycling nutrients from one to the other. The carbon dioxide, which I am breathing out, the plants and trees are breathing them in to grow; the oxygen that plants and trees were breathing out, I was breathing them in to renew the cycle and the supply of the chemicals I need in order to remain alive. Like me, every living creature is entangled in a web of life for their subsistence and growth. The bacteria in the soil, the pansies and the lilies, the rhododendrons, the chestnut trees, the animals and birds seen and unseen inside and beyond the domains of my visions...far... far away... over the Himalayas ... the glaciers...under the seas...in the deserts... in forests teemed with flowers and insects, I have never seen, and may never see ... are all breathing with me.

This breathing does not stop here on Earth. It is breathing beyond the limit of the sky, that my eyes can reach, in the realm of the stars, galaxies, clusters and super clusters of the galaxies … and the entire universe! From the tinniest structure to the highest form that spans billions of light years, there exists the same breathing in and breathing out … the same force that has created everything in the universe! Like the entanglement of bacteria to my own existence, every structure in the universe is entangled with each other in order to supply the ground for existence of the other. There is a universal pattern and order, in which every existence is anchored following the vibrations that animate the universe.

It is amazing that I am awake in this world and is able to sense this wonder that cannot be grasped by any word and language. Touching the petals and the leaves, I know that I am one with this wonder of life! By perceiving the world outside me through vision, touch, sound and smell I know that I am one with the other creatures of my own species and those from whom we have once evolved.

What creates these emotions of wonder and awe? Where is the source of the mind that sees things beyond the boundaries, where seeing through the visual cortex of the brain appears rudimentary and crude? Who speaks in me in silent voice to create poetry and art? How does the brain create the vision of marvel that is common to mankind in all ages and cultures?

Are there really channels within every being that must be opened to receive the forces that can connect awareness with the universe? Do the bacteria too possess "consciousness" when they swim through the microscopic realm by using the flagellal wheels that rotate? Are the galaxies and the clusters of galaxies turned by the same force that turns the wheels of the human body? Are we children of Earth and Heaven? Are we children of the same "parents" who have passed on their traits to all species and life?

Like a bee my mind flies from flowers to flowers. At every petal I land I see an amazing beauty that penetrates down to the network of the pathways filling the vascular channels carrying water and nutrition to the cells. The petals that look violet, white, yellow or red, carry so many hues of colours, interlaced at every corner, that no painter would ever be able to reproduce them. It is like entering into a world of dream - a universe of colours that reproduces the subtlest vibrations of light. Everywhere there exist patterns of mesmerizing beauty that absorbs from the mind all ecstasies that life can produce. What a heaven! What a paradise! What a fortunate chance given to the eyes to experience this marvel!

The bees and butterflies are, in fact, among the giant creatures in this wonder world of so many different insects of varied forms and colours – some with wings flying fast, some that could fly only a short distance before they needed to land, some were without wings moving in different speeds: Beetles, spiders, mantis, flies, lice, ants in many varieties, colors and sizes. Most of them have gathered in this paradise in order to nourish themselves either by absorbing the nutrients that the petals are carrying along the fractal pathways, or feeding on the species that are feeding on plant juice, or the excrements of the other insects.

Like the punishment of Prometheus, with the rising of the sun, they are all thrown into the struggle of gathering foods for survival and thus facing suffering of life. They are condemned to this battle and struggle for survival life after life. Different species of insects have different roles to play in nature. Some live on eating on the insects that sap juice from the plants as if to protect the plants from these evil creatures. Some are selfish: they eat the insects that feed on the plants in order to keep the plants safe for their own consumption. The tiny Lady Beetles and Ear wings, in incessant haste, move up and down the pistils and stamens to keep them clean of the insects that could endanger the life of the flowers. They are preying on insects that try to enter into this paradise of beauty.

Children of Satan or Angel, whatever roles they may play, in this insect world everybody breathed in and out the energy deep inside the flowers as the stars and galaxies did. According to the Darwinians these insects were set into competitions against each other to make best use of the environment in favour of their own survival. The evolutionists believe most of the activities in nature are driven by self-interests. The ants are moving around in this Paradise to protect the evil lice, sucking the life force from the flowers. They are protecting the lice from the hands of beetles and spiders, who like to feed on lice. The ants protect the lice because they love to feed on the honeydews that these lice secrete. On one side the ants are acting in self-interest, while they also collect the fungi from the plant and harvest them. The fungi act against the parasites and diseases in plants. In that role they serve the purpose of life against evil threats of nature. So what is evil and good?

In every corner of this living world, one's life is the source of other's food. Every creature is trying to avoid the predators that are preying on them by creating camouflages, or secreting obnoxious smells and poisons, or developing claws and stings to defend them against the predators. Some take the shapes of their predators in order to avoid being hunted: The ants, who eat the beetles, are in turn eaten by some kind of beetles, who camouflage themselves by taking the look similar to the ants. Thus they escape their predators and in turn prey on the ants. In one side the nature has released the force that attacks life and growth, and on the other side it has created the predators to eat those creatures who do harm to life. There is a constant battle between life and death, with massacre and killing going on side by side burgeoning of new life. This results in a world, where those who can take advantage of the natural conditions and develop means to escape the predators and, in turn, become efficient in their methods of hunting, without endangering themselves, increase their numbers and become the winners. They grow and multiply by devouring the others.

The primary foundation of reality of life is based on this biological sphere of struggle and battle for survival. However, what we call "reality" has many other layers, which are colored by knowledge, experience and awareness of the possibilities that may exist outside the things one knows, or experiences through the senses. Human concept of reality is based on what they know and perceive mixed with portions of beliefs, imagination and fantasies. Thus myth and dream become inseparable aspects of the reality.

Right in front of me, on the other side of the street, I see a lamb carved as a relief in stone decorating the portal of the Church, which faces the apartment. Behind the lamb is the image of the sun spreading rays in all directions. Christ is often depicted as the Lamb of God, who is sacrificed for the atonement of the sins of Adam and Eve, which has thrown humanity in the path of perpetual suffering life after life. By eating the flesh and drinking the blood of this lamb one may achieve contact with the Divine realm. In the end of every mess the priests offer bread and wine. It is believed that by divine intervention transubstantiations occurs, in which bread becomes flesh and wine turns into the blood of Christ.

In this Christian world, the humanity is depicted as creatures undergoing suffering due to the original sin of Adam and Eve. Christ took this sin on himself by sacrificing his life on the cross, so that his blood and flesh could bring salvation to all. However, the atheists view things in a different way:

"......what a sado-masochism! God incarnated himself as a man, Jesus, in order that he should be tortured and executed in atonement for the hereditary sin of Adam…The central doctrine of Christianity is vicious, sado-masochistic and repellent. We should dismiss it as barking mad. But its ubiquitous familiarity which has dulled our objectivity. If God wanted to forgive our sins, why not just forgive them, without having himself tortured and executed in payment – thereby, incidentally, condemning remote future generations of Jews to pogroms and persecution as "Christ-killer"…. To cap it all, Adam, the supposed perpetrator of the original sin, never existed, in the first place: an awkward fact – excusably unknown to Paul (but presumably known to an omniscient God and Jesus, if you believe he was God?) – which fundamentally undermines the premise of the whole tortuously nasty theory. Oh, but of course, the story of Adam and Eve was only ever symbolic, wasn`t it? Symbolic? So, in order to impress himself, Jesus had himself tortured and executed, in vicarious punishment for a symbolic sin committed by a non-existent individual? As said, barking mad, as well as viciously unpleasant…," I hear Dawkins, the author of the best-selling book "The God Delusion" screaming.

It is a grey day. The chestnut trees in front of the Church portal are covered with white clusters of flowers. Several weeks have passed since the sun has crossed the Vernal Equinox, when it rises vertically above Earth's equator heralding the coming of spring. In this city the activities have taken a new pace and vivacity after the Easter holidays. The open air restaurant under the balcony, which was closed during the winter months, has started receiving guests.

Easter is the most popular holidays in this city. It is the time of the holy feast celebrating the resurrection of Christ from Death. According to the Christian faith, after Jesus was crucified and buried in the tomb, he had risen from the death and appeared to his disciples on the Easter Sunday.

Hardly anyone, possessing rational mind and scientific knowledge, believe anymore in the story of the resurrection of Christ in blood and flesh as Marry Magdalena had reported. According to Dawkins, *"Presumably what happened to Jesus was what happens to all of us when we die. We decompose. Accounts of Jesus' resurrection and ascension are about as well-documented as Jack and the Beanstalk"*.

However, this is the time when life, which had passed into a lifeless world during the winter, resurrects again - like the myth of the death and return of Eurydice and Idun from the underworld in my paintings. The celebration of resurrection has originally a root in Egypt, which goes much earlier than Christianity. This Egyptian festival was celebrated several thousand years before the beginning of the Christian era. Still today it is celebrated in Egypt as the festival coinciding with the vernal equinox. The ancients associated the day of vernal equinox with the time of the beginning of new cycle of life.

The story of the virgin birth of son of God by the Divine Father existed from the time of the agrarian civilization in the Nile Delta more than four thousand years before the story of birth of Jesus by Virgin Mary. The story of the birth conceived by a virgin mother impregnated by God existed also in Babylon, Syria and among the Druids in Ireland.

According to the Egyptian legend, Assur (Osiris) was the inventor of agriculture. The evil god Set had murdered Assur and put him into a casket and floated it in the Neil to an unknown destination. When it finally reached the Phoenician coast a tree grew around the casket, which was cut and then used as a pillar in the palace of the Syrian king. Isis, the wife of Assur, went to Syria to fetch the wooden pillar, where Osiris remained entombed. After Isis retrieved Osiris`s body, evil Set hacked Assur into pieces. Isis gathered the dismembered parts, and put them back together, and resurrected Assur from the dead. Set became Satan, the god of evil.

When the Phoenicians were brought under Egyptian control, the Syrian counterpart of Osiris became Baal. Statues of Baal showed him in the stance of the Giant Orion/Osiris wearing the Leo/Gemini as Crown. In his left hand Baal held the Tree of Life. The Water of Life ran beneath his feet. A bull`s ear was attached to his Crown, which represented the dawn of the Age of Taurus.

The Baal Cult was associated with the Bull. He was the god who died and rose again. Baal became the seasonal god of vegetation, dying in the autumn and having his resurrection in the spring. The Ancient Egyptian culture was also assimilated by the Sumerians. The god Bel derived his name from the Ancient Babylonian counterpart of the Syrian Baal. In the Age of Taurus, Bull reigned as the supreme god. Similarly "The Lord" during the Age of Aries became Ram in the Old Testament. It followed Jesus in the Age of Pisces.

Celtic/Druidian Hesus (also known as Hu) was not unlike Osiris. Hu was the celestial Sphinx, the creator of the precession of the equinoxes. Druid mythology relates that Hesus was crucified, and his soul survived after Death. The period following his crucifixion was referred to as the "Golden Age". In the Beltane ceremony Hesus was crucified on an oak tree which was symbolic of the Tree of Life. Just as Osiris became one with the tamarisk tree, in which he was encased, so Hesus became one with the oak tree. Both Osiris and Hesus were representative of the Axis Munde around which heaven revolved. These trees were the World Pillar, the link between Earth and the celestial worlds.

This ancient symbolism of the Tree of Life survived in Christianity until today as the Christmas tree.

In the Druid religion Hesus was fathered by God and born of a virgin mother whose body was enveloped by light and who wore a crown of twelve stars on her head representing the Constellation of Coma Berenices, adjacent to the constellation of Virgo, traditionally associated with Isis in Egypt, and Isthar in Babylon. Druid virgin mother Mayence kept her feet on a serpent, the constellation of Hydra. Hesus belonged to the Age of the Ram, when the Sun was in Aries. The virgin birth of Hesus was an allegorical myth to explain the movement of the Sun out of the sign of Taurus into the sign of Aries. Hesus was the new-born Son/Sun of God in the Age of Aries.

Jesus belonged to the Age of the Pisces, when the Sun was in Pisces in the vernal equinox. He was born of a Virgin Mother and a Heavenly Father. And like Hesus his virgin birth heralded the Dawn of the Age of Pisces. The virgin birth of Jesus was nothing but another myth around the movement of the Sun exiting the Age of Aries (the Old Testament) and entering into the Age of Pisces (the New Testament). The Virgin Mary was the constellations of Virgo and Coma Berenices combined. The Father was the Sun in the Age of Aries. The Child, Jesus, was the new-born Son/Sun of God. The myth of Jesus in the Christian era became a continuation of the similar myth associated with the precession of the equinoxes as it had been before.

The movements of the sun and the moon, in the backdrop of a starry sphere, have colored imaginations and fantasies of the earthlings since the beginning of human civilization. Thus the existence of the celestial sphere, existing outside the boundary of the Earth, has added a new dimension to the consciousness of reality. Since the ancient time the human beings have associated mythical stories with different constellations, which do not change their shapes for several thousands of years. They have observed the appearance of the same groups of constellations in the sky in different seasons and thus associated seasonal changes as caused by the influences of the starry world, which brings the destiny of life and death. They have noticed that the polar star remains fixed in the sky while the other constellations move around the fixed point. They have associated the Gate of Heaven with this immobile point, lying at the apex of the Tree of Life, in which the Son of God was crucified. The constellation of Dragon guards this Divine gate while it moves as a coiling serpent around the Tree bringing life, death and resurrections years after years. The changing positions of the stars bring floods, hurricanes, storms, wintry cold and blazing heat that hurl mankind to suffering and pain. They have fantasized about heroes like Hercules who fought with the Bull, the Hydra and the Scorpions, which brought storm and cyclones, flood, diseases and plagues. In the myth of Prometheus they have found hope of liberating themselves from the power of the starry sphere controlled by the gods. Like the myth of Christ, Prometheus had to suffer for his good acts in trying to help the mortals.

Darwin's theory of evolution has taught us that neither we are progenies of Adam and Eve, nor the creatures whom Prometheus have created. We are nothing but progenies of the chimpanzees, who have learnt to walk on two feet about a million years ago. Our immediate predecessors are Homo sapiens. The modern human have originated about 200 000 years ago from these Homo sapiens. Insects and flowers appeared on Earth about hundred million years before Homo sapiens had evolved from the chimpanzees. Bacteria and virus were the first signs of life that had developed nearly a billion years from now. Life on Earth started in the sea. Then algae and mosses spread on land. The amphibians rose from sea and learnt to walk on lands. The flowering plants started to emerge in a world dominated by non-flowering species. During the last few million years the flowering plants and insects have dominated the life existing on land covering the surface of Earth. Today, the volume of only one insect like the ants alone is many times larger than the all human beings on Earth. The species, which have been able to develop the best strategy for survival, by adjusting to the changing climate, and developed intelligence to escape the onslaught of the predators, have become the dominating species on Earth.

The Newtonian theory of gravity has explained to us why the sun changes its position at the equinoxes and moves from one constellation to the other with every 2000 years, and what causes the seasonal changes that move through spring, summer, autumn and winter. Science has clearly explained why the polar star remains fixed while all other constellations move around the polar axis and why different constellations are seen in the sky at different seasons. It has also explained the nature of the constellations, which were associated with mythical figures in the past, and shown how human imagination and fantasy, governed by ignorance, have dominated human understanding of reality.

The geological science has revealed the mystery behind the climate changes, the formation of mountains, eruption of volcanoes, and upheavals that have formed and deformed the terrains on Earth. It has enlightened us about the dynamic crust, moving above a molten core. On the solid crust the species are evolving or disappearing according to their abilities to adjust to the stress and strains generated by the balance of forces operating and sustaining the climate where mountain chains, volcanoes, seas, clouds, and all living organisms, spread through all realms, are competing for their places in a living cosmos. They have shown how chemical reactions, taking place under different conditions of temperature and pressure, are eroding the mountains, forming new landscapes, making once irrigable land infertile, and turning infertile fields into fertile lands. They have shown how the continent which once existed in the southern hemisphere, hundreds of millions of years ago, has now moved to the northern hemisphere, and spread insects, plants and animals throughout the globe. All these changes on Earth and the cosmos are occurring following fixed mechanical and chemical laws. Where is the supernatural in this reality?

The picture frame rotating over the piano is most probably not supernatural, though I do not find a scientific explanation behind this phenomenon yet. It must be my ignorance and lack of knowledge of the relations of things and their movements, which I have not yet been able to decipher. One day, I may find a scientific explanation for this. But the audio-book, about Tathagata`s Journey which I have been listening to… how could it evolve without any plan and ideas from my unconscious mind?

169

The idea of the journey of the wanderer, sailing between the islands of the sun and the moon, had descended in my mind accidentally while I was visiting Ånun`s grave. Since then I was possessed by a mental state similar to a kind of trance for several years, while I had been writing the book. It was difficult for me to identify who was the real author – me, or some supernatural existence external to the conscious mind. I had started the book without knowing what I was going to write, and how it will develop and where and how it may end. I was only a medium through which someone was relating the story of the journey, that all human beings of all ages were destined to make. It was difficult to grasp this mental process using scientific logic.

Similarly was the process of the creation of the paintings, hanging on the walls in this apartment. I had received the ideas of the art project from the inner guide, who had asked me to:

*"Engage in representing the realms of dream and myths in art. Know them as other "realities" of human existence. Pursue the light, the dream and thoughts that appear in the mind through mythical allegories about the creation of the universe and life. These are far more complex than deep than what you may explore with mathematical structures constructed by your mind. Bring forth the unborn and the unseen in the images of the world that can be seen and known. Pursue the inner light that may bring the images of beauty, awesome marvel of dreams that float in the inner universe. Thus know yourself, know your relation with the mystical, magical and be a part of the existence which is eternal."*

After the epic was written in Geneva and we moved to Seoul, I had taken up paintings once again which I had abandoned for many years. The project called "Art without Beginning and End" too started in an accidental way. In Seoul Ragne got her first posting as an ambassador. She was not so happy with the art works hanging in the residence and therefore asked me to make a few paintings that would fit the furniture and carpets in the living room and the dining room. These paintings became so popular that I was offered an exhibition space in the Art Gallery at the Seoul Arts Centre.  It was a pretty big gallery and I needed nearly 50 paintings of large sizes to fill the walls. I did not know what to do. Then I heard from the inner world what I should create and embarked on creating "Art without Beginning and End Moving through the Cycle of Life, Death and Resurrection". The winter painting of the Svartskog Churchyard (Ånun`s resting place), where the ideas of Tathagata`s Journey had appeared in my mind, became the central painting of this project. It was followed by another winter motif "Angel Sleeping in the Graveyard". From this winter theme of death the project unfolded through the resurrection in the spring, the vivacity of life in the summer and the struggle and decay of life in the autumn that returned to winter again.

In this project reality, myth and dream were inseparable. I made use of the stories of Orphus and Eurydice in the Greek mythology and Idun and Brage from the Norren mythology to weave the theme of life, death and resurrection. Both Orpheus and Brage were the musicians of Heaven, who went to the underworld to fetch their beloved Eurydice and Idun back to life. It was a story of the coming of beauty in spring, who was destined to return to the world of the dead in the winter before resurrecting again in the next spring.

After we moved to Oslo "The art without beginning and end" received a brutal treatment. Because of the lack of space only a few paintings could be put up on the walls. The choices of the paintings were decided by the colours of the carpets and the furniture in different rooms. Two paintings from the summer and one painting from the autumn have found their place in the library room. "Sol-maiden in her profane and divine aspects" is decorating the wall above the piano. It depicts the landscape from our summer house by Sognefjord. In this painting the sun-goddess (sol-maiden) is riding her chariot drawn by white steeds through the clouds above the mountains covered with glaciers, while scattering spangles of rays that have illumined the fjord. In her profane aspect she is holding an apple in her hand, as a symbol of temptation for the mortal world and bathing in the sun by the rocky beach by the fjord. Besides this painting Prometheus is undergoing punishment. While being tethered to the sun he is screaming in pain. An eagle is devouring his liver. Prometheus had stolen the fire of Heaven from the gods and given it to the mortal. By transferring this knowledge

171

he had made the mortal creatures smart. They could now win over the vagaries of nature and defy the power of Heaven. As punishment for this crime the gods had put Prometheus in chains. An eagle came during the day to feed on his liver and left in the evening, leaving Prometheus to suffer in the cold wind blowing over the mountain. During the night his liver grew whole again. Next morning the eagle returned once more. Prometheus had no respite from this perpetual suffering. The autumn painting "Idun`s Fall" is hanging on the opposite side of the piano. Idun has fallen from the tree and lying dead surrounded by colourful leaves shredded from the trees getting ready for the winter. From here she will enter the realm of the frost and remain away from life until spring.

Did the way the ideas of this project had unfolded and paintings had come into existence indicate that something supernatural exist? When I was offered the gallery space at Seoul Arts Centre, I had no idea what I was going to exhibit. I had just finished writing the last part of the book "The Dialogues on the Mountain", which was the most weird writing of all what I had written so far. Hundreds of pages had flown through my hands as automatic writing springing from a source beyond my conscious mind. This peculiar process of the mind continued as I started the painting project. The ideas, that never came to me before, flowed through me and I saw an "art that had no beginning and end" around the most central theme of all religions - life, death and resurrection. I visualized a mythical journey of life through the endless cycle passing through all four seasons. Individual paintings also became equally weird creations. Though I was holding the brushes and mixing the colors with my own hands, I could not be sure how the individual paintings would finally look like. In those paintings, where I could free myself from the constraints of the conscious mind, I saw a supernatural world emerging through the canvas. For example, while I was painting the piece that finally became "Angel Sleeping in the Grave", someone took over the control of my hands and a grave opened up, from where an angel rose in the world and rested on the head of a lion bedecked in snow. The theme was surprising, and the painting appeared so beautiful that I got overwhelmed (till today it is one my most favourite paintings) and thought that God was behind its creation.

Does there really exist any ghostly world "outside there" not discernible in time and space? Or, is everything a process generated by the human brain that is constrained to function following the mechanical and chemical laws of nature? Could the brain itself be the site of the most supernatural of all –beyond the scientific comprehension of the human mind? Does the supernatural, existing outside the mechanical and chemical spheres, manifest in the mind through the processes occurring in the brain, or the brain processes phenomena that may appear as supernatural?

Or, are there really channels within us that must be opened to receive the supernatural forces that can connect our consciousness and brain to a greater realm of existence than what science has been able to reveal to us? With the beginning of the new millennium, when the sun has entered the new constellation at the equinox, astrologers have been predicting great spiritual upheavals on Earth. Depending on the interpretation what the sign of Aquarius stands for, there are different opinions about how this great change will come. Some believe that it is the beginning of a New Spiritual Age, the others believe that it is the Age of Science and Technology and the end of the age of the spiritual nonsense.

During the first decade of the new century both sides have done so well that it is tempting to believe that the New Age is going to encompass both: Rising spiritualism, rising scientific knowledge and rising awareness to get rid of the dark forces of religious dogmas. While on one shelf, the bookstores sell the best-selling books written by the scientists and atheists like Dawkins, who makes fun of God and his spiritual angels, in the shelf beside it the stores stack books on New Age spiritualism in such a huge number that any attempt by the atheists to dethrone God would seem impossible. The interest in Angel Power, Yoga, Ayurveda, Acupuncture, Healing, Kundalini, Energy Medicine, Hypnosis, Homeopathy, Qi Gong etc… are so overwhelming that one should believe that the balance is tipped towards the New Age spiritualists. This explosion of spiritual interest seems totally contradictory to the Aquarian Age of high-tech communications and people`s lack of faith in the traditional religions.

One may wonder are all these spiritual seekers insane, or do they belong to the failed group of the human species who are seeking their annihilation in the hands of the competing forces of the powerful bearer of science? Won`t natural selection eliminate this group of new age "parasites" leading life on the basis of the irrational functioning of their brains? Were they not affected by the mental viruses that originated many thousands of years ago in ancient cultures and later spread through the rest of the world? It appears that the new age spirituality has become endemic by threatening the Age of Aquarius that many see as the age of scientific rationality. To cure the world from this expanding virus the atheists and the scientists have rallied against God. The evolutionary biologist, Professor Richard Dawkins of Oxford University has become their ring-leader.

Dawkins has every reason to fear the rise of the "anti-factual, counterproductive fantasies of religion"... that make people doubt scientific explanation, and instead let them lie supine under the microscopes of the mind of the healers, who can see tumours and viruses and the blockages of flow of universal energy. While the scientists are trying to convince the public that the healing, clairvoyance, prayer etc. are fake, people are more and more rushing to the Taoist masters or the Indian Yogis, or the local healers to open the channels through which they may receive the energy that lies outside the knowledge of science. By tapping the cosmic energies, that create harmony between Heaven and Earth, human being is looking for physical and mental life that will help them to prolong the life span.

The interests in this New Age spirituality has multifolded during the last few years and now regular fairs are being held in Oslo where people can see how the practitioners work. The spring fair was held a few days ago. It was arranged by the National Research Centre for Complementary and Alternative Medicine. The headlines included "Do you need help of angels?" "Those who can see virus and tumours"; "15 000 practitioners are ready to treat you" etc. In such a festival one can see the practitioners holding their hands of their patients and detecting the virus, bacteria and tumours that may have taken dwelling in the bodies. In one fair, I remember, a couple, experts in spiritual surgery, was busy in operating a patient. The male practitioner kept his elbow on the stomach of the patient while pressing the elbow with his full body weight. The female practitioner kept the palm of one of her hands open as antenna to receive the spiritual energy, while she transmitted the received energy through her body to the elbow of the man, who then passed it to the area that needed surgery. The woman`s other hand was used to complete the circuit of energy transfer from heaven to the internal organ of the patient. In such fairs, among others, one can buy many weird things like feathers of birds hanging from loops, that have the power to catch and fulfil one`s dreams, or Feng-shui lamps of salt from Himalaya, by the help of which one have the opportunity to create a balanced and harmonious chi in his/her surrounding, and thus attain a happier, healthier and wealthier life. Or, one may invest some money in purchasing crystal balls that have the power to track down the paths of energy helpful to one`s physical and spiritual health… !

According to the newspaper report about the last fair in Oslo, there were 200 such stalls and 300 events took place during one week-end. Many of the names of the alternative treatments were unknown to me. Among them craniosacral therapy seemed interesting. These therapies recognize that all living tissues breathe and create rhythmic pulses. These "breathes of life" include the cranial rhythmic pulses, which can be detected by sensitive hands of the practitioners. The cranial rhythm is the shortest tide that moves through the tissues. The longer tides bring the first stirring of life as the Breath of Life emerging from a deeper ground of stillness at the centre of our being. These biodynamic rhythms carry waves that disseminate the ordering forces in the body and the mind and form patterns. Under stress and traumas these natural patterns can be affected down to the cellular level. Biodynamic craniosacral therapy claims to resolve congestions in the rhythmic patterns that may cause disease of body and mind. The therapists "listen through their hands" to body`s subtle pulses and identify places where tissues are unhealthy. Then they redirect the body`s natural healing power to heal itself. Thus they help to enhance body`s own self-healing and self-regulating capabilities.

The main reason for this spreading interest in the alternative therapy is the realization of the presence of an energy field around biological systems – which are given many different names – like bioplasma, human energy field, universal life energy, prana, chi etc. It is recognized that this energy flows along the spine from the sacrum to crown of the cranium in both directions carrying different vibratory frequencies. It is known as craniosacral movement in craniosacral therapy, kundalini power in Kundalini Yoga, and "chi" in Taoist Inner Alchemy. Different therapists profess different methods to tap these energies to improve the conditions of the health and the mind without being able to find a scientific rationale behind what they profess.

However, one common thing among these different branches of alternative practices, related to the bioenergy, is the existence of three sources of energies – one is universal spiritual energy not related to the material energy the scientists talk about, the second is the cosmic energy in which every living and non-living beings are immersed, and the third is the source of energy that is tied to earth, water, fire and the physical environment around the living beings. The human beings receive the universal spiritual energy through the crown in the cranium, which then descends along the spine to the physical body. The earth-borne energies ascend from the sacrum towards the crown. The interactions of the heavenly and the earthly energies form the foundations of the biological and mental life of the human beings. Taoists masters profess that cosmic energy enters through the direction of the prefrontal cortex - the so-called third eye lying between the eyebrows. It empowers the mind and the brain with the capacity to connect oneself with the higher self. Other schools, like Kundalini for example, are nothing but different variants of the same. Scientists consider them as humbug and bogus. How can these people prove the existence of such energy unless they can be tested under controlled experiments of the scientists? One fails to measure these forces with the available instruments at the disposal of the scientific community and therefore the practitioners withdraw from scientific reasoning and assert that science cannot explain everything. They argue that science is still in its primitive stage as regards the understanding the mystery of the life and the mind.

Instead, they claim, as the sages of the ancient world did more than five thousand years ago, "The universal energy or Prana, the breath of life, is the basic constituents of all forms and life; all matter, animate or inanimate, are composed of and pervaded with this energy moving through the duality of Yin and Yang – one moving from earth to heaven and the other from heaven to earth. Life is a dance of molecules and atoms in this sea of the energy field. It supports, nourishes and gives us the essence that we call life. We sense each other with it; we are of it and it is inseparable from us."

"Can you prove that this energy that cannot be detected by scientific instruments really exists?" the sceptic may challenge.

"The easiest way to observe the energy field is to combine the body and mind together and use it as an instrument. Then simply relax on your back on the grass on a nice sunny day and gaze at the blue sky. After a while you will see squiggly patterns floating against the blue sky. This will bring an expansion of the vision and with training you will be able to see the whole field pulsating in synchronized rhythms. Now you should shift your eyes to the edges of the treetops against the sky. You will see a green haze around the tree. If you look closer you will see globules at the edges of the green haze changing their squiggly patterns and flowing into the aura of the tree…" I have heard this explanation from a healer who heals patients by reading their auras.

"Such visions can be caused by epilepsy of the visual cortex. Anyway, what you see, are all happenings in your brain", skeptic may charge back.

"So use your brain as an instrument to observe. You believe that every experience of the mind is driven by ionic transports that follow mechanical laws that bring accidental outcomes through a complex set of chemical interactions. It is purposeless and blind in whatever it sees. But if you are a good scientist you should know that ions themselves do not follow definite paths. Their existence fluctuates in many energy states at the same time. How the fluctuations of trillions of such fluctuating ions coordinate themselves and realize as a particular vision of the mind may not be so easy for you to explain. How do the ions, dancing chaotically everywhere in an indeterministic way, create the order that you perceive as a vision? Aren`t everything dancing in a sea of energy? Isn`t this energy the source of the order that emanates as the world in the end? If you know science well, you certainly know that the reality observed and the one who observes the reality cannot be separated from the definition of reality of the world. How can you subtract the functioning of the brain from the reality itself? The brain is also an integral part of the dance of everything in this sea of energy. Why the experiences of vision appearing as a reality to my brain should have less reality than what you define as a reality where the brain is not an integral part of what you claim to observe? Why, what I see cannot be called real? " the healer rebuts.

"Energies contained in the cells can be measured by scientific means in terms of actions and work they are able to produce. But your fictitious energy cannot move things and produce actions and work." skeptic would not like to give up to a healer´s argument.

"This is exactly what it does. It sets up the foundation of the pattern and order that hold in place all those fluctuating ions dancing randomly in a sea of energy. The ions rest in the network formed by this universal energy field and become the source and sink of the physical energy of matter that you talk about. In our language we call your form of energy as the Earth energy which is tied to the existence of the material forms. There exist forces in the universe that transcend the form-bound world that you call reality. Understanding of the true reality may be gained where mind and spirit are seen as an integral part of all existence. Do not make an ad hoc assumption that everything can be reducible to the energy that imparts forms to the material world."

I see the healer lying supine and gazing at the blue sky and watching the aura moving around the trees that have already turned green. The spring has come. The sprouts have emerged as leaves around erect spikes that have transformed into cluster of white flowers on the chestnut trees. According to the healer, before the leaves have opened like fingers around palms, energy fields have grown in the shapes of the leaves before the physical body has anchored in that energy field and filled them with biological tissues. This energy field, on which the physical leaf has anchored into existence, can be observed in Kirlian photography. The Kirlian photographs were first made by Semyon Kirlian, when he took contact photographs of the whole and then the cut leaf on photographic plates subjected to high frequency high voltage electricity. In the cut leaf the image of the whole uncut leaf was visible, which was interpreted as the representation of the underlying energy body of the leaf.

This Kirlian photography has become popular in the fairs of alternative therapy. It is believed that with the help of this photography one can make images of the auras of different colours around human beings and things. These photographs are now understood as being caused by discharges from ionized gases that follow the energy pattern of the body. The practitioners can read information about the health by studying the auras, which are sensitive to mental and physical state of the patient. These auras, that have many layers spreading from the edges of the body to the outside space, are results of the flow of the energy along the spines. According to Kundalini Yoga these auras are related to several vortices, which are known as chakras that move like in a cone from the spine to the outer surroundings of the body. Through these vortices the earthly, the cosmic and the spiritual energies enter the physical bodies. Different vortices are connected to different physical organs and mental states like reasons, emotions, love, compassion, spirituality etc. The diseases of the body and mind are explained as being caused by locking of the vortices and their misalignments. The healers can open up these energy channels by using their own energy fields.

After a program in the main TV channel that presented a healer of Norway, lately the interests in healing have sky rocketed in this country. This healer could even heal through distant communication without any need of transferring energy through nearness. After this program the interests in the esoteric have multifold at the dismay of the atheists. The interest in healing has become more dramatic when the Minister of Health has openly confessed in the TV that he believes in the healer and he himself has consulted him and got good results.

The interests had started building up after the princess Martha Louise of Norway announced the opening of a healing centre called "Astarte Education" where she offered the participants in the training course in coming in contact with the angels. About two years ago she had opened this centre in Bygdøy Alle. Now the whole nation is gripped by this esoteric world. People now say that they do not believe in religion but believes in the healer instead.

Are there channels that must be opened to receive the forces that can connect to the greater consciousness? I try to connect to the human beings who pass by Bygdøy Alle. Some are fat, some are lean, some are muscular and some have features that attract the eyes and arouses the appreciation of beauty. The specialists studying human auras see different colours around them depending on their physical features and mental makeup. However, once one moves away from the immediate vicinity of the bodies and sees auras that envelop all other auras lying close to the body, the outer auras reveal more universal colours and form. The healers call them the astral and spiritual bodies that become more and more pronounced in human beings with higher awareness of life. The auras have different colours depending on the chakras they emanate from. The aura emanating from the chakra lying at the crown of the head is believed to be golden in colour.

My vision cannot penetrate the realm of the auras around the human being. Like Dawkins I also see the human beings as evolved chimpanzees walking on two feet whose bodies terminate at the epidemis level, where skin breathes in and out moisture and air. It is now established that the Kirlian photography are created by the electrical discharges released by these moisture. So colours of auras depend on the emotional state controlling the dissipation of the moisture around the body. However the auras are structured and have patterns which can give information about the inner physical and mental state. The healers say that it is the underlying energy body that brings this structure and pattern in place. If one can open one`s chakras to receive different energies the auras corresponding to those energies become stronger, orderly and more organized.

The search for such a hidden world behind the living realm has lately led me to study the fractal structures in leaves, petals and flower heads. My interests have been mostly asters and daisies belonging to the sunflower family. I have been studying the fractal patterns in the microscopic scale and been interested in finding out if I could find similar world in the flowers as I have discovered in the cosmos. Are those fractally embedded spirals that carry the mystery of creation of the cosmos, present in the flowers too? I have found spirals under the yellow clusters of florets forming the disc heads of these flowers. Behind these spiral patterns there exist the mathematics related to the Golden number, known as the Divine number by the mystics in the antiquity. Similar spiral formation exists in tens of thousands of species belonging to the Asteracea family of flowers, who are the late comers in the evolution. I have been following the development of this spiral formation with the passage of each hour of the day. It is as grandeur as a cosmic experience in watching how the florets open and reveal a universe that fluctuates and changes every moment. In the centres of the tiny florets there exists a world very similar to the structures that appear, at first, as chaotically oriented pattern, similar to the objects in the cosmos. The images of the cosmos and the flowers are so similar that it will be hardly possible to guess which one belongs to the cosmic structures millions of light years in size and which one belongs to the world of the flowers in the scale of microns.

My primary motivation for this study has been to find a new realm of art. The world in the cellular level has opened a realm of art I have never seen and could not imagine before. They have lifted my mind in an ethereal domain bringing a sense of mystery and wonder beyond my comprehension. How could the cells arrange themselves in such organized and planned way without the guidance of an intelligent mind? How could such a design be possible?

The movements of the chains and patterns follow the direction of the sun rays. So the sun is behind this intelligence…or what? This movement needs water supply and passage of nutrients that the bacteria are producing in the soil. Apart from the hydrogen, oxygen, and carbon, that the plants gathered from air and water, they need mineral nutrients like nitrogen, calcium, potassium, and phosphorous to grow in vigour and beauty. The minerals, dissolved in water, are carried to the cells against the force of gravity. Who empowers the plants to defy the force of gravity that have carved the massive fjords, rivers and mountains on Earth? Is it the force of life - the "prana" and the "chi"? Botanists explain it as the results of transpiration from the cells that breathe out moisture from the cells and create a pressure in the vascular system that transports nutrients to the leaves and flowers. In the Kirlian photography one can observe this transpiration as discharges moving out from the leaves and creating an aura that constantly changes, vibrates and moves as an animated object representing the force of life. What has set everything to respire and transpire and brought forth this extremely intelligent way to overcome the pull of gravity and move upwards? Once the nutrients come, the "eyes" or the openings through which the plants respire and transpire, inhale oxygen and then by the help of the energy pouring out of the sun, set extremely complex chemical processes that generate energy necessary for the organelles of the cells to form and renew themselves.

It is said that there are about seventy different chemical reactions involved in such photosynthesis. Is there any intelligent mind, who has set all these motions and reactions in place? Or are everything just caused by chance? Can such immense complexity of planning and design arise out of accident and chance? Is it not too awe inspiring to have come into existence by chance?

Is it natural selection as the Darwinians argue? According to these scientists natural selections reduce the problem of the immense complexity into problems of lesser and lesser improbabilities as one breaks the problem into smaller and smaller scales. According to the proponents of these ideas the things in smaller scales are not as highly improbable as the one that exist as a larger system. Thus breaking things in smaller and smaller units one may reach the scale when things are tractable and may be only slightly improbable. The complexity, that appears as an intelligent design, can be nothing but a result of stacked up improbabilities of increasing order with stacking of smaller units to form larger units in a hierarchical manner ending up into an objects of irreducible complexity as a macroscopic object like a flower, for example.

But are the cells, which are thousands of times smaller than the florets in the daisy less complex and slightly improbable and more tractable to understanding as the evolutionist would like to believe? What I have discovered in the cosmos goes against this view. The Universe appears to image itself in smaller and smaller scales in a very similar way without reducing the complexity that exists in its manifestation in the highest order. This realization has now led me to look into the microscopic world down to the levels of the cells and the DNAs.

Of course, though the organelles in the cells are extremely complex and their interactions with each other appear immensely and, may be, irreducibly more complex, they are all made of the same elemental stuff – mostly hydrogen, carbon, oxygen and nitrogen. These elements, once produced in a sun like star, is the building blocks of the amino acids and proteins that form the backbones of all living creatures – from bacteria and algae to the creatures of any size and intelligence that live on Earth, or had ever lived before or, going to live anywhere in the future.

So all are made of star dusts! Somehow these dusts have come to form the amino acids and proteins on Earth and with it the process of life has begun following the principles of natural selection. How amazing that in the cellular level the cells of the human body and the cells in plants and trees – even the bacteria are very similar! They all possess the similar organelles that have similar functions. What makes a human different from a plant are the different genetic codes that remain uncoiled inside helically moving spiral structures. Even in the level of proteins and the DNAs that are built by assembling different amino acids, or nucleic acids consisting mainly of carbon, oxygen, nitrogen and hydrogen, the structures are very complex. Do these cells and organelles breathe? Are the protein and DNA formations activated by a mechanism outside the chemical properties of the molecules, like some kind of vibratory energy like "prana", or "chi"? Or do the molecules bind themselves into complex designs following the blind laws of physics?

The healers say that the all-pervading "prana" or "chi" can act upon the chemical buildup of cells and organs and with the use of such energy one may heal the wounds and diseases of the body. The human mind is the instrument through which one may access this unphysical energy that has escaped the detection of the measuring instruments of the physicists, chemists and biologists. The scientific medicine uses a different view about the working of the body and the ways to treat the diseases. In this view the way the cells in the body function are results of nearly a billion years of experiences of the cells in seeking a path of survival amidst constant stresses and strains impressed on them by the changing conditions of the climates and chemical elements dissolved in the air, the water and the crust forming the Earth. It is the need to survive in the evolution, based on natural selection, which has set these modes of functioning as automatons programmed by the nature driven by purely mechanical laws. This function can be hampered with the scarcity of the elements that go in forming the amino acids, proteins and the nucleic acids. It will result in the imbalance of the production of the energies, which are released in different chemical reactions. Without the supply of these chemically generated energies the cells and tissues in the body won`t survive. When some chemicals are over produced, or under produced, the body reacts by showing symptoms of diseases in the form of cell dysfunction or cell growths, which may threaten life. The way to cure is to find out the particular chemicals to be set in balance in the body by supplying it in the form of medicine.

With the entrance of the sun in the Age of Aquarius, the world has got polarized into two opposite camps: On one side the rational science, that interprets everything in the universe including mind, consciousness, spirituality, God as the products of the material world. In their view the mind is nothing but chemical activities in the brain cells. The character of the mind including feelings and emotions can be changed by rewiring the cells so that they may fire differently in face of given physical responses. The artistic and musical abilities, as well as power of the rational reflections, required for scientific endeavors, can be manipulated by genetic means. According to them religious feelings are caused by mental virus, the spiritual vision is nothing but epilepsy of the visual cortex, the hearing of voice from a spiritual realm is result of damaged Wernicke`s and Broca`s area in the left cortex, which is the mechanical part of the brain specialized in sound and language recognition.

In this scientific understanding of life, there is no higher purpose and meaning than what nature has bestowed on us as an animal that has evolved from more primitive ancestors by accidental mutation of genes. Moral is a derivative of the selfish genes which do not act without the goal of achieving positive results beneficial for its survival and reproduction. The smarter genes avoid and discard environments and associations that may make them less competitive in the battle of gaining evolutionary advantages. In this Darwinian rationale, only meaningful altruism is reciprocal altruism. Dawkins has explained this nature of this altruism in his book:

"… *The hunter needs a spear and the smith wants meat. The asymmetry brokers a deal. The bees need nectar and the flower needs pollinating. Flowers cannot fly and therefore they pay the bees, in currency of the nectar, for hire of their wings…both side benefit from transaction. ..Vampire bats learn which other individuals of their social group can be relied upon to pay their debts (in regurgitated blood) and which individuals cheat…For there will always be cheats, and stable solution of game theoretic conundrums of reciprocal altruism always involve an element of punishment of cheats. The mathematical theory allows two broad classes of stable solution to games of this kind. "Always nasty" is stable in that, if everyone else is doing it, a single nice individual cannot be better…But there is another strategy…goes under various names, including Tit-for-Tat, Retaliator and Reciprocator. It is evolutionary stable under some conditions…"*

In this scientific world nothing is considered rational enough unless one can formulate things in a mathematical language. The smarter species of the Age of Aquarius have started making mathematical models of morals and interpersonal conducts that would be more stable in the face of competitions and battle for advantage for oneself and one`s own progenies.

Another product of this rational thinking, based on Darwinian theory of evolution, is the free market economy, where everybody compete with everybody for economic gains and survival without any plan, intention or purpose except making profits and strengthening one`s personal wealth. In this free market capitalism prices of goods follow the rule of demand and supply. More the supply than the demand, the prices sink; more the scarcity but higher the demand, the prices rise. Higher the prices higher are the profit which attract more investors. More investment generates more supply and in turn brings down the prices, which repel the investors. It is a yo-yo game of the money seekers. They flow money from one area to the other, in one part of the globe to the other in order to find the best opportunities to make more profits. Wherever there is loss they abandon, and whenever there are opportunities of gain they gather as bees. The flow of money and investments pass through the banks. Once this flow gets bottle necked, the economic activities suffer. It is another scientific area where game theoretic models apply.

About a year ago the monetary flow has got bottle necked throwing many big banks and investment companies into bankruptcy and out of business while creating shock waves throughout the global economy. The share markets, where the speculators buy shares of companies with a hope to make profit later by selling them when the company's profits will be higher, went into disarray all over the world. All economies plunged at the same time while needing interventions from the governments to save the economic health of the respective countries. It revealed the danger of economic Darwinism that can bring global economy into ruin and thus endanger life of millions of human beings dependent on the production and supply of goods across nations and continents.

Another side of the free market economy is the modern consumer culture. It has exponentially exploded during the last few decades. In the open air restaurant by Bygdøy Allé an advertisement board has been carrying the picture of a young man surrounded by headphone, i-pod, mobile, Bluetooth etc. It entices the young passersby to enter the new information age: "Access to information can change life of millions of people..." Now one may download from the net in the hand held mobile, or the i-pod all the music that one may wish to enjoy. The most popular music for the young generation is the Metal Band. In the official main website of the Metal Band, that advertises "Cannibal Corps-

Style: Brutal Death", "Cradle of Filth","Children of Bodom" (named after the multiple homicide of children by the lake of Bodom in Finland) at the top of their music list, young people are invited for Unlimited download "...Download anything you want...No bandwidth limit... No content limits..." This is a world of death, terror and horror, which is sending out its tentacles to paralyze the human mind by using the power of technology and the media available in the communication age. They belong to the opposite camp of the New Age spiritualists and the healers.

The world has transformed so much within the first decade of the Age of Aquarius that no fortune teller could have ever predicted these developments. The traditional Easter festival in Oslo has got a parallel festivity called "Inferno Festival", which has become a yearly event of this city during the Easter time. The participants of this years` Festival were "Nocturno Culto", "Revolver", "Kill the Christians", "Paradise Lost", "Pestilence", "Septic Flesh", "Swallow the Sun", "Execration", "Terrordrome", "Vicious Art", "Vulture Industries", "Death Hammer", "Blood Red throne" etc. These are the names of the music bands who are as a group is called the Metal bands, that are subdivided into different genres like  Heavy, Black, Death, Doom, Thrash, Power, Speed etc. The fans of these metal bands are usually the young people, who have their quarter in this city that bustle with outdoor cafes, restaurants and night clubs. This generation has no fear for Heaven and God. They have the mission to bring down the religion belonging to the Age of Pisces to its ruin. Now man can marry man, woman can marry woman. In this liberated society no one - even a bisexual, or a blind, or a cripple - can be discriminated against the full right to enjoy leisure, pleasure, promiscuity or anything they may desire as their life`s goal. Those who worship Satan have full right and benefit to practice their belief as the believers of God do. In this New Age moral and values are synonymous with what individual ego can pursue. Everybody has the right to consume, abuse, and squander as much they can afford.

The changes brought during the first decade in the new millennium is so far reaching and unprecedented, that one may wonder how human beings would be able to adjust with this accelerating technological changes and to which direction the human beings may evolve from here. All knowledge of the world remains at the fingertips at any place or any moment where the connections to internet are available. One can even access it by a tiny handheld mobile phone from anywhere in the world. One can encounter each other in the virtual space and chat and discuss as in a real meeting where one can see each other. One can visit millions of shops of all kinds all over the world and order things that one may need. One can enjoy music and films from anywhere in the world, without any need to step out of the place one chooses to remain. With this New Age mortals seemed to have gained total control over his/her destiny. It is the Age when knowledge of science has triumphed and revealed how our brain and perceptions work in relations to mechanical signals that we receive which can be digitized and transmitted anywhere we wish. We can transmit sound and image of anything that can be received and perceived by human beings around the globe.

It is an age of the miracle of science that sees no God –but only the mechanical laws that bind the atoms and molecules together as chunks of matter possessing different properties. The mechanical laws also destine the paths that the particles must follow when they conduct through such matter, and control the electromagnetic waves when they propagate from one time and place to another time and place in the speed of light. The signals arrive to the brain, which use similar mechanical laws to transcribe and decode the digital data back to audio and visual forms. Thus the reality existing at far distant places and time appear as something happening in front of the listeners and the viewers.

For me this library has become my new Time Hall, where as a part of Tathagata I meditate and reflect about the spheres of reality that enwombs me in layers after layers of different levels of consciousness. I see myself immersed in the realm of consciousness bound to the biological necessities, the realm of myth and dream, the cosmos that activate the processes of evolutions of life, the intelligence that appears through the activities of the human brain and the supernatural, that I cannot comprehend, who breaks forth as vibrations and waves in my mind.

I feel fascinated by both of these sides of the Age of Aquarius. The imperceptible vibrations and the cosmic power, that enter the brain, expand the consciousness beyond the realm of things one can only understand by the power of reasoning and knowledge, are something that confirm my personal experiences since childhood. They draw me to the realm of wonder and awe beyond my comprehension and open imaginations and fantasies that elevate experience of life beyond the grasp of knowledge, symbols, languages and thoughts. It creates the urges to seek a world "out there" beyond the human intelligence.

After returning from Seoul, my eyes opened about the realm of arts that existed "out there". While working on the project "Reality, Myth and Dream: Art without Beginning and End" I had sensed the existence of the realm of experience that I called the realm of the "Poetry of Light".

This project had lifted my consciousness into a new level. Now the vision of an even greater art emerged in my mind. The project had revealed that once the paintings stand as a group around a theme, the individual paintings transcend the meaning that they bear as lone pieces. They gain a new level of beauty and meaning once they stand as parts of a whole. Similarly when a collection of groups of paintings can be assembled together to form a larger art, the themes related to the individual groups may transcend the meanings affixed to them and acquire beauty and meaning far greater than when they may convey as individual groups. In this way the beauty and meaning of individual art pieces can be enhanced and given an ethereal dimension by making them parts of larger and larger groups embedded in a hierarchical manner. I saw a new unseen world emerging with each level of transcendence towards larger and larger embodiment into a whole. With it my consciousness too expanded beyond the activities of the brain that processes information in the visual cortex lying above the temporal lobe.

In my imagination I could see a painting that will be so huge that it will be practically impossible to build any gallery, or museum that can exhibit such an art. But once my mind was ignited by such ideas and visions I was looking for a way to realize such an idea of art. I saw the possibilities in the technological development of the Age of Aquarius. I got possessed by the idea of building a virtual gallery in the computer that had no such limitation of space that one faced in the real world. In such a virtual sphere it was possible to embed any number of hierarchically assembled groups of paintings. Only limitation was the power of the computers to process and store such information.

In this virtual world, art, music, dance, philosophy, religion all could be woven together in a whole, that would be more representative of the true reality that embeds us in different layers of consciousness, like the one I experience in this Time Hall. It cannot be experienced by the power of the eyes, or ears alone.

Thus I wanted to create art in order to see the greater realms existing in myself – those unknown realms, which do not appear in thoughts, words and languages. Art became a way to penetrate into this reality which was rich in emotional contents. Here the real visual world fused with the invisible psychic domain colored by one's imagination, belief, fear, angst and the state of the mind which expressed one's relations to the world, that remained hidden but whose existence one could apprehend. Art existed in the boundary that divided the self between the realm that was revealed through thoughts, languages and perceptions and the greater world which lay hidden as a ghostly invisible sphere beyond the realm of languages and thoughts. Through art now I attempted to grasp the content of the invisible in the visible forms, and thus tried to penetrate the sphere from where urges and visions of supernatural world arrived and interfered with the so-called real life. It was an attempt to take  inside out, as if, standing in front of a mirror and looking at one's own image: Here one entered the other world and remained absorbed in the realm that was normally inaccessible to thought ridden life. The image of the one, one looked at, was not a replica of the image of oneself, which one normally saw in real life. It was an image of the self as one would see if it was seen as parts of the greater body to which one belonged.

It is this greater body, this greater image, one confronts while one stands in front of this magic mirror of art. In this greater body I see myself as the part of the protagonist, who is making a journey within himself through many territories of imaginations and feelings, known or unknown. On the other side of the mirror, one moves and mingles with the creatures and beings of mythical origin, as well as confronts challenges to overcome fear that sets the mind to ride in territories of unprecedented ecstasies of joys. It is the realm where the self, revealed in the conscious realm, meets the other nature of the self, which is hidden under the veil of an imperceptible nature. By encountering this self one encounters one's imaginations of the higher and lower powers driving life and nature as instruments of will and desire.

So, art became a meeting ground, a platform or a stage, where one could dance with oneself. In this dance I danced with me wearing masks of gods, devils, angels or whoever appeared from the realm of the unknown. It was a dance of the soul with itself, a confrontation of oneself with oneself moving on the other side that remained hidden and veiled.

It was a drama of meeting oneself alone with the crowd of characters, who were parts of oneself. It was a drama where there was only one character, divided into many images. I created myself. I threw away, or wore masks of others and taking the roles of the others or me, swirled around the stage where gods, goddesses, devils and angels entered and from where they exited. Thus art became a lonely play, where I acted and enacted again and again the role with my counterparts on the other side of the mirror that divided my real life from the one, where I moved with characters existing beyond the reality of life. It was a stage where I created a plethora of images and characters out of myself in order to avoid the crowd who encircled me on the stage that one called the real world of life.

I wanted to entangle all in my dance, and let them swirl in the play where I was the actor and the author of the play. It was my own dance, my own drama, and search to go beyond the limitations which the crowd and the so-called reality imposed on life. In this way I wished to bring forth all colors of visions which existed within me in territories where I was a part of the whole.

To find a platform that would give greater freedom to express one's emotions and visions, and bypass the constraints that lie in the real physical world, I got absorbed in mastering the virtual reality of the high-tech computer world. I embarked on this project where, by using videos and digital techniques, I sought to merge the characters and landscapes of the virtual worlds with real ballet and dance, mixing the multimedia production with my paintings and drawings. Thus I was set to penetrate worlds inside worlds that were inseparably enmeshed as the inner life of all human beings on the rotating stage.

This project, that demanded high skill in digital techniques, led me to master several computer software related to virtual characters, landscapes, architectures etc. and I had to learn several graphic, video and audio editing techniques. As I got possessed in this digital world the doors to the mystery of the universe opened. It came through the understanding of the way human vision works. The digital techniques extended the capacity of observing the reality far beyond my imagination, and thus by an accident revealed a totally new universe that had no beginning and end.

# Chapter 6

# UNIVERSE AND GOD

After Geneva we went to Seoul, where my wife was appointed as the Ambassador of Norway to South Korea. This change of place brought a change of activities. I resumed paintings, through which I had maintained a contact with the inner being in my childhood. By then the age of digital technology had entered the daily life of people. My renewed interests in arts led me to get more and more interested in the graphic software and image processing methods and techniques. This, in turn, became the steps in discovering the universe, which had obsessed my mind since the cosmos had appeared in my vision in the adolescent age.

In Seoul I got an opportunity of holding an exhibition in the prestigious Seoul Arts Centre. This opportunity led me idea to create a painting that consisted of many paintings. Every individual painting was a part of a single painting that had no beginning and end. Each painting returned to itself after moving through the cycle of life, death and resurrection. With this movement darkness descended and devoured light, the beauty that once seemed Divine, disappeared and returned as earthly maiden possessing power of seduction and temptation that drag life in the biological and sensual world of struggle and suffering. Similarly, when everything sank into darkness, the light broke forth, spring followed winter and the spirit of love and life resurrected from the world of the dead. The beauty transcended the boundary of the senses and appeared as muses who drew the mind to an ethereal domain. In this dream world the earth-bound creatures aspired to ascend to Heaven, from where angels, gods and goddesses descended as mythical figures to mingle with the earth-bound women and men. The tranquillity of Heaven existed side by side the turmoil of the mortal world: Chaos gave birth to tranquillity and from tranquillity chaos and turmoil reappeared again and again.

The paintings for the exhibition were done on large canvases so that the painted figures had the sizes of the women and men in the real life. I got the idea of integrating ballet and music with paintings, to bring forth the world I had been visualizing as poetry and opera in my mind. In the exhibition the mythical figures in the paintings came out of the canvases as dancing figures and mingled with the real world of the mortal visiting the gallery. After the dance these figures returned to the dreamy world of myth once again.

While painting for this exhibition "Reality Myth and Dream in the Norwegian Lanscape: Art Without Beginning and End Moving Through the Cycle of Life Death and Resurrection" I saw the arena of the mind where not only reality, myth and dream were one, but also the virtual worlds constructed by the pure imaginative power of the mind and the advanced digital technology, available in the new computer age, could expand the reality in a newer level of consciousness.

The interests in creating 3D virtual reality by digital means took me to explore the possibilities of various computer software and computing techniques. At the same time, I returned to pursue the mystery of the universe once again. By this time, due to the availability of more and more powerful computers, studying nonlinear systems had become possible.. heralding the age of doing mathematics with the help of computers. With it, chaos theory and fractal geometry had become popular scientific subjects. Mandelbrot had popularized it and had an idea that the universe could itself be a fractal.

It attracted my imagination. With a professor in Seoul I started studying the possible chaos theoretic model of the universe. Then I returned to Norway and started a collaboration work with a friend and former colleague at the University of Trondheim who was studying neutron stars. He brought to my attention the phenomena called the gamma-ray explosions occurring every day in the sky. These small bangs were outpouring enormous amount of energies in gamma-rays. As I started looking into it, I got convinced that these explosions could be extra-galactic. Thus I was drawn in studying the large scale structures in the universe like galaxies and galaxy clusters.

Soon the quest for an answer led me to study quasars and my eyes fell on a special galaxy known as the Cartwheel galaxy. NASA's Hubble telescope had already taken close up pictures of the inner ring, and deciphered comet-like structures inside the nuclear region of the galaxy. It was very bizarre. I decided to use my newly acquired computer knowledge to explore the nucleus of this galaxy in details and thus to my amazement entered into a new universe!

The structures I discovered were truly fractals, as Mandelbrot had speculated. Very similar ring like structures were embedded inside the nucleus itself. This ring, inside the nuclear ring, enclosed an even smaller ring in turn. It became a tremendously fascinating journey that led me to discover the universe without any beginning and end. The universe has never appeared at any moment of time in the past. So there is no question of coming from somewhere in the past or going to somewhere in the future. It lives in eternity while carrying an unchanging design as its foundation of existence. Through the manifestation of the most perfect order, it can self- regulate all that are coming into forms and disappearing outside the realm of forms by a processes which we call death and birth. It rises from itself and becomes manifest in form and then through renewal of its parts it remains ever-unchanging in all scales from the tiniest structures to the largest that can ever form. It is the only way the universe can self-create itself from itself and thus exist forever.

In this timeless universe the most central dynamics lies in the way every structure regulates inflow and outflow. This mechanism is enacted with the help of a three-armed spiral form, which sits at the centre of all cosmic objects. It ejects material along the spiral arms and then creates a mechanism to attract the outgoing flows, so that all outflows merge with the incoming streams and return to the centre again. The three-armed spiral is a fractal structure, which is embedded inside a large spiral, which in turn is embedded inside an even larger spiral and so on. In every scale the similar mechanism of outflow returning as inflow are activated while creating an extremely complex entanglement of filaments knotted together.

This universe had little in common with the idea of the universe on which the Darwinian atheists based their understandings and views about the meaning of life. The standard model of the universe says that the universe started from a singular point 13 billion years ago. Before that no time, no space existed. The newer versions of this model now envisage many universes existing as bubbles. Our universe has risen by the collisions of two such bubbles by accidents. All these bubbles exist as purposeless accidental happenings. The Darwinian variant of the multiverse theory expands these ideas to propose that the daughter universes are born out of the mother universes in black-holes. The fundamental constants that decide the nature of the material universe in a daughter universe is slightly mutated version of the constants that existed in the parent universe. Those universes, which have the values of the fundamental constants that are fit to survive and reproduce in a competition among the universes, predominate the multiverse scenario. Those who last enough can reproduce a daughter universe in black-holes.

What a limitless freedom of fantasy! What a marvellous example of blind faith in a theory and a model that may have nothing to do with the creation of the universe!

Before Copernicus, the Earth was believed to be surrounded by circular bands with hierarchically arranged circles of kings, bishops and angels of higher and higher ranks. All these bands were encapsulated in a world of stars. The whole, including the stars, was in turn enwombed in a transcendental unmoving space of God. In this cosmogony the powers of the kings came from the providence of God, sanctioned by the earthly representatives of the Divine world, like Popes, the cardinals and the Bishops. These religious men interpreted the words of God and the creation mystery. They also raised people to wars and crusades against the nonbelievers and played power games with the kings and their mighty men while amassing wealth and gaining controls over the faiths of the common women and men. As the image of the universe existing around the Earth with the planets, and the sun and the moon orbiting around the Earth, as the prefect creation of God, crumbled with the rise of the Copernican view, that displaced Earth from the centre of the universe, the human beings rose to understand their true positions in the cosmos and began to challenge the teachings of the churches. After being displaced from the centre of the universe, man started to project itself in the realm of the cosmos as a creature in search of its true identity. The idea of the universal harmony related to music took roots in scientific enquiries. Kepler associated the orbits of the planets with the spheres circumscribing the polyhedrons embedded inside each other in a concentric manner. The universe was music of proportions existing among these spheres. The other theories of the planetary orbits were based on the musical vibrations arising from the celestial monochords. Athanasius Kircher described the six days of creation as results of a polyphonic organ music played by God. Thus the attempts to understand the mystery of the universe moved towards universal harmony, proportions and geometry.

The role of God was further diminished after the orbits of the planets could be described by the laws of gravity discovered by Newton at the end of the 17th century. With it the age of the mathematical physics was born. Now, instead of Earth the sun became the centre of the universe as a star surrounded by innumerable other stars forming a celestial sphere. Only by the end of the eighteenth century it was discovered that the universe consisted of not only stars but there also existed a few nebulae within a disc like shape. Though philosopher Kant had speculated that the nebulae could be clusters of stars forming galaxies like the Milky Way, the observational evidence of the existence of a galaxy outside the Milky Way did not come before Einstein had formulated a new theory of gravitation. Newton believed gravity was a force created by God. Einstein brought that Newtonian God down, and replaced it by a very sophisticated mathematical theory. According to this theory, the source of gravity is matter itself moving in a reality where space and time were intimately connected by forming a four dimensional world. The presence of matter creates dents, i.e. curvatures, in space-time, which acts as a force surrounding the matter and generates the attractive attributes associated with gravity. So, no Newtonian God was necessary for explaining the origin of mechanism turning the celestial objects in orbits.

The mathematical equations explaining gravity as space-time curvature were very difficult to solve. Attempts for a solution succeeded in 1928 with the assumption that universe was like a sphere filled in a homogeneous manner with gravitating matter, so that any sample picked from any part of the universe was similar in properties. The solution of this model indicated that all matter in the universe were concentrated at a point in the beginning of time. The universe had taken birth with an explosion and been expanding since then. By then Hubble had already detected several galaxies outside the Milky Way and found out that they were all receding away from us. It fitted with the results of the solutions of the mathematical model and thus gave birth to the modern cosmology. The truthfulness of this theory was further strengthened by the discovery of a ball of radiation enveloping all corners of the sky. It was interpreted as the remnants of the hot fireball that had once risen with the explosion. The formations of galaxies were explained as the results of the fluctuations in the fireball.

Though this model was accepted by the majority of the scientists and publicized as the truth about the universe, the voice in me had always spoken against this scenario of creation. My attempt to build a higher order theory of gravity in the 1980s ended in drawing ridicules from the experts. In the cosmic journey of Tathagata Angel had explained the mystery of creation. However, the views expounded by the Angel had no empirical foundation. They appeared as knowledge pouring forth from a supernatural realm. He was like a supernatural agent, possessing all knowledge of the universe, breaking forth in the mind to deliver the mystery of creation to the ignorant man.

The doors to understand the cosmic mystery in a scientific way, that confirmed much of what I had heard during the comic journey of Tathagata, opened after I moved into this apartment in Oslo. It opened through a series of accidental happenings. After finishing "Tathagata `s Journey" when I had returned to the mathematical model I was pursuing during 1980s once again, as results of errors in my calculations I ended up in finding very unstable solutions, that fluctuated widely with slight variations of parameters. Before I found out my mistakes these wide fluctuations led me to believe that the universe could be chaotic. Therefore I plunged into studying chaos theory and attempted to build a chaos theoretic model of the universe. While I was deepening my interests in chaos theory and fractal geometry, a former colleague from the University of Trondheim contacted me. He suggested to me if I would be interested to look at the phenomena known as gamma-ray bursts. The satellites detecting gamma-rays from cosmos were observing explosions coming from different directions in the sky everyday without leaving any counterparts that were visible in the optical wavelengths. There were speculations that these explosions could be caused by merging of colliding neutron stars. However, observational evidences were indicating that they could be coming from outside the Milky Way galaxy. I got involved in this project in the middle of planning the multidisciplinary art project involving music, ballet, paintings and virtual reality 3D. The knowledge about the computer and the digital imaging techniques turned out to be a great help in understanding the nature of the universe. Soon my interests switched from the neutron stars to the extragalactic arena and to the realm of the dwarf blue galaxies where new stars were being born. With it, the rapid expansion of the internet facilities became a god given opportunity to access data taken by the telescopes and satellites making observations in different wavelengths. Thus a new scientific journey in the cosmos began again!

Soon I discovered a universe that was in conflict with the big-bang cosmology. The beauty and profundity of this newly discovered universe was so immense that no religious experience could match it. With the help of the computers I was discovering a universe of utter awe and splendour that I could never imagine. Such a universe was beyond the capacity of my rational thinking and power of imagination. It contradicted with all what I had been doing as a mathematical physicist. Gradually steps by steps I started understanding the mystery of creation that had no beginning or end. It was so overwhelming beyond words that I kneeled before the sky :

*"O Infinite! It is not possible to comprehend Thee. But I see and comprehend Thee!*

*From every place I see matter being released into space and moving away from the centre of creation. From wherever I stand and watch I see the centre from where things are moving away. From everywhere I see you emanating as the world.*

*O Infinite! I cannot comprehend your true nature; but I see Thee through the veils of creation that you have woven in the universe. Everywhere the same, every where you are working; at each place you are moving within yourself embedded in self-similar structures in smaller and smaller scales.*

*O Infinite! I see Thee in the tinniest of all; I see Thee in the largest structure that is possible to see with the observational instruments mankind possess; I see you unfold in my mind creating an amazing awe!*

*O Infinite! I see Thee as the Wheel of Eternity. I see things emanating from Thee and returning to Thee. This Wheel of Eternity contains wheels inside wheels in a never ending order in every structure, sub-structure, sub-sub-structure...and so on. I see the burning rings enclosing one another. From these rings the universe is being born. The rings are falling into pieces and carrying your eternal form, while the images of the disappearing rings are being born in the womb of the created things.*

*O Infinite! I see this process as the movement of the one existing in two. I see motion that is moving in order to contradict itself; I see you as two opposing coils merging and forming the shape that is you, who is always remaining the same.*

*O Infinite! I see the collisions, the merging, the spirals, and the ellipticals as the manifestation of the same dynamics. From the pieces moving from centre of everything, I see you forming the same motion in smaller and smaller domains. I do not understand Thee; but I see order in the apparently never ending chaos.*

*O Incomprehensible! I see you being manifested as the highest and the most sublime order, while things may apparently be moving in a state of disorder, from the point of view of my existence from where I observe Thy wonder.*

*O God of infinite wonder! I see Thy compassion creating the world and in Thy womb all are moving back as the Children of God.*

*O Lord of eternal motion! I see you as the end and the beginning of ALL."*

Since then I got totally absorbed in studying the way the structures in the universe have come into existence.

In this universe without beginning and end, everything existed as parts of the whole, which exist always. A star in the universe, like our sun, exists as a part of a galactic system; a galaxy exists as a part of a cluster structure; a cluster exists as a part of the super-cluster structure; a super-cluster exists as a part of the universe, which is timeless. Structure belonging to a particular scale like a star, or a galaxy, or a cluster, or a super-cluster does not pop up at a particular moment of time in the history of creation to be used as an assembly part to create larger units. If the structure in the higher scale does not exist, the smaller structures would not come into being. So, like the whole universe, structures in all scales - from stars and planets to the clusters and super-clusters of galaxies - have existed as long as the universe has existed. Although the stars, galaxies, galaxy clusters etc. have existed as classes of cosmic objects, the individual stars, galaxies, clusters etc. Are not eternally shining objects. As individuals they all come and go in an eternal universe. The individual objects take birth (or die) as results of the evolution that occurs in the higher object of which they are parts. The evolution from birth to death in the higher scale, in turn, is a consequence of the evolution taking place in the next higher level. The birth and death of stars are consequences of the evolution taking place in a galaxy, the evolution of the galaxy is a result of the evolution in the cluster, the evolution of the cluster is destined by the evolution of the super-clusters to which the cluster belongs, the evolution of the super-cluster results from the evolution of the universe. So the eternal universe evolves in the sense that everything embodied in the universe moves and undergoes changes and evolutions. Though things are born anew, or they die following a path of evolution everywhere, that bring forth the concept of time, the universe self-creates itself from its own death and decay. Thus it remains the same in the way it sets forth the dynamics of changes and evolutions everywhere, and maintains its own existence as an eternal entity. The universe exists in time in a timeless arena.

In this timeless universe the cosmic structures of different scales, from the largest to the smallest size, have existed always as expressions of the existence of the Being, who is never born and never dying. In this ever existing reality, that appears as the universe, the individual objects are all ephemeral. They all come and go as dance of life and death in order to renew the universe everywhere in all scales. The destinies of the individuals are orchestrated to fit into the eternal waltz of existence where things appear and disappear here and there to renew everything again and again, without disappearing forever into nothing, or appearing from nowhere and nothing.

It was a universe where spiral structures were the central elements of the formation of all cosmic objects appearing in different scales. In the heart of all creations there existed a structure similar to the triskelion, which for the Celts is a symbol of the triple goddesses Danna, who is their most ancient deity. It is most possible that the Christian Trinity came from this Celtic symbol. This triple spiral in Celtic religion means wisdom that brings life, death and rebirth. She is the Divine creator, who brings all things into being. The Celts saw her as the power of Earth that brings fertility and growth, as the water and sea carrying flow of her magic Divine energy, and the source of inspiration and intellect in her aspect as the goddess of Air. She is the source of Divine knowledge, the knower of the secrets of the Divine Alchemy and Magic that encompass all into a universal structure forming an inseparable knot. This knot is a representation of the infinite that encompasses all into one.

This knot has no beginning and end and portrays the timeless nature of all existence. Spiritually, the symbol is interpreted to represent the connection that the humans beings have with the infinite universe that exists on the outside, but is also present within every creature. Some historians also interpret as the symbols representing an uninterrupted life cycle, wherein the soul continues to make its journey from one body to another, until it merges with the source of all things in this universe. The knots having continual looping patterns represent eternity and interconnectedness of all.

Amazingly the new universe I discovered by analysing the recent data from different satellites sent to explore the cosmos in different wavelengths, turned out to be a complex "Celtic knot" where the triskle were the source of all birth, death and regeneration. The design of this knot turned out to be universal and timeless. It embraced all existing structures in the universe in the same network of weaving – however small or large. There seemed to exist a universal cosmic intelligence that surpassed all imaginations and intellectual comprehension, as regards its complexity. It held everything as an "inseparable One", which created everything from itself. In this universe life could not exist without death occurring simultaneously somewhere else. Like a Phoenix universe emerged from its own death and decay.

It was only a more complex knot than what the Celts had been able to imagine. It was a fractal knot, made of similar knots in a smaller scale, which in turn were made of even smaller knots and so on in hierarchically descending scales, starting from the structure representing the whole universe to the tinniest objects that one could observe. In these immensely complex networks of knots, which in turn are made of network of smaller knots, which in turn were made of similarly complex network of even smaller knots and so on... built inside smaller and smaller structures in an unfathomable way, the universe remained similarly complex at whatever size one studied it. In this entangled universe what happened here and now was intimately connected to what were happening there and then. The universe acted as an organism communicating with all parts at the same time, so that every occurrence of things at one place and time had its place in the universe`s complex design.

The discovery of this universe came from the search of the origin of the gamma-ray bursts. The search outside the Milky Way galaxy convinced me that the strong bursts were associated with dwarf star forming galaxies moving at high speeds. It led me to study the quasars and the related objects. While studying the quasars I came across phenomena that indicated that these so-called quasars could be ejected objects, as the Astronomer Halton Arp had been professing since 1960s. It brought me to study Cartwheel galaxy that had two companion galaxies nearby. I was interested to find out if those accompanying galaxies were ejected objects or not. By that time Hubble Space telescope was taking close-up pictures of the nucleus of the Cartwheel galaxy that appeared puzzling to the astronomers because of the comet like structures that were seen inside the nucleus. This Cartwheel galaxy possessing an outer ring as the rim of a wheel of a cart, and an inner ring surrounding the nucleus and joined by spoke looking structures with the outer ring aroused my curiosity.

I discovered more rings inside the nucleus and finally was taken aback by discovering a fractal structure, which I called the "Design of God". The galaxy was made of similar structures embedded in smaller and smaller scales. At the heart was the knot formed of triskelion, which controlled the ejections of matter from the centre that emerged in the forms of the so-called "comet-looking" structures of thousands of light years in dimension.

I threw myself in studying other galaxies and found similar fractal networks in most of them. They all bore a universal way of embedding the knitted pattern in smaller and smaller scales running deep inside the nuclei. In every scale the pattern was made by weaving of the filaments of gases falling towards the centre while gases were streaming out of the centre. All that moved outwards were pulled back to join the incoming flow. The interactions of the incoming and outgoing flows created the seeds of structures along the pathways carrying gases along the woven pattern. The similar pattern repeated to occur in a fractal manner inside the womb of the same pattern existing in a larger scale. The incoming and outgoing flows of the patterns exiting in scales after scales formed a much more complex knot than the Celtic mystics had envisioned. Wherever, in whatever scale, the incoming and outgoing flows had met, the new structures were generated that carried the same pattern resembling the whole.

This fractal nature of the building of cosmic structures appeared also in the scale of clusters of galaxies as well as the clusters of clusters of galaxies, known as super clusters, in a very similar way as in the formation of the galaxies. The whole universe turned out to be very similar to what the Celts have represented in their religious symbol – though more complex and amazing, beyond human comprehension.

I discovered the area in the sky from where the super clusters of galaxies have emerged from the "void". This place is known as the "Local Void" to astronomers because very few galaxies can be observed in this area compared to other areas of the sky packed with galaxies. In this "void" there existed a triskleion structure. The super clusters emerged as cosmic objects ejected from this three-armed spiral form. They were all moving away from the "Local Void". After being ejected from the centre, these structures were on a journey outward to join the structures which were moving towards the centre. The universe, while ejecting structures on the one hand, was pulling structures towards it centre at the same time on the other hand. The universe was an arena where implosions and explosions were going on at the same time. On one hand the universe was regenerating new structures and on the other hand breaking down the old structures and pulling the material towards its womb to recreate the world anew. By upholding these movements from inside out and from outside to inside, the universe remained unchanging and the same. It was feeding on itself as the fuel of its own growth, while breaking itself apart into its own fodder.

These movements created a fluctuating world, appearing and disappearing from everywhere, and then reappearing as new object …again and again … as the dance of life, death and regeneration. However though fluctuating and ephemeral in all places, the universe remained the same by upholding the same pattern of weaving in all cosmic scales that never changed with this constant flux of life and death. The fluctuations created the consciousness of time in a timeless arena where the dynamics forming the whole and its parts remained eternally the same. It was a universe where time existed in a timeless arena woven by an eternal design.

In complete contradiction to the big-bang cosmology, in which the universe has risen at a moment of time as an accident and chance without any purpose and meaning to fulfil, and without any intelligence to steer it course, this new universe has not risen at a particular moment of time, and its existence is not accidental. It has existed eternally as a self-regulated system that rises and sinks within itself again and again in order to recreate and renew itself everywhere in all times. Like the "Celtic knot" neither it has any spatial beginning and end, nor it has any beginning and end in time. The time rises in our consciousness as the results of the fluctuations that keep the material universe dynamic and ever moving by reshuffling and rearranging matter from place to place. These rearrangements follow the dictates of the "intelligent way" that generates the image of the whole in smaller and smaller structures.

In this way the universe is the realm of perfect order and beauty, as the Neo-Platonists had once philosophized about. The Christian Platonists, Boethius, living in the fifth century, had described this beauty and perfection in a poetic prayer (Consolation of Philosophy)

*"Thou who dost rule the Universe with everlasting law,*
*Founder of Earth and Heaven alike,*
*Who has bidden time to stand forth from out of Eternity?*
*For ever firm in Thyself, yet giving movements unto all…*
*Thou makest all things follow that high pattern.*
*In perfect beauty Thou movest in thy mind a world of beauty, making all*
*in alike image,*
*And bidding the perfect whole to complete its perfect functions.*
*All the first principles of nature Thou dost bind together by perfect orders*
*as of numbers,*
*So that they may be balanced each with its opposite: Cold and heat…"*

The discovery of the new universe supports many of the philosophical reflections expressed in this poem: Everything emanates as the image of the world in forms from the perfect "One" that creates and embodies all. Everything is created to reveal the perfect "One" in alike image however large or small the existing objects could be. There exists an eternal pattern that manifests as the world. The triskle sitting at the centres of all cosmic structures bring the movements unto all as death, birth and regeneration. However, it itself never changes in form and remains firmly existing as a three-armed spiral for forever. Through this dynamics mediated by the three-armed spiral, the universe binds all existing beings in an orderly network formed by the outgoing hot gases and the incoming colder matter.

The existence of the Divine pattern becoming the world has been the central idea of the Platonists and the neo-Platonists since antiquity. In this new universe the "Diviner pattern" is the fractal weaving of filaments that appear in a universal way in all cosmic structures. It is the fractally embedded complexity of incomprehensible nature that cannot be fully grasped by the human mind. It is a network of networks of networks... of unfathomable depth, forming a complexity that appears as an immense chaos. This chaos hides the beauty and order, which have brought forth all creations.

In this universe things exist to create the foundation of time, animated by the constantly fluctuating motions of life, death and regeneration. One may wonder why things exist at all! The mechanism by which the universe sustains its existence may give a clue to an answer: In the entangled knotted universe, nothing can exist without the existence of the whole, and every existence is an image of the whole in different scales. The existence of the macro-worlds is intimately tied to the existence of the micro-worlds as inseparable foundation of the existence of the whole. Things exist because others may exist, and thus the universe may uphold its existence as the whole. One may question: "Why does universe exist? Has it any meaning beyond that it exists as the embodiment of all - and that`s all? Or has it any deeper meaning? Such questions are, of course, reflections of human quest for meaning of existence, and seeking purpose of being in relation to the universe. In that context, the universe fulfils the role of the embodiment of perfection, which ensures that the image of the "One", whose dynamics binds all into the whole, is revealed in all in the same way. By being in existence through innumerable beings, and reflecting its universal image in all, it realizes the existence of the cosmic consciousness that sees all as "One", which exists in infinite diversity. The meaning of human existence is to realize this consciousness as the power that flows through all, and experience it as the emotion of love for both animate and inanimate worlds existing as parts of the same whole.

However, this "perfection" that emanates as the cosmos is much more profound than what the Platonists, neo-Platonists and Christian-Platonists have been able to express. It is not a fixed template, which the mind of God accesses through ideas, and which God uses to create an image of the world, as Demiurge does in Plato`s Timaeus. There is no such simple "template" of building the universe by finding the hidden geometric properties, that connect all things in unity and then modelling the universe by following a mathematical procedure. This "template" exists as a bigger package which includes many other items than only the template consisting of the Platonic pattern. Instead the package comes with the following items: The fixed conditions that may give birth of things in one place at a particular moment of time; the template of the fractal pattern that all matter must follow in the universe while forming any structure; the dynamics of simultaneous implosion and explosion that follow the triskle, that appears at the heart of all things being born; the universal program that charts the paths of evolutions of things from birth to death; and the method by which the creation passes into annihilation and returns as the source of creation again. One needs to possess the knowledge of all these items, put in this package, before any Demiurge will be able to create the structures in the universe. However, the conditions that may bring forth things in place and time, the pattern that follows the seeds of creation, the dynamics that arises from the triskle and generates the fractal pattern, the program that drives evolution of the pattern, and the methods of destructions and regenerations are universally the same everywhere and all times in all scales. This "bigger template" is the foundation of a more profound perfection and beauty than the Platonic beauty and perfection.

By using this bigger template the universe is eternally rising from it-self and sinking in itself, bringing life, death and regeneration while creating the consciousness of time. Where ever the in-flowing colder material meets the out flowing hotter material it creates the seed of formation of structure. At the heart of structure the spiral appears, en-suring the mechanism of both inflow and outflow. The matter flowing outward from the centre and moving inwards towards the centre forms a fractal network of knots inside knots. After taking birth the object evolves to maturity by moving from a more chaotic state towards a more orderly structure. The knot becomes more and more compact and thus stores more and more energies locally. As it becomes self-sufficient by supplying all the energies needed for its existence by channelling the fuels outside from its centre and then circulating them throughout the structures like a perpetual energy generator, the pro-cess of decay starts. As it tends to shut itself out from the network that has supplied the conditions of its existence, it breaks up by ejections of structures and dissipation of energies into space.

Is there anything called chance in this universe, which may acciden-tally happen without any relation to anything else occurring in the uni-verse - a mere blind happening without any need to fit into, or comply with any other happenings in the world? Is there anything called blind fate, that occurs. But why does it occur and where does it take is its ori-gin cannot be known by any means? Which means: Is there anything that can rise from outside the creation fashioned by using the "big-ger template"? When the material universe is concerned, the answer is: May be "no". Nothing can occur that falls outside the universe made by following the "bigger template". Any appearance of structure is deter-mined by the inter-relationships that exist among the different items forming the template package. So called accidental happenings are re-lated to the complexity hidden in the fractally embedded networks of patterns, like the movements of filaments in a whirlpool, which may appear as the perfect embodiment of chance and chaos. Once one knows the nature of the whirlpool as a fractal structure made of simi-lar patterns, embedded in scales inside scales, the problem of accident and chance reduces to the problem of the degree of entanglement to be resolved. All entanglements are purposeful in the sense that every movement of a filament has a purpose to fulfil inside a greater network of filaments, which in turn similarly fulfils its purpose of existence in an even greater network of structures.

In this universe everything appears and disappears because they are not caused by accident and chance, but they are destined to live and die in order to fulfil the purpose of existence of the whole. Things come into existence in place and time as events occurring in a greater arena in which it is embedded as a small part. The evolutions occurring in the greater arena determines the conditions of coming into existence as a small part and evolves in a way that will serve the greater body to evolve following the program of evolution destined by the template. So the evolution of the greater body determines where and when the things will appear and disappear, i.e. when and where the things will grow and die. The greater body sets the environment around the small parts that constitute it and generates the conditions of evolution of the smaller constituents. Thus the big destines the evolution and fate of the small. The evolution of the big structure in turn is decided by the evolution occurring in the universe in the next higher structure, which in turn is determined by the evolution going on in an even greater structure and so on… ultimately ending in the highest structure, that we may call our universe. So, every tiny happening has its relations with what are going on in the entire universe, and nothing can be detached from this network of evolutions occurring everywhere. Thus every happening has its role to fulfil in the cosmic arena. In this universe nothing can be called blind accident and chance. The things appear as accident and chance when it does not fit into our understanding of the relations of events seen through a small window of happenings around our immediate surroundings. Once such events are projected in the universe in greater and greater scales one may understand meaning of the events that once appeared as accidental.

It does not mean that things like tipping over stone and falling and breaking legs or a flint on the road hitting the window pane of the rushing car, or an asteroid getting out of the asteroid belt and hitting a nearby planet, follow any cosmic plan. They are accidents which bear no purpose and meaning. However, all such accidents take place in a world where things are bound together following laws and rules that absorb everything in an intelligent order, that we call harmony in nature. The accidents may punctuate the existing order, and may temporarily perturb the harmony, in which things remain absorbed. But the intelligence of the system brings new reordering to absorb the accidental happenings and bring everything back into order and harmony again. In other words, the nature bears the intelligence to heal itself from the impact of accidents and chances. The accidents do not shape the nature of the world. Instead the intelligent designs of the nature absorb accidents and place them in its purposeful scheme that brings order and harmony to serve the purpose of the whole.

When it comes to the human world, one may speculate how one may understand the accidental happenings that may turn the course of one's life. Is there any intelligence guiding us and forming our lives, or are we living by responding to blind accidents and chances appearing on our way?

These questions are harder to speculate about because the mind and the brain in an integral way are enmeshed in the relations external to us, which are arbiters in the evolution of happenings in the world. One needs to understand the nature of the brain and the mind before one can speculate about the way the accidents may play roles in the reality bound by the natural order and intelligence existing in the material sphere.

For example, how should I understand the occurrences of life that have deflected my life in different paths since my childhood? Are they accidents, destiny or design of a supernatural mind. All answers relate to the brain, which remains absorbed in an environment created by the intelligence in nature. The brain interacts with the nature, of which it is a part, and thus produces our consciousness of reality, which is multifold. The brain is an integral instrument that defines the nature of the reality, in which we try to find meaning and purpose of life. The complexity of this meaning and purpose lies hidden in the fact that the brain itself is made of material components, like the rest of the environment that surrounds it. The functions of the brain are rooted in chemical reactions and mechanical laws. However, it is also the source of our mind, which is hard to understand. By interacting with the world it defines the nature of the world, and generates consciousness of reality, that in turn decides our modes of interaction with the world. It is like a loop: The consciousness feeds back interactions with the external world, and these interactions create consciousness in return. Thus the world and the mind become parts of an inseparable whole. Without the existence of the world mind has no ground to form consciousness, and similarly, without the existence of the mind, we cannot have any consciousness of reality. More evolved these interactions, more complex becomes our world and more layers of reality open in the mind. Higher awareness entails complexities of brain activities that lie outside the immediate constraints of the biological needs. The brain seeks its foundations in a greater world that surrounds it outside the boundary of the species to which it belongs. It may even expand its capacity to connect to the realm not yet detected by science.

How do I understand my own mind? Has it any existence outside the material world? It is hard to answer because, though mind is an integral part of the brain, it can shape the development of the brain at the same time. Its existence belongs to brain matter that mind itself can affect and change. Without matter it does not exist; but confined in matter it can shape matter and appear as a power that exists beyond the confinement of matter. One may wonder if it is the cooperative intelligence of all matter in the brain, that transcends the behaviour of matter and appear as mind. Or, is there anything outside matter, that takes seats in the complex network of the brain and appear as mind - for example, a spirit who enters the material sphere and controls the activities of the brain?

It is the second alternative, which has ruled my thoughts since my encounter with God over the Ganges. I have experienced the existence of a power that moves as waves leaving messages in the mind. I have interpreted it as the spirit which has entered my mind and affected the functioning of the brain by creating the wavy movements. Sceptics may explain them as the results of psychological stress that have released chemicals, which have, in turn, created rewiring of the brain circuits, that simulated the wavy experiences. Under critical amount of stress, the brain may create experience of different identities, as in schizophrenia. Or, was there any supernatural being interfering into the normal brain activities? Being myself the possessor of the brain, which was observing the world and the activities of the mind, I was entrapped in an absurd task of understand the phenomena arising in it.

Was it an accident that had led me to this mental trap? Or was I psychologically disposed to such mental abnormalities? I was born in an atmosphere, where spirituality was never discussed, and no form of worship related to any divinity or religious celebrations ever took place in our family. Instead, existentialism and Marxism were the ideologies that defined the cultural atmosphere in which I was brought up. How could I become psychologically disposed to spirituality in such a surrounding? However, since I was a small child, I have heard "someone" whispering in my mind, telling me that I was one with a spiritual world that existed outside my vision. It had started with a pantheistic understanding of the presence of the spirit in all – in animals, birds, plants, trees, clouds, wind, the sun, the moon and the stars etc. The whispering voice was coming from all that existed around me and not from the deities whom people worshipped. So I never worshipped any deity, never bowed down in front of any temple, or places of religious worship.

I had my private world where I touched God in plants and leaves, listened to the voice in the whispering breeze and the twittering of the birds, saw the beauty of the supernatural in the wings of insects and petals of flowers. Above all there existed the starry cosmos! The greatest mystery of all!

A new form of encounter came with the activities of arts. It opened a new dimension of the mind, through which I could visualize the invisible world that had penetrated everything. The artistic activities started with a few dried out water colour tubes, which an uncle of my mother wanted to throw. He had bought these colours when he had visited Switzerland many years ago as a young man. However, he had no brush to throw. So I made my first "brush" by winding threads around a needle from my mother's sewing screen and created my first paintings. My parents appreciated abstract arts and therefore I got involved in exploring my talent as an abstract artist. This revealed a new realm of the mind. More I experimented with abstract art, more I got in touch with a psychedelic world swirling in a realm that seemed to arise from the same world from where the nature was whispering in my mind.

So I became psychologically disposed to the supernatural! However the turmoil did not start until I attended a session where some friends were calling a deceased spirit to know about the happenings in the future. I joined this planchette session for fun believing that it was nonsense. However, I got entrapped in a mental phenomenon, which I could not reject off hand. More I wished to understand about what could be really happening, when the so-called spirit appeared and moved the objects, I stepped into a quagmire of the mind. It finally ended up in the incident of encountering the Spirit over the Ganges. Since then my life had taken a dramatic turn.

The spirit calling session became a destiny of my life. Since then I believed that my life's course was already destined by a supernatural power. Was it a foolishness of a gullible mind? I had been trying to get an answer to this question since then! What happened? How did I get into the trap of the mind? Could I have steered myself away from this psychological quagmire?

Was it my brain, which had deceived me and drawn me to understand reality in a way that was delusive? Or was there any supernatural power acting behind the scene, whose meaning and purpose I could not understand with my intelligence? I had chosen to believe the second and thus dug myself in a peculiar mental state believing that I may be able to understand its meaning one day in the end. Was it the brain which was fooling itself in order to escape the stress and strain of life that required more power and intelligence to resolve the challenges of reality? Was it a way to escape the harsh battle and struggle by pouring out irrational ideas and thoughts and creating a cocoon to protect oneself from the predators?

When I am the origin of my own brain, how shall I be able to answer these questions that will be rational enough and transparent to scrutiny of a sane mind, not perturbed by irrational leanings? Through my own reflections I can never know it. I only know how puzzled I feel!

So, how do I understand the accident and death of Ånun, which seem so bizarre and meaningless! What were those premonitions of death? Why such coincidences of happenings that led us to the mountain top where the accident occurred in the most absurd and improbable way! Was everything just blind chances? Were all coincidences only mere projections of thoughts not related to the reality in question? I do not know.

They are projections of thoughts in my brain. What is the origin of those thoughts, how did they appear, how did they fall in a pattern to coincide with happenings that really occurred, and confirmed the fear that appeared as premonition before hand? Could everything be an intelligent way of the brain to spin and weave thoughts and simulate a consciousness which is delusive and false? I cannot know. The brain is too complex, which is impossible to be understood through my own scrutiny. It can be deceptive and create delusion, or it may relate itself to a reality that is not accessible to logic and thoughts that can appear in the human mind through symbols and words.

I have been believing in the last possibility. The book, that I wrote about Ånun, where the beginning became the end of the book, where the cycle of life, death and resurrection continued without break through realms of dreams and myths, sprang from a strange mental process. A few days after the cremation ceremony was over I began writing that book, without any plan of the structure in my mind . I just continued writing. It evolved and took an interesting form which I had not envisaged. The story of the life and death of Ånun was woven in a way where it was difficult for the readers to distinguish what was real and what was dream. In this world, where dream and real were indistinguishable, the life passed into the realm of death and resurrected once again in cycles without beginning and end. After the book was finished, I was surprised by the complex way the book was woven together. How did it happen? How could my mind conceive the whole structure in such a complex and intelligent way and unfolded a story without the interference of my conscious mind? It seemed mysterious.

Similarly with the writing of "Tathagata`s Journey Between the Islands of the Sun and the Moon". The idea of the universal wanderer sailing between the islands of spring and the islands of death goddess had descended in my mind by the grave of Ånun. When I had started writing it in Geneva, I had no idea how the journey would evolve. I even did not know who the main character of this book would be. As the writing continued I understood that all of humanity was the character of the book. Individual human beings appeared in life`s journey as parts of the universal being, who comes and goes life after life. In search of meaning and seeking a way that will release man from the cycle of life, death and regeneration, the universal wanderer was set to explore different dimensions of the mind that formed the human consciousness of reality. He moved through many spheres in an attempt to reach the realm where he would find meaning and home. In the end it passed through the cosmos and the realm of cosmic consciousness, where he met the Divine Being and held the "Dialogues on the Mountain". This encounter with God revealed the knowledge that could not be gained by any other means. The dialogue appeared as automatic writing, where the role of the conscious mind was restricted in posing questions. The answers came from a world that existed "out there" beyond the realm of comprehensible of the human mind.

Was it delusion? How could the brain conceive such an immensely complex work of literature, philosophy, mythology, religion... and much more... in such a structured way as if everything existed in a higher mind before it was written down? It is difficult to believe that I could ever structure and conceive such a book through my limited intelligence. It embodied experiences and knowledge that were still unknown to me. While writing, I was enlightened about a greater world, about which I did not know before. Was it just another spin and treachery of the brain? Was I only deceiving myself by believing that it was not me, who was the author of the book, but someone else "out there" breaking through my mind and writing it by using my mind as a medium?

I believed it to be so. I let the happenings be overtaken by this inner force and followed the development of the book, which took more than seven years to complete.

After that, a vision of "art without beginning and end" opened in my mind. Again a similar process took over the control of the activities. I saw the realm of the "Poetry of Light", that was immensely vast and beyond the capacity of a painter to realize it in the traditional form. The mind span again new territories. New realms emerged, which could not be represented by using colours and forms on canvas. Therefore I plunged in exploring the realm of the virtual reality, where one could bypass the limitations of the physical space and time. Brain realized the possibilities to "see and hear" in new ways, that were not confined to the limitations of the physical organs of the body. Was it the brain, who was rewiring itself and finding new connections to form new experiences and understandings, like an intelligent automaton, or was someone "out there" in the cosmic arena who was stimulating the brain to expand its activities by setting up new circuits and controlling the machine?

I believed in someone "out there", who had asked me to fulfil the tasks of my life. He was steering the course of destiny. Then came the greatest surprise: The mystery of creation of the universe opened to me. First it appeared as the voice of the Angel guiding the wanderer through the cosmos and explaining it in a poetic language. After the writing of Tathagata`s Journey was finished, through a series of accidental happenings I was drawn to study the large scale structures of the universe. First it drew me to study chaos theory and fractal, and then I jumped to study gamma-ray bursts, star-forming galaxies and quasars. Then I came to study the Cartwheel galaxy which revealed the fractal nature hiding in the large scale cosmic structures. Thus I discovered a universe built in a fractal manner, where the large universe imaged itself in similar way in smaller and smaller structures. The entire universe was an entangled system of similar structures embedded in smaller and smaller scales embedded within each other. Here nothing could be separated from the others. It was an immensely complex intelligent design, which seemed beyond the intellectual comprehension of the human mind.

In this universe, a universal dynamics was bringing cosmic structures in life, and leading them to a universal path of evolution and growth, before destroying the structures in the end. The central element of this dynamics was the formation of spiral at the centre of all cosmic structures in all scales. How could such an idea of a spiral universe break forth in my mind long before I had started studying the data? How could it be possible that what the wanderer had heard from the Angel about the universe during Tathagata`s cosmic journey, could be confirmed by observational facts. Was there a supernatural mind that was transferring knowledge and guiding the brain to discover the mystery of the universe?

I thought so…

# Chapter 7
# GOD: IS IT A DISEASE OF THE MIND?

After writing the epic, discovering the mystery of creation of the universe and creating arts that revealed the world that lies outside the realm of the senses in the domain of the "Poetry of Light", I discovered myself entrapped in a world completely different from the reality where others lived. While I was grappling with many layers of realities, embedded in different levels of consciousness, and seeing myself as a wanderer moving through these spheres as a part of a Divine Being, the world was spinning in a different reality.

When I again and again listened to the audio CDs "Tathagata`s Journey" which reminded me of the higher spheres of human existence, people out there watched soap opera, James Bond, criminal and action films, or science fictions, or fictions that involve conspiracy, murder, espionage, or vulgar banalities of comic nature. With the advent of the Age of Technology the virus of freedom to wire the brain to these sorts of entertainments was spreading all over the globe in a lightning speed and changing the reality of the human life. It was the reality of the New Age of Aquarius when a new sun had taken birth.

How should I communicate across these barriers that define my reality and the reality of the others? I feel alone and imprisoned in my own world, where I find no other companion to share my reality than the Divine Being. Similarly when I believe in the presence of the cosmic mind, that has created the universe with an unfathomable intelligence, which holds everything in a timeless arena, the world out there is sunk in the belief that the universe has risen as an accidental happening as the result of a big-bang. Where I see the universal spiral sustaining the dynamics of the cosmic bodies in different scales, most scientists believe that there exist black-holes – the objects, which verge on science fictions and can satisfy any one who has the psychological leaning for the weird and the absurd. The big-bang and black-holes have received so much attention and popularity through the mass media that it seems impossible to convince people anymore that they could be wrong. Any attempt to promote the ideas of the timeless universe that exists without beginning and end seems to be in vain.

The art, I have created, is another area of frustration. The arts appreciated by the world out there have totally different meaning and character than what I have been trying to create. Most art works are design oriented abstract art, or provocative art that either provoke the sexual morality, or religious themes, or represent unconscious fear and trauma of terror, blood, death and destructive impulses. Some are representation of extreme banalities of daily life and expression of utter chaos of the mind. They are promoted because they reflect the true spirit of the time. Among others, five hundred kilos of hair formed as a cube, and a plastic female nude pissing on a dog were presented in the last autumn exhibition of arts in Oslo. Moreover, the art and art exhibitions have become a business of money makers in a Darwinian market driven by investors, who possess a consciousness of reality and esthetics governed by the intentions of making economic profits.

After realizing that there was no way to cross the barriers that separated me from the world out there that decided the destiny of the man of modern time, I sank in a depression. I went to see the doctor, who took blood test and found that the prostate specific antigen value was high. To eliminate the possibility that it could lead to prostate cancer he sent me to take a biopsy of the prostrate. Biopsy results showed no anomaly. However it caused infection, which resulted in blood poisoning. I was admitted to the hospital, where I received intravenous penicillin for nearly two weeks. The antibiotic and pain killers caused damage to the intestines and it had to be taken care of. It was followed by an operation and so on… I was caught in a whirlwind and spent several sleepless nights. I woke up experiencing nightmares….In one dream I saw myself being hauled to a gallows, where I was standing in front of an executioner. When I pleaded to return to life, the exterminator questioned about my motive to return to life again. On the condition that I shall serve mankind, I was granted permission to return.

The doctors treated me with medicine as if I was nothing but a bio-chemical factory. The blood cells were invaded by harmful bacteria, which had entered the blood stream through the urinary tract. These bacteria managed to break through the defence system of the body guarded by white cells, which protected the body from undesired bacteria that may intoxicate and kill the healthy cells. However, when I saw that the doctors by injecting antibiotics could incapacitate the bacterial killing mechanism, and finally managed to make me free of symptoms, I understood the power of scientific knowledge. Could a healer gather and transmit "prana" or "chi" to the infected body and strengthen the cells of the immune system so that they could win over that life threatening bacterial invasion, remained a big question in my mind.

Life was definitely a battle of contending organisms seeking their survival at the expense of the others at all levels – from macro-molecules, forming proteins and DNAs, to the animals roaming on lands, fishes swimming in water, birds flying in the air and the humans. By knowing the working of the nature at the level of the molecules, atoms and even deeper, which goes down to a millions of times smaller than the molecular and atomic sizes, the human beings can manipulate the power in nature to their advantage. By splitting the nuclei in atoms they have learnt how to release energy stored in nature that can annihilate all species on Earth many times over. Similarly they know how to generate radiations and waves by mechanical means and transmit and communicate signals across continents and seas and even between planets in the solar system. They can meet and discuss with each other by bringing everybody in a physical room by projecting their real-time animated images and voices on screens.

So what were those waves and voices I had been experiencing? I got alarmed! Now I started observing my own mind as a scientist and tried to find out the circumstances that could trigger such false signals in the brain. Were they related to the physical and social environment and the psychological state? When the waves appeared could I stop them by just denying their existence and telling myself that the whole thing was nonsense? With the power of the will was it possible to control this phenomenon in the brain?

I realized that the waves appeared when the mind was open to experience such phenomenon. When the will seemed to be overpowered by a spiritual surge I wondered if I was trying to escape the realm of struggle for survival by creating such delusion. Was I trying to negate the reality that engages every species, even the microbes, in wars? Was I just unfit to live and therefore creating such hallucinations with a hope that something supernatural would come to my aid? But why had the brain wired itself in such an inefficient way that called for its annihilation in the face of competitions with others? Was it based on false judgment and misunderstanding? Anyway, who was making these judgments? Wasn`t it the prefrontal cortex - the site of such understanding and comprehension – that one called the site of the self? Did it mean that my prefrontal cortex was not developed enough to make a proper reflection and therefore I was making such erroneous choices destructive to my survival? Anyway, who was choosing?

"Where was God in this picture?" Was it all foolishness? Was it all psychic aberration? How shall I know? Was it me...totally entrapped within myself? I spoke as God, answered as God. What a mess! What a wonder! How impossible to know oneself! ...However, how grand! How magnificent! What a brilliant trap of the mind where one exists as two! ...What a dilemma! What a pain! How tumultuous it is!

God...God...God... Someone always appeared in my mind and

claimed He was God. I was bleeding in agony and pain without knowing a way how to escape this state of existence. Was it caused by insanity of the mind, or were those words truly messages from a Divine world? Doubts tortured me without end.

What nonsense to believe that I could receive knowledge about the nature of the world, mind and brain from an omniscient God just by directing my will to talk to Him! How gullible a man must be to believe that "God comes bursting through from whatever other-worldly domain, crashing through into our world, where his messages can be intercepted by the human brains – and this phenomenon has nothing to do with science?" There was no way to verify if any of these ideas appearing in the mind, as if from an omniscient being, could be wrong or right. Human thoughts and emotions emerge through exceedingly complex interactions of physical entities that comprise the brain. This complex functioning of the brain can broadcast such nonsense into the head if one does not take guard of oneself against the possible erroneous modes in which the brain may misfire. This misfiring occurs more easily in brains where the prefrontal cortex, which is the site of intellectual judgments and reflections, is not developed enough to take guard of the false processing of information using thoughts and feelings as vehicles.

Were not such communication and tapping of profound knowledge from a Divine realm, without making any effort to acquire any other knowledge and verify the experiences in the light of that knowledge, demonstrative of mental illness? Was I mad…psychotic and delusional? The Dawkinian atheists point out that the brain possesses a formidable power of constructing visions and visitations of the utmost veridical power. To simulate ghosts and angels would be a child`s play for a computer software of the sophistication that the brain uses to simulate images and sounds. Such simulations appear as dreams in the state of sleep and imaginations and day dreaming when one is awake. Was my brain falsely wired to create such a weird simulation that could generate information by simply "wiring" the will to a ghostly realm?

Then I came across the work of Eric Kandel, a Nobel-laureate in medi-

223

cine and Director of a research institute devoted to the science of the brain and the mind. He was seeking to uncover the biological nature of the mind. This new science of the mind is based on the principle that mind and brain are inseparable. The brain is a complex biological organ possessing great computational capability, which constructs the sensory experiences, regulates thoughts, speech and emotions. It is responsible for creative acts in language, music and art that are carried out by specialized neural circuits in different regions of the brain. These circuits are made of elementary signalling units called nerve cells. The specific signalling molecules have evolved through millions of years of evolution. Some of them were present in the cells of our most ancient ancestors and can be found in our most distant and primitive evolutionary relatives like single-celled bacteria and multicellular organisms like worms, flies and snails. These creatures use the same molecules to organize manoeuvring through the environment as the humans do in their daily lives.

The visual representation of objects, scenes or audio experiences of sounds and melodies need cellular and molecular mechanisms to store information in the brain. Different circuits are critical for different sorts of memories. It is believed that once the complexity reaches the network of proteins or nerve cells the faculties that one calls mind beings to emerge. The interactions among different neural circuits generate pattern of activities resulting in the aspect of the mind we call cognition. Attention of the mind and awareness can shape new pattern and reconfigure neural activities in these networks.

There are modules in the brain that must be turned on to generate such attention. These modules can be activated and manipulated by changing the proteins and amino acids, which may lie behind social behavior? The biology of the mind acknowledges that every mental state and attitude is a brain state, and all mental disorders involve dysfunction of the brain. Some scientists have found that memories required for many forms of learning, are regulated by some regulatory proteins, which are similar in snail and flies and the human.

Was I selecting with my free will a mode that put the brain in disorder and malfunctioning? By giving attention to a special emotion, that has wired itself in the brain as an experience of the spiritual world, was I engaged in a counterproductive act that was harmful to the evolution and survival of the specie? How to get out of this wrong wiring and re-structure the pattern, set in the brain circuitry that generates attention towards a non-existing world that one calls spiritual?

I started observing how the letters were randomly appearing in the mind, as if churned by a machine used in a lottery. Each letter imme-diately drew a set of other letters stored in the brain and formed words by chance. Each word formed this way drew from memory a complete sentence and appeared as a heavenly message swirling in the mind. A sentence drew other sentences stored, in the mind and formed a group of sentences, that carried the content of an emotion and thought. Thus I was communicating with the spiritual being.

Were not the proteins in the brain cells responsible for this retrieval from the storage system to work so efficiently? Was I not just delud-ing myself in believing that something outside the brain existed in the form of a higher mind? How to bring an end to this disorder which has turned obsessive? Each time I could not resolve a question by rea-soning and knowledge, I reverted to the method of connecting to the spiritual domain again and again. I was obsessively hard-wired into the delusive world.

Now being aware of what might be happening in the brain, I put the mind in scrutinizing the process whenever the messages from the in-ner world appeared. With the scrutiny the process halted and the mes-sages disappeared. So I concluded that the voice had no reality out-side my own mind. I had not been clever enough to discover it before, and therefore I had let myself be fooled by this delusory phenomenon. More I got involved in analysing the brain with scientific knowledge, more I was getting frustrated.

"Where was I going?"
*"To your father`s home"*, the spirit again returned and replied.
"Why am I so tormented on the way?"

*"Fulfil the tasks that I have asked you to accomplish. This is the way you will be able to return home. I have given you the vision to see the realm of love and the direction to go. Your task is to awaken and uplift mankind the way God has awakened and uplifted your mind.."*

"Can I change anything in this world with my thinking and reflections? Staring blankly at the world and reflecting deeply about the essence of things, as I do, will not even cause a fly to change its course around the garbage bin where it searches its nourishment. Meditating deeply about human affairs will only cause mental depression. Trying to teach about things that academic and religious institutions do not condone, may prove hazardous. In the past they have sent the sanest man to mental asylum. So paradoxical is this world!"

*"By seeing yourself as a part of the body strewn in all, realizing the state of consciousness that can lift human mind out of the lonely wandering, participate in life. With every object you touch, every word you speak and hear bring the news of the Paradise existing in the human mind, from where warmth of love of God radiates.*

*Embrace all, teach all what you know, tell others about what may make life precious and pleasant to live by winning aggression and bear compassion and love for all. Letting aside the arrogance of reason and the greed for personal power ask human beings to help others to flourish and grow and thus move towards the greater being. It is the path of coming home."*

I have experienced the effulgence of the poetic mind; I have written the epic about human wandering life after life, created arts that may uplift the human vision to the realm of light, and discovered the mystery behind the creation of the universe that you have entrusted me to do.

I have created my world and lived alone in it by ignoring the forces of the world spinning it around. Now I feel dejected, abandoned and alone. Do I have anything else left but the dream to hold on to? Dream!…dream!...dream!... so treacherous dreams! … Shattered.... torn... and bleeding like a tortured animal imprisoned in a cage! As a prisoner of myself in living I am dead, in trying to wake up I fall back in sleep and return to a new dream in the same way as I have done so many times since my childhood. In believing that I am going somewhere where the sky will open to clear all clouds of the mind, I have lost directions and entered dark alleys of the mind time and again.

I want to get back a life driven by reason and free myself from the mad psychotic... delusional world. Who to attack, how to attack and how to free myself from this mental virus when I am a captive of my own brain? I have dug my grave, created my ruin, and fallen in a hole of despair...how could I return to the world where human beings live as rational creatures enlightened by scientific knowledge that could be tested and proved?

In every direction I move I enter the ghostly alleys, where the spirit returns again and again. I see at a distance the executioner waits. But why did I plead for life? What shall I do? Where shall I go? I always return to the same place, in the same alleyway. Where shall I find the Window of Light that will open the vision of the path where the sky remains ablaze in the clarity of the mind, where there is no doubt, conflict and bloodshed as in the realm where I am entrapped?

A few days after I returned from the hospital the sun was about to reach the vernal equinox – the spring was about to break out. I was looking for a new rebirth and with a hope to discover a new spirit of life; I went out for a walk along Bygdøy Allé. The same waves, which had enveloped me more than forty years ago, and led me along the streets of Calcutta, descended again in the same way as they used to do then. I was moving along the footpath in a zigzag manner tracing a serpentine path, as I used to do every time the spirit took over my power of walking along the streets of Calcutta. The time had not changed, the same reality was repeating once again in a world that had not changed its character. I was not going anywhere. I was standing still in a world that was invisible and immovable in my mind. Only the objects around me were changing. The weather, the landscape, the culture, the features of the women and men walking around – their clothes, speech, beliefs were changing in different points of time enwombed in an invisible reality. I was searching a way out of this invisible trap, seeking a new renewal and rebirth in a world where the others were experiencing the movement of time and life.

Where shall I go to find the way? I did not know. If it was forty years ago I would have asked the waves, guiding my steps, to bring me to the place where I might find a clue. I may have followed the weirdest suggestions then. But now, when I wish to get rid of these waves, I do not again want to fall a victim of the same psychological power that has entrapped me in a hole of despair. Who could help me? I have no belief in any guru, pundit or religious preacher. Nor do I have much respect for science a la Big-bang and scientists like Richard Dawkins and the clans addicted to the dogmas of the evolutionary theories. Only way left is to dig oneself in one`s own brain and like a desperate man seek an outlet to escape from the conspiracies of the brain which keeps the human mind engaged in the network of neurons and cells.

So I returned home after a short walk in the neighbourhood feeling even more frustrated and torn. "Searching home?" Devil taunted. "Searching meaning?" Devil laughed. "Searching God?" Devil pointed his index finger to himself. Was life truly a Devilish complot? Or was it a test of God?

But why should God be so merciless and cruel? Is he not a compassionate father, who loves all? Why does he uses so devilish methods to torture souls who seek meaning and home in the realm that the conscious mind may not comprehend? If God exists in all why did he punish the young man for believing

*"He is in me as me. God is energy and the "Will" that has created the cosmos. He is impersonal, abstract, without ideas, languages, assumptions and thinking. He is the radiant vibrations eminent in the billions of galaxies strewn in time and space and still beyond time and space. He is in the solar flares, the cosmic dust, and the radiation that enwombs the universe. He is on Earth, in the serene beauty of the sky, in the currents of air and water where there are life. He is the green leaves of the trees, the blue eminence of the sky, the smell of the ocean, the touch of the wind on the rocks and stones. The heat of the lamp, the warmth of the flesh, the lights scattered from the eyes are all His warmth. The flying birds, the reptiles on the land, the amphibians, the mammals, millions of species of insects animating water, air and earth on seas, mountains, deserts, hills and glaciers have evolved from Him. The flares of lightening, the*

*rumbling of the thunders, the splashing of rain, landslide, eruptions of the volcanoes etc. is the manifestation of the force that He unleashes in nature. This Earth -our home- with immense beauty and warmth of life is made by the touch of the loving hands of God."*

If the young man was wrong and foolish why God had to make him a greater fool by breaking into his brain and sending the messages of love and compassion for all and misguiding him to live a life in delusion? Why he had to mislead him:

*"Transcend the bounds of your earth-bound consciousness and elevate yourself to God. Love man...and thus merge in the love God. The meaning of life exists in pursuing the life with love, knowing that through love God manifests in you.*

*Just as the meaning of being the flowers is to attract the eyes to experience beauty and invite the creatures to participate in the carnal existence of love that suffuses the world, the meaning of life lies in the participation in the eternal festivity that we call life and be one with the beauty of the nature and the cosmos. In the moonlight, in the murmuring breeze, or on the vast expanse of the deserts there lie the love of God, who comes to touch the souls watching the world alone as part of the whole.*

*Travel around the world. See as much as possible. Know that in the shivering of the leaves in the forest, in the warbling of the hearts as the chirping birds, in the ringing of the emotions God speaks to you. See, touch, listen and know the mystery as much as possible to see, feel, listen and touch. In stones that you touch know that music of the eternal world remains frozen on Earth.*

*Go... Experience the immense joy that exists in loving the world. This joy will bring the experience of God.*

*I am He and you are me. Return to me. In wandering through the world make a journey in search of God."*

So I did...And as reward received a life full of suffering and pain.

Or, was everything just nonsense? God was just a product of hallucination created by the brain. He did not exist. The young man should not have paid heed to such messages appearing in the mind. May be, it was Devil who was playing games with him and eluding him to fall in a treacherous trap from where he could not get out anymore. But why the Devil should be so devilish? What benefit he can derive from fooling and torturing souls who are kind, benevolent and bear love and compassion for all? Moreover, if God does not exist, why should Devil exist instead? Aren`t they both equally fictitious and nonsense products of the mind?

Once one gets rid of the both God and the Devil, what are left? The brain of pure causal connections twirled by the forces of the mechanical world? The molecular bindings assembling trillions of helical chains by mechanical means, each of which is as large as ladders running from Earth to moon (if the space between steps is the same as the ordinary ladder we use). By breaking and replacing the helical steps with different chemical compounds one can create the feeling of the existence of God and Devil in our brains. So, may be, God is nothing but chemical secretion and ionic transport through the neurons!

If it is so, why the hell the ions have to speak simulating the voice of God to announce

*"Knowledge is the path by which one may transcend and move towards the knowledge of the true self. Knowing unveils the image of God, who is a transcendent above all transcendence. Knowledge is a path to be united with God. Knowledge is the way towards me, towards my lost identity - my Godhood."*

How do the chemical compositions make such a devilish complot to fool and mislead human mind about something that does not exist?

Dawkins says it is a mental virus inherited from the parents, which cause these phenomena. It is just disease and nothing else. It should be treated before one may recover one`s mental health that is clear and dazzling. Prescription he proposes is to believe in the Darwinian theory of evolution and slaughter and plunder others as the insects and the animals do in nature for their survival. According to him the theory of Big-bang has enlightened mankind about the mystery of the universe, which has no purpose behind its creation. It happens to have come into existence by chance. Though life is an extremely improbable occurrence in the universe, we still exist and we must assume it as the foundation of truth and go ahead in enquiring about the rest from the stand point of an anthromopic principle.

While fumbling in the darkness, I peep through every opening and hole I find. Each hole opens different realm of the mind, weaving different dreams in the stream of time. I meet the angels and children of the Devil on the way. The road is illumined by a chiaroscuro of light and darkness. Moments of joys are interposed with moments of sorrows and despairs. While bleeding on one side I experience a tranquil world – ethereally serene and beautiful above senses touch in another realm.

By the shore of life where I walk I see the mythical Odysseus, Orpheus, and Prometheus, and I pass by the islands where beauty and beasts haunt and excite the forces of life. The fears of death and annihilation resurrect again and again. Somewhere I see myself torn, broken and dispersed in the sand and dust collecting the pain and suffering of a windblown coast. Somewhere I see the wholeness of a meditating mind reflecting about the cosmos in molecules and atoms. Somewhere blood and flesh penetrating the mind create pain and wound; somewhere in the broken mirror floating in the blood stream I see the supernatural mind vibrating in great splendour and joy. I do not know who creates these fluctuating and contradicting visions and emotions from place to place, from time to time.

How can I find my way? It seems I am lost in the darkness of the world created by the mechanical force. In this darkness I dream of the angels and muses beckoning me to follow paths I am trying to avoid. Where does the myth end and reality begin? Where is the end of the cosmos and the beginning of the boundary where I may find home? Where is the borderline between me and the surreal world? Who is walking and who is remaining still?

Where is that Window of Light I am seeking? Is it mythical, surreal, invisible substrata of the mind, remaining to be opened by a magical force? Or, is it just a delusion - a fantasy ridden act of the brain lost in the chaos of the universe? Only thing I know for sure is that I cannot know the mystery of life. It is too complex, and indecipherable by the power of my mind!

Everywhere I step the cosmic vision penetrates, the angels and the devils appear – some rob, deceive, and lead the soul to darkened paths, some caress and assure the soul that this suffering has meaning and purpose. I see no end to paradox, contradiction, and absurdity that confuse me at every step. But still I carry on. Still I search the Window of Light – the illusion to go beyond myself in a realm that exists within me! I want to be illumined by my own mirror, by my own light – with or without God, demons, or angels!

After a short walk I returned home. As usual I entered the library room framed by the four walls of the Hall of Illusion where I write, dream and paint. I wished to tear myself inside out. I wanted to open all blood vessels and cells, the neural circuits forming the cortex and the links between the cortex and the midbrain. I wanted to watch what was going on inside the person who is me. I wished to take apart the conscious world from the unconscious, free ego from the delusion of the self, and thus separate me from God. How could I do it? The ego, self and God all were swimming with the molecules, bathing in the chemicals, drinking from the fountains of acids forming enzymes and proteins. With breathing in and out they were growing and forming in one moment and dying and disappearing in the next instant.

The molecules bound in chains moved, cohered, disintegrated and restored to structures again and again to create colours, forms, perceptions, imaginations and thoughts. Like magic of life, once one modified the protein chains the music rose, arts unfolded, poetry reverberated through the mind, and the whirlpool of chaos turned into a symphony of the mind existing in the cosmos. By changing the secretions of the brain chemical, called acetylcholine, dreams and fantasies flared and by bringing together random cortical activities they concocted stories that brought the contents of the hidden world into the visual sphere.

Windows of Light opened one after another as series of dreams in the awaken state.

It became a new project of art where the young man had now become older. Through these windows he watched many bizarre scenes: He was falling through a bleeding torso… sitting at the root of the flesh from where innumerable bodies were taking their nourishments to rise upwards… after crucifixion being taken down from the cosmos in a field covered human skulls where three angels were standing and watching the descend of life into death… colourful souls were whirling in agony and pain over his dead body…tearing his face he was attempting to see through himself and walking over a burning mirror… as a blind man trying to untie the knots of the blood veins in which the soul was impassioned… and so on… and so on…there was no end to the power of the unconscious to concoct images of life and death battling against each other in dreams….

Both Freud and Jung mean that the origin of such visions and dreams lie in the infantile experiences in the first years of one`s life. For Jung unconscious part is the self and conscious part is our ego. In the beginning years of life all is self, which is the centre of unity of the total psyche (conscious and unconscious). It brings forth order out of a chaotic dynamics characterizing the psyche. The Self appears prior to the birth of the ego consciousness. In earliest infancy, at the stage when ego starts taking shape, the self is perceived by the ego as a deity representing wholeness and perfection. This deity brings mystical communion with nature and cosmos. As one grows older the ego rejects the wholeness and totality and focuses instead on individuals` demands and necessities to cope with the reality of survival. In the adult the ego separates from the self. It brings the feeling of banishment from the Paradise of the childhood satisfaction. In Jungian psychology it is known as alienation. Repeated experiences of alienation continue throughout the adult life.

According to Jungian psychoanalysis dreams carry the messages from the unconscious self. The contents of dreams express in mythical-poetic language the meaning, needs and desires to connect with the self, from which one has been alienated. It is a dialogue between the ego and the inner life with a desire to return to the Paradise of the infantile stage when ego has not yet fully emerged from the self. The dreams carry the symbols representing the archetypes of the anima or animus, and the shadow self.

Freud describes mind to have three categories of functions: Id – the unconscious, Ego – the conscious and the super-ego that censors the Id to float up to the conscious level. The superego suppresses the unconscious drives that are in conflict with a civilized norm of life. The unconscious is believed to be empowered by illicit sexual urges like the Oedipus complex. Freud meant that most mental processes that create thought, emotions and volitions have roots in these unconscious urges. His central idea is infantile amnesia that cannot be recalled to consciousness any longer in the adult life. However it plays great role in forming the emotions and feelings in the adult life. In the state of dream the censorship, imposed by the superego, may break down, and the unconscious may come afloat – often cloaked in the disguises of symbols.

Newly dreams have been found to have neurophysiological origin. Hobson claims that dreaming has its origin in the region that generates REM (Random Eye Movement) sleep. This region lying in the brain stem produces signals that force the forebrain to concoct a random synthesis of images stored in the visual cortex. According to such observation there does not exist any censorship mechanism coming from the prefrontal cortex, which disproves Freud`s censorship theory. Another neurologist named Solms, claims that the basis of dream are chemicals released in the midbrain. These chemicals are also activated in connection with pleasure seeking emotions. He supports Freudian theory of sexual pleasure seeking motives behind dreams.

How do these different theories apply to my own fantasies and dreams? Is sexually motivated pleasure seeking hidden desires a la Freud the source of my creating God and Man who remain engaged in dialogues about everything - from cosmos to molecular basis of brain activities? Can God be a product of repressed sexuality as the Freudians claim? Or could it be caused by the reduction of aminergic activity and increase of cholinergic activity in the brain stem sending signals that activate visual cortex which randomly fetches images of God to allow the forebrain to concoct a narrative?

However, I never see God in any image, or conceive him in any language I know. He appears from the depth of the mind, more akin to the Jungian idea of the Self. My own analysis of personal dreams point to the conclusion that psychoanalysis of Freud, Jung and the observations of neurophysiologists could all be partially wrong and right. The main themes of the dream contents are very often the tension between the force of life, which seeks fulfilment of pleasure and joy, and the fear and anxiety of suffering and death that looms at every step of life. We certainly have inherited these instincts of life and death from our mammalian ancestors, whose brain stems are similar to ours. Therefore the origin of dreams in the brain stem seems quite rational to believe. The power of life brings sexual motivations, which may appear as Jungian anima or animus in the disguise of gods and goddesses. The fear of death and suffering could be the shadow archetype of Jung – like witches, demons, ghosts or fearful grotesque animals. In some cases the death and life may appear in the same imagery – like a killer goddess who is the source of life at the same time. Dreams could be interpreted as a religious procession behind the deity who kills and gives life. The pilgrims in search of bounty and happiness in reproductive life celebrate her/his festival, and then wakes up and screams when they discover his/her fearful aspect of a killer and harbinger of death. A dream I noted in my diary in 1983 is a nice example of the essential messages that most of my dreams probably signify:

*"A man was being punished. He was sitting at the top of a huge metal spike with very sharp head. He was screaming. Close by, there was a well full of blood. A soldier, clasping a sword in his hand, was standing in a corner guarding the entrance to this dark place.*
*The scene was visible through a hole in the wall.*
*One could hear the sounds of drums getting louder and louder as a procession was passing through a village and approaching closer to the vision. People wearing masks formed the procession. They were dancing while holding burning faggots in their hands. Some were blowing out fire from mouth that they had devoured. At the end of the procession, the fire dance was followed by a dance of a horse. Two dancers formed the figure*

*of the horse hidden under a colourful horse cover. A man was ridding on the horse. A small sword pierced his mouth. In the head of the procession a priest was throwing money. People were frantically running around to pick the money pouring from the sky. Behind the priest people were carrying on their shoulder a deity sitting on a golden throne. It was followed by a group of women carrying food for the festival.*

*In this crowd a young man was searching for his little brother. He was asking everybody if anyone had seen his brother on the way. After his brother had woken up in the morning he had not seen him. He was afraid about his life. Everybody he asked gave negative replies. However, one of them pointed towards the hole in the wall. The young man looked through the hole and started screaming. A man wearing the head of a wolf passed by his sight. Plugging his ears with the fingers, in order to avoid hearing the screaming of the man being punished, in fear he ran through the hole and passed by the soldier-guard. He noticed a young girl standing naked on the way. The man sitting on the spike was being punished for sexually violating this virgin. The head of the man being punished resembled the head of a grotesque bull. The young man succeeded in escaping from this dark world through the hole. He came out in an open space where an artist was sculpting the image of the goddess, whose image people in the procession were carrying on their shoulder. The artist was fashioning her from clay. There were many replicas of the same image that lay scattered around. Like the naked girl none of the figures were draped in clothes..."*

The death fears and sexual fantasies are often censored by the conscious ego – otherwise, it would be difficult to meet the challenges of the daily life that requires attentions to the factual conditions forming the basis of reality that throws everybody in the competitions for survival.

The above dream appeared to me in New York. It had no link to the reality in which I was living there. Instead it wove inside it many memories from my childhood, which I can still recall.

The screaming man sitting on the spike is the same man, who scared me when I was about the age of three. At this age I wanted freedom to explore the world on my own and be independent from the care of the parents. A lady in the neighbourhood used to give me lot of goodies each time I visited her. Now and then I made my way to the neighbours' house alone without informing my parents. Therefore my parents concocted the story of the punishment ground that existed behind the neighbour's house. I was afraid of the screaming man being punished in such a horrible way. This childhood fear did not go away after 35 years.

In the same age I had experienced my first day of "freedom" in life. I remember I got hold of a kite. To try it out I had gone out of the house without asking for the permission from my parents, who were often worried that I may get lost if I was allowed to enjoy freedom. The joy of running with the flying kite along road flanged by flowering golden coloured Mahua trees on both side, in a small town about hundred kilometres from Calcutta, is still vivid in my memory. It was like experiencing the joy of flying in the sky far above those flowers that hang high over the buildings standing around. While experiencing this joy the kite dived on the ground. When I was trying to get it up again in the sky I found myself standing in front of a sculptor`s hut. He was making the masks of a goddess from clay. There were many replicas of the same mask spread on the floor. I left the kite and got fascinated by what the artist was doing. While I was watching him at work someone whispered inside me "he is making my image". I asked the artist whose image he was making. And got involved in a chat with him. The artist got fascinated by the little boy`s curiosity to know about the goddess and gave a mask as a gift to take it home. I ran in joy...

I stopped only after reaching the football field near our house, where another man was putting finishing touch on the image of the goddess in full size. The puja festival was near. He was putting the finishing colours on the image made of clay. It was the image of Kali- the goddess of death. She was naked wearing a griddle around her waist made of decapitated hands and a garland of skulls around her neck. In one of her four hands she held a huge dagger ready to execute anyone anytime. On another hand she held a bowl collecting the blood from a decapitated head while holding with the third arm a head from where blood was dripping. In the fourth he held the trident of Shiva - her consort.

Her companions were Dakinis and Yoginis – who roamed among the corpses scattered in Kali`s killing field, and lived on flesh and blood of the victims. She was a frightening goddess creating fear and horror. But someone in me whispered "I am not there. It is just a fantasy image. I am within you. They are worshipping you as me." It was this image people were carrying in my dream in New York.

Jung calls it inflation of the ego in the childhood, when ego identifies itself with the Self – the archetype representing the totality and unity of all life in a deity who holds in his/her hand the power of life and death. The fire and horse dances are also pieces of memory from that age, when I had seen people dancing in religious festival like those in the dream. The dream truly contained childhood experiences of fear, joy and pleasure.

The mother goddess followed me when we moved to Calcutta. I was then ten. The house where we lived was built on the premise of an ancient Kali temple. However, there existed no sign of the temple. A new building was erected on that spot. The main deities worshiped in this part of India were Kali and Durga. Durga is Kali in her life giving aspect. She is represented as the sun-goddess, who delivers energy to all living beings. She rides on a lion, and holding different weapons in her ten arms besieges Assur, the green bodied competitor of the gods for the power of Heaven. By slaughtering a bull Durga releases the vegetative force of life hidden in nature and wins over this demon.

The house, where our family of the atheists moved in, was in a locality where a farmer cast living on the production of betel leaves lived for many generations. It was about ten kilometres from the centre of the town in north of Calcutta. The Indian Statistical Institute, where my father got a posting, was within a short walking distance and a school was nearby. Therefore, though the social environment was backward, my parents decided to move in here. Here my father introduced us to the literary work of Dante, Goethe, Nietzsche and Rabindranath and regularly brought from the library new books of philosophy, psychology, anthropology etc. Here he also translated highly advanced books of mathematics from Russian and was a voracious reader of scientific books from various fields.

We became acquainted with the names like Karl Jaspers, Buber, Heidegger, Marx, Hegel, Freud, Jung, and Huxley, Russell etc. before we knew much about Indian philosophy, culture and religion. Here my brother bombarded us with Paul Valerie, St. John Parse, Baudelaire, Rimbaud, Camus, Kafka, Sartre and Jean Genet among others. Our house became a living stage of an absurd theatre full of books from avant-garde dramatists like Ionesco, Beckett, and Bertolt Brecht. We were living in an absurd island of intellectual paradise surrounded by the devotees of Kali and Durga, and shanty quarters of destitute and prostitutes all around.

Here my dream to unveil the mystery of the universe rose. In the dimly lit corner of the house, for the first time the contours of the surreal landscapes of the human mind, existing as a parallel reality in another world, unfolded. The surreal world, where no human, beasts or plants existed, started emerging again and again whenever I took a pen to write, or held a brush to paint. The unknown and the invisible world swirled and rose from the unconscious world revealing masks and forms that had no similarity with the ones I had seen before. They seemed to arrive from the world from where "someone" had whispered again and again in the mind of the child "I am within you. Come…find me!"

This "play" soon followed visions of doom and destruction like the one below: I was walking alone in a lonely landscape of huge expanse. It was all deserted - not a single tree, or plant, or any sign of life existed anywhere. Only massive hills were looming at far distances. They engirdled the landscape as chains. This loneliness made me feel insecure. Suddenly I got frightened by this lonely surrounding and started running back to the place from where I had entered this deserted field. As I started running a cosmic catastrophe began. As if I had a premonition. The hills changed colors and turned bluish green and began glowing as surreal hills from another world. Then volcanoes erupted from their mouths. They threw blood towards the sky. Thousands of such volcanic mouths opened and filled the cosmos with fountains of blood. In fear I continued running. I found no place where there was any object which could give me a shelter. I looked upward to the sky filled with stars, hoping that I may find a shelter there. As I was seeking a way to escape this catastrophic event, the stars, which were glittering as huge diamonds a few seconds earlier, all turned red. They too became full of blood. The laws of the universe, that had held the stars in places, collapsed and the stars started moving in random directions in the sky, indicating the imminent destruction of the universe. As I was desperately seeking a way to save myself, the stars started pouring down on the landscape. I knew if any one of these stars hit me I would die. I suddenly found myself in a market square where people were screaming and running to escape from death. Many were being hit by the pouring rain of blood and dying instantly. I found a shade of a small shop and was waiting for my turn to die. To my surprise I discovered that this shade stood beside a colossal statute carved from white marbles. It was a statue of a Divine mother. She was a beautiful woman wearing finest clothes. She gradually turned alive and took my hands. We walked together in the rain. All fears disappeared. The universe appeared beautiful - tranquil and serene. I fell in an ecstatic joy of meeting the Divine! The dream broke…"

She was the anima of Jungian psychology. But the association of the divinity with the female figure changed after the encounter with the waves after the planchette session in Kharagpur. Divinity turned into a father figure instead. Planchettes are often explained by psychologist as ideomotoric effect, where mental suggestion directs muscular movements independently of the volition of the subject. The movements, which appear to be generated by the supernatural force, in fact, result from the occupation of the mind by ideas which have been suggested to it. These ideas exert unconscious motoric activities of the muscles, which lead to movements experienced in planchette. Unconscious or not, it was definitely a puzzling phenomenon for the conscious ego to cope with!

After the encounter over the Ganges this "unconscious" appeared as a Father figure. These waves were definitely phenomena resulting from the activities in the brain. But why were they activated? Who was activating them? From the perspective of psychoanalysis the unconscious was activating the occurrence of such phenomena. According to Freud it was run by an infantile pleasure seeking motive of the unconscious. Jung says that this unconscious is trans-personal and universal ground of archetypes for all human beings. It possesses structural and ordering principles which unify all unconscious urges to a common ground. It is the supreme authority to which the conscious ego must accept its subordinate role.

So if God exists he must be hiding in the unconscious. The neuropsychiatrists say that the limbic system and midbrain that we have inherited from more primitive species are the sites of the unconscious where signals are activated by chemical compounds. But who is causing the chemical secretions? Is mind manifesting by acting upon the chemical states of the brain, or the chemical secretions bringing the mind to come into existence? Is the unconscious being activated by an external agent that is not bound to the chemical laws, or alternatively, the chemical laws are building those ideomotoric effects like the ones experienced in a planchette? Do the willing and volition have trans-material existence outside the neural circuits, and precede the motoric activities in the brain stem? Or, the ionic and chemical transports in the brain cells cause the experience of will and volition?

According to the inner guide

"*Mind is not body. They are two separate entities. Mind chooses time and place, partner to reproduce before a child is born. The parents carry the seeds that transform into living beings amidst immensely complex processes of the associations and dissociations of what the light, air and the nutrition bring to the womb. Once the forces of growth are released they whirl in the motion of the unseen world where human mind has no choice to intervene. The climate, the food, the strength of the forces counteracting with each other on the surface of the earth, the sky and the air all determine the body that is formed*". The Guide engages me in a dialogue again.

"What is mind? What drives human beings to choose? What governs the mind and makes man think? "

"Human bodies are structured and formed in order to withstand the natural forces of time acting in the places where they are born. Once the conditions transform the bodies face challenges to cope with the new conditions in times and places where they are. The forces carried by matter interacting at a time in a place adjust themselves to develop modes of functioning of the bodies to keep alive the living structure as a method of seeking unity in the forces released. The body stores the codes of information brought by the new condition in order to build its system of adaptability to newer conditions. More complex a biological system, more complex is its system of codification and responses to adaptability and defence of life. These systems of defence against the forces of time is encoded in signals and stored in the physical body of the living beings. Once challenged by a condition body is triggered by these signals in order to defend its existence. As soon as the condition appears unfamiliar and threatening, the mind comes into play. However, mind is not body. Mind activates the process of thinking and reflections. It exists to cope with the whirling forces of time in order to bring harmony and unity in all forces moving the world".

"What is thinking?"

"Thinking is a process by which it is possible to associate objects and their relations with each other in connection with the phenomena triggering the senses. It is a cooperative process of the brain cells by which the body is able to analyse the perceptive world in need of defence and security of its physical existence."

"How can human being think although no outside signal triggers the sense perceptions?"

"Then thinking is based on the perceptions already registered by the body. In that stage thinking is recapitulation of the relations revealed to the body in different circumstances. Body remembers and stores in linguistic form the essential ingredients of the objective reality in relation to its existential needs. Mind is able to stimulate the objective image of the previous experiences without the presence of the objects themselves".

"What is language?"

"All thinking is born in languages. Language carries sound patterns to encode the content of thoughts. Sounds trigger the associative chains of experiences, perceived through sense organs, and act as image generators for objects, and relations and processes that may have ceased to exist."

"What is imagination?"

"*Thinking can be an idle endeavour. It is possible to build a world of association through the use of language. Mind is able to trigger thinking that can generate associations by the help of language or symbols and patch up experiences together and construct an image in the mind that has no counterpart in the material reality. This is imagination.*"

"What is doubt? What makes human beings doubt?"

"*Doubts are awareness in the mind about the possibilities of failures as one builds, on the basis of thoughts and languages, a pattern of choices in a condition, and projects the choices in reality. Doubts develop when the choices are based on imaginary constructs.*"

"What makes man choose by using his/her free will?"

"*Choice reflects the existential uncertainties that exist in every moment. By choosing one tries to secure one's existential condition against the motion of time.*"

"But human beings also make choices between to act or not to act, think or not to think, believe or not to believe, be or not to be. How shall I understand these choices?"

"*Human beings possess this higher form of will. By the use of this will they are free to negate or affirm any relation - imaginary or real. Will is the source of the freedom that you mention, which distinguishes human beings from other living creatures.*"

"Describe the nature of this will."

"*The will resides in the mind. I have implanted this will in all human beings. By the use of their will they may free themselves from the dictates of the material world, or sink deeper into the material bondage. Will drives them to seek the unity with God, or separate oneself from God. It is the power of freedom to separate oneself from me, or return to me.*"

"What is reason?"

"*Reasons are relations in human mind. With the help of reason the mind is able to discover fallacies brought by thoughts. Reason is like a fire. It burns in all human minds in order to show the right path of action that can free human beings from the bondage of the material relations.*"

"If reason is the right path, why have you asked me again and again to sacrifice reason?"

"*Your path is not the same as other human beings. You possess light much brighter than reason. Follow that light and serve the will of God.*"

"You have said before, you have no will. How shall I understand your reply?"

"*Read me through you. Your will emerges from me. Your mind is working to project the will of God in the human sphere. I am the source from which your will is derived.*"

"Is my will your will?"

"*God has no will. I exist in you. Read my will through your will.*"

"Your answers are difficult to understand. Enlighten me so that I may comprehend it."

"*Refrain from questioning the mystery that I am. Read in your mind the will of God and bring to the world the messages of light that I am.*"

How shall I know that if any part of this dialogue makes any sense? It could be a nonsense babbling arising from the unconscious where I myself am suggesting the answers that seem to be coming from God? Am I insane?

To believe Freud this dialogue with the unconscious is a product of a neurosis rooted in unconscious pleasure seeking motive. According to Jung it is a result of the infantile inflation of the ego, where ego identifies itself with God and wishes to return back to the paradisiacal state of wholeness, with which it had identified itself at birth before being separated from the Self. According to neurophysiologists they are caused by unbalanced secretions of acetylcholine in the brainstem, sending signals to the cortex that generate and structure this dialogue in order to fool the mind about the nature of the will and the mind itself.

Anyway, since the day I learnt to connect myself with the inner self, the unconscious had appeared as a father and a guide. He again and again brought the message of doom and destruction:

"*Earth will be undergoing a violent cataclysm and the world will suffer from a movement of war that will make man shudder in fear. Doubt not that your work will be the world's end and beginning of a new world. Doubt not the movement of the power that is going to destroy. Doubt not that mountains will move, the world will be shaken by the rumbling of* the mass that forms the world's crust. Reality is not what you believe it is. World is not in reality what you feel and touch. Reality of the matter-spirit is far deeper than what you can know by your senses. Doubt not that the mountains are already moving all around the crust, and soon they will erupt to fill Earth with mountain dust. My Will is working to make the mountains move to bring the destruction of Earth.

Doubt not the doomsday is moving close. Doubt not the movement of Earth that has already set in the process for the day when all parts of the continents will be thrown into turmoil of water, air, fire and earth. God has ordained the fate of Earth that will see its end. God will be reborn and then a new world will come. Get ready for the doomsday that will move as you will finish the dialogue between God and Man. Eruptions of the mountains will start, the water of the sea will bulge, the wind will bring hurricanes and massive streams will overflow the banks. Death will rampage the matter-spirit world and make man lowly and feel distressed. Doubt not the Words that move from the Will that makes the mountains move, the weather change, and create death.

Europe will be severely destroyed by moral chaos; Asia will experience massive mountain movements; Africa will be devastated by malnutrition, disease and death; America will experience the turmoil of the surge of water, wind, streams and severe heat and cold. God's Will will work to make Earth move towards massive annihilation that will eradicate much of the population. God's fearful words will be spread all over world and God will move as the Will behind all creations and the meaning of life on Earth.

God's Will is working for the renewal of man. The women and the men will be making a new world, that will no more be based on the understanding of science of matter and the endeavours of man in trying to find meaning of existence in the material sphere. The destruction will be moving as a force to renew Earth. Once the matter-spirit world will be ready for a new world that will move with the Will of God the destruction will be working as the forces of order amidst chaos. Bear in mind that destruction is not chaos. The chaos brings a transition of the world from one state to another with the force that is uninhibited by the will of the man and out of man's control.

Reality is not what you believe it is. Reality has a Divine meaning and is governed by a force that is working to bring order and chaos in the movements that are worldly manifestations of the Will of the Divine. The mountains are moving as the results of the will that is working behind the order and chaos working in union with the whole. God's Will is not order or chaos. God's Will is world's meaning that is bound in world's order and chaos. Order is implanted in chaos, and chaos is the state before any order. Therefore the chaos and order are working together at all times. Both are worldly matter-spirit bound forces that cannot be separated from the whole. Doubt not the mountains are going to make this order into chaos a reality soon. God's Will is working to bring the doom.

God is the word of all words. Search in these words the force that will make man understand the meaning of order and chaos. The process of transition to the new world will not be abrupt. It will work for world's renewal for many generations to come. Do not doubt My Words. Your Father has sent you to spread this message of renewal before the mountains will move and spread destruction on Earth."

Above messages of doom, came about fourteen years ago. I was then writing the "Dialogues on the Mountain" in Seoul. Since then no doom had fallen on Earth. Only doom that has fallen is the destruction of my life as a scientist and a social being who has failed to integrate with the world in a successful way, and ended in finding recluse in an alien world.

Such doomsday predictions have been made many times before by different doomsday cults. Social psychologists explain such phenomena as caused by cognitive dissonance, which rises in human psyche when two contradictory ideas compete for place in the mind simultaneously. The dissonance occurs when the subject perceives logical inconsistency between his/her two contradictory modes of cognition. They may manifest as anxiety, stress and dreaming of a violent end of the world.

Undeniably, I had been a victim of such a dissonance where the rational ego could not find meaning in what were pouring forth from the unconscious mind. They were in total contradictions with each other. However, I could not refute one in favor of the other. In one side there was the desire to defend the rational ego, while on the other side there was a drive to confirm the existence of the unconscious power as a

Divine Being.

I went back to visit the house in Calcutta where these doomsday messages had started erupting for the first time around the age of twenty. Those messages, which had appeared as automatic writings, were so frightening and scary that I used to keep them hidden in a corner of the house where no one would be able to discover them. After a few years these material disappeared. The moles in the damp place, where those papers were hidden, did the job. And I was psychologically relieved of a great anxiety!

I went to see this house in North Calcutta to understand the social psychological context in which this doomsday scenario had occurred in my mind. To my surprise the house did not exist anymore. It was demolished. There was no trace of the building where I had confronted the unconscious through arts, writings and colourful dream and had flown in the starry cosmos. The window where I used to sit and write poems only existed as an invisible window in my mind; the rooftop that had once opened the gate of Heaven to my mind had vanished in the void enwombing the cosmos.

Only prophecy of the doom that had come true is the catastrophe that had psychologically devastated me. My father, who had inspired me to explore the universe, opened the realms of philosophy and science, and got me interested in great classical literature of the world had become a victim of the Killing goddess. The brother, who stimulated the passion for unconventional thinking with his love for avant-garde writers, died in an early age. The house where I had sat with him to call a spirit in a planchette to convince him about the existence of an invisible realm of the mind had now turned into a place looking like a graveyard where Dakinis and Yoginis roamed. The frightened face of my brother, when the spirit, we were calling in the planchette, declared himself as God, was still hanging in my mind above this graveyard. "What is reality?" he wanted to get an answer from God. "The reality is created by orientation of the finite elements", the reply came. It still reverberates in my mind. Neither I nor my brother was sure what was the meaning of this answer. Anyway....

What is reality? I still grope for an answer. Was the reality, in which God appeared, only an illusory construction of the brain? Anyway... what is illusion? Is everything emerging from the unconscious an illusion? Is unconscious itself is a delusion and hallucination created by the chemical substances produced in the brain stem? I am still equally confused now as I had been most of my life.

Anyway I understood that I need to come out of the state of dissonance of cognition if I wished to get out of this alien world where I was entrapped. I got convinced that everything was being caused by the brain activities. God was nothing but a dream and delusion of the mind, created by misfiring of the circuits in the brain. The wirings in the brain were results of the evolution and experiences of complex interactions with the whole during the millions of years of history of the species. These memories are stored in the genes that may manifest as the archetype of Jung. The ego and consciousness emerge to cope with the challenges of environment and competitions of life at the moment when one finds oneself. The collective psyche suffusing a particular moment of history creates the foundations of anxieties and fears and may generate the visions of doom.

Equipped with this knowledge and understanding I was now set to get rid of God from my mind. Like a mad man I shouted foul words to the spirit that tried to surface in the conscious mind again. When the spirit tried to tell me about the supernatural world I screamed. I wanted to uproot God for ever from my mind.

But how to kill the unconscious without killing oneself?

One day, when the sun was intensely blazing in this room I tore into pieces the paintings where I had depicted that Divine Self. I wished that these images won`t appear in my mind any more. It was an attempt to break down the spiritual bubble in which I was captivated by erasing and attacking the processes of the brains which have created the delusion of God.

When the belief in the existence of an unearthly power, beyond the realm of reason, that can illumine the mind, disappeared from the mind it threw me into a realm, where I saw nothing but darkness. With it the feeling of nothingness and meaninglessness became so intense that I felt paralysed and lost every desire to engage in any pursuit. All activities, which had given meaning to life before, now appeared totally foolish and meaningless. Since then, dark thoughts had been swirling around like ghosts taking flights from everything that had anything to do with the unconscious mind.

With it I was caught in a whirlwind raging in an inferno: Torments rose as hellish wind. I was thrown in a meaningless universe, where chemical and physical laws decided what I am, how I think, what I dream about. This dark hellish wind not only shattered all, I felt it was also blowing through the entire universe, where things rose and fell driven by random accidents and chance. Here things flew meaninglessly. No one controlled anyone, no mind planned or scrutinized anything, and no soul remained after the bodies evaporated into gas and dust. It was dark…dark…dark… so dark that even the darkest part of Dantian Hell would be a more desirable place to seek a refuge.

After returning from the hospital I had fallen in this dark hole that seemed to slip nothing from its womb. Only howling wind of despair and shriek from a bleeding soul, seeking a way of escape from this Hell, was echoing from all walls of this room. I was gripped by an unbearable psychological turmoil, where everything had fallen apart: God, universe, me, the spiritual companion … The foundation of the reality itself, that I had built so assiduously by using my knowledge, experience, reflections, introspections, mediations, rational judgments, feelings and intuitions, had collapsed like a catastrophe drawing me into a hellish world.

While I was desperately seeking a way to escape this terror of the meaningless world, I got  an escape route through writing this book and started  the project "The Windows of Light".

# Chapter 8
# BORN AND UNBORN

The sun has passed the vernal equinox twice since that day when I had gone berserk in destroying anything that brought spiritual thoughts. By destroying writings and works of art that gave any association with God, I wanted to clean myself of the delusion. I got a mad urge to destroy everything that did not conform with the scientific view of the nature of the body and the mind.

The spring has returned twice after that day. The bees, butterflies, insects, and bacteria have invaded nature to support and protect the foliage and flowers in plants and trees, as well as the invaders who are harmful to life. During this transit of the sun across the constellations – moving from Taurus to Gemini - the life forces are on the winning side of the battle for life.

The same forces were acting when the darkness had suddenly covered light of heaven from my mind two years ago. Then the sun stood in Taurus and was about to enter Gemini. However, except Uranus, Neptune and Mars other five planets have now entered different constellations: Venus has moved from Cancer to Aries, Mercury has moved from Gemini to Taurus, Saturn has transited from Virgo to Leo, Pluto has crossed Sagittarius and entered Capricorn, Jupiter has moved from Sagittarius to Aquarius. Uranus is still in Pisces; Neptune is still in Aquarius and Mars has come back to Aries again. The planets were more scattered in the sky then than they are now. Except Saturn, all have gathered in one part of the sky.

With the sunrise, all planets, except Saturn, are above the horizon and moving westward. Right at this moment the Mercury is moving together with the sun, the crescent moon is about to get completely covered with shadow cast by the Earth. In ancient cultures people believed that the positions of the planet destined the courses of events on Earth. Even today the astrologers predicting happenings in the future on the basis of the positions of the planets thrive in large numbers. Many people in the world, including politicians and businessmen still consult the position of the planets before taking important decisions! What a delusional world! According to Dawkins the brains of these people are attacked by a mental virus.

In an attempt to cure myself of any such virus, when I was about to fall apart and disintegrate, sinking in a turmoil that I did not know how to cope with, one morning I woke up hearing the following words:

*"Die bravely. Do not collapse and rot as you do. Live your delusions fully and if you believe life had been a tragedy for you, complete the tragedy with honour and grace. No way is true: All ways could be fallacious. Though you have chosen a way, which has deprived you of the glory, fame, recognition and any meaningful integration with the world of women and men who you see around you, you are the only foundation of your existence, that you must exploit in order to find meaning in your life. There exists no such meaning that can be applicable to all life in general. Meanings reflect the choices the individuals make. Your choice has led you to the path, that you call delusion. But which other choices that human beings make are not delusions like yours? Your delusion has led you away from the world that trumpet the glory of the senses and reasons derived thereof. But many forms of delusions, which enter through senses, stream and form a whirlpool of chaos, which one calls life in the real world "out there". Don`t shriek and yell in fear and pass away from the world as a loser who does not possess the courage to face the reality of your own choice. You have chosen to climb along a path, which has slid*

*away under your feet, leaving you hanging in the air in a lofty sphere of dream. You see no ground where you may set your feet and experience the so called reality of life which is solid and true. But why should it be so frustrating? All life must end sometime in some way. It is your way of ending your life in a dream. How does it matter if God exists or not? If He existed you would have never understood the nature of His existence. If He does not exist, by believing that He existed, you have only created someone who you wished to create for your existential need. If you think that what you have created has no reality, you should know that no reality has any reality outside one`s own sphere of delusion. Your delusion is your reality. Live with your delusion and defy the realities that other may call real: They are realities of delusions of other human beings. Why should you put more meaning to those realities than your own? Create your own reality out of the delusions that you have created yourself, and live fully with this reality that appears to you as a dream. Live in the lofty height as a bubble of dream, and disappear with the clouds in the invisible arena that no one can perceive. As clouds need not complain why the earth is so solid and green, where flowers grow, trees stand upright and human beings dance and feast, that they call life, so you should know your own makeup, and float above the earth and move towards the mountain top, where you will meet the birds, and the light that do not come down to the realm of Earth. Fly with the angels, swim with the ethereal light. It suits your nature and do not weep because you are not one of the ferocious beasts that roam in life`s jungle, who dominate over all other earth-bound beasts. Knowing your own nature subject yourself to the pain that is required to perch on the height above the realm of mud and clay, where you will never be able to build your nest. Why seek home in a place where venomous serpents will strangle all your dreams and hopes? Fly in the realm where you may feel free; wander in the realm where the earth bound beasts dream to soar; feel comfortable with your own conditions, though it may not be composed of earth and mud; breathe the lofty air around, and find your destination above the clouds in a realm that no one can reach. The beasts may not know where you are going, but why their knowing your way, or not knowing the path of your flight should bother you so much that you won`t seek freedom of your way? Go where you have been going; don`t look down on earth to find out if the beasts know about your destination, and understand the mean-*

*ing of freedom that you enjoy along your flight. Should a bird ask a fish "follow me to my destination above the clouds?" They are species of different nature meant to swim under water. The fish won't understand where you want to go. You are a bird of a rare sort, whom most creatures on Earth won't be able to recognize as someone they may have seen before. Should this be your reason for not to fly and live in the realm where you are? Fly in the realm of freedom where you are flying beyond the view of the most animals and birds. Go to your destination where the mountains dazzle with light, and the reality and dream are one. You grieve because you wished to meet God there. This meeting will make your lonely journey meaningful, you thought. Now you doubt and think that there may exist no God. Therefore you are caught in the despair with a fear that the journey will end as an utterly meaningless flight. Fear not! Land on the mountain top. You yourself may turn as a being who is one with God, who you are seeking to find. God is no being outside you. Find Him within you, and stand alone confronting the dazzling light. You will find your God. If you sink in despair and darkness and stay immobile after reaching the height where you are, you will freeze and loose the power in your pinions to ascend higher. Go higher; fly beyond the view of all. You may attain the realm that no one has attained before. You may grieve that no one will see you, no one will know about your existence, no one will ever understand the realm that you have sought. Should a bird of paradise grieve because it is so rare and not visible to all and does not stroll as close as the pigeons do? Will the meaning of living be to live stripped off and exposed to all, in order to get clapping for the acrobatics one may be able to show? The clapping, the warmth of caressing touch and nearness to those who only care for the birds who come their near, and have no knowledge of the birds of the rarest beauty ... is it what you are looking for? Aren't birds of paradise are of different categories of species? They fly in the realm of God. So, fly towards the mountain top. Those human beings, who will be able to climb to that height where you will perch, will discover in you the light that will dazzle as the light of God. You may argue that God is a delusion of the mind and has no reality. It may be true, but do you know of anything else that is not a delusion of the human mind? Things, which you call real, have colours, odours and forms. But those colours, odours and forms are devoid of reality unless they are created by the delusion of your mind. They are all products*

*of the way of seeing and perceiving the world. So is with God. God mani-
fests in the mind in various images, experiences, visions and forms. He is
a product of the mind, who takes various illusory forms depending on the
power of the inner vision one possesses. Like the fact that the world exists,
that no one may observe it in any color, odor and form, God has His existence beyond the qualities of things as a power that animates things and
minds. God cannot be perceived. God can be known only through the
power of the mind. You thought you knew God and believed in His existence, because something or someone always stirred your feelings deep in
your mind, which you could never understand and grasp. It had appeared so real that you had submitted the course of your life to this inner
force. Now you are afraid that it is not God; it is you yourself who has
dictated the course that has led you to the brink of a psychological disaster. The life, you thought, you have not chosen yourself but God has destined for you, now appears to be your own choice. You feel that you have
deluded yourself and ended up in a world of not your choice. If you knew
that God was not there you would have chosen differently according to
your true nature. You repent in submitting your will to someone so delusive and hidden within you. Now you wish you could undo everything
and choose the way you would have otherwise chosen if you did not believe in the existence of God. You feel so unhappy because the choices
imposed by the delusory specter have led you to live a life where you feel
alone, as if an alien in the world. The world moves and runs in its dynamic course where you find no role to play. You wished to play a role, in
fact, a role as big as God, and hoped to be able to change the course of
events in the world according to your visions and dreams. Now just the
reverse appears to be true. You are no one in this world, nothing you can
affect or change with your involvement in life. The world does not even
care if you exist or not. You discover how meaningless and insignificant
your life has turned in the reality where you find yourself. You will like to
put blame on someone for this tragic end. But you find no one to blame
but yourself. You realize that you yourself has created God, and drawn
you to the illusory trap of the mind, from where you find no way to escape any longer. Even if you manage to escape, there is no way to reverse
the course and get the life, which is lost, back again. Therefore you have
fallen in such a great despair. But what has really happened? You have
deluded yourself by creating the belief that God existed and you were act-*

*ing in fulfilling the will of God. Now God has disappeared as an external agent. Whatever has happened in life is cause by your own choice and belief in something external to you, which appears to be non-existent now. You realize that it is your own choice that has led you to such unhappy circumstances of life. You feel unhappy because you feel that all doors of actions, that may make you an important actor in the world, are closed by now. So you must accept it as a catastrophe and a doom fallen on your life. You believe that if you had not let yourself be driven by such a delusion, and instead taken control of life through rational reflections and understanding of the realities of nature and life, you could have done better. By believing in something that does not exist, you have disabled yourself and made yourself useless to the world. This cannot be reversed. The path which is left to you is to follow the delusion, or suffer the immense despair as you do. If you let yourself be driven by this intense despair you may lose mental sanity. So retreat to God again. Even if God does not exist, it is the only path that can bring in you the forces of creativity and make life livable in this alien world. It may be a dream, a delusion, a spectre, or a hallucination, as you say – but it is a nice dream, a colourful illusion, a friendly spectre, and a hallucination indistinguishable from yourself! It is your own self split apart, which is appearing as you and playing the role of God. So the drama should continue. Let characters, who are not you appear as you; let you appear as not-you. Anyway, you do not know yourself: Your mind has territories far beyond the territories where the rational mind operates. So losing a rational grasp of life, should not lead you to live a life that may jeopardize the entire realm of the self. Enter the unknown realm of the self where you yourself may enter as God and angels, or your compassionate friend willing to serve man in suffering and need. Play the role of God; elevate your mind to the plane where you wished to see God and look through yourself. Stand alone and recreate God, whom you have tried to erase from your mind. Fly to paradise; see your incarnation as the one, whose death you repent. Be God; fulfil your illusion as the bird flying to Heaven. Do not sink down and let clouds sweep through your mind as cataclysmic turmoil destroying whatever is left in you. Create colours, create visions, and recreate yourself in words, images and sounds. Like the bird of paradise fly high…generate waves that will return from the mountains as the music of Heaven singing the hymns of life … God or no-God, be the foundation of life that knows no other bond than the bond to the inner light. Recreate God... recreate yourself."*

These words struck with such intensity that they changed the course of my life once again. I got in the pursuit of recreating the existence that I have tried to erase from the mind, and embarked on writing this book. I wanted to reconstruct in words the existence of God and the wandering of the man walking in the shadow of the Divine. I wished to return to the reality where I once lived and wanted to fly again towards the mountain top where I once dreamt to meet the birds of Paradise.

But now the power of the mind has dwindled, the vision has weakened. The reason has demolished the capacity of imaginations to see the unseen, to perceive the unperceived and create that being that exists beyond the power of words, colours and forms. I cannot see the image of this Being clearly any more. It appears hazy and torn into pieces, scattered through the multilayered reality. Though I apprehend the presence of that incomprehensible existence immersed in the reality of this room, where I paint and write, the image I wish to reconstruct in my mind seems to have spread and dispersed far beyond the confinement of its walls. It has merged with spaces known and unknown - even far beyond the realm of the stars and the material universe.

The mind appears like a sea beach where innumerable waves arrive every moment and make me conscious of the presence of the world "out there" in the realm of God. Striking the objects, that exist around, they break into thoughts, and generate visions, colours and forms. These illusions have no end. The unceasing streams of the reality, passing by vision and thoughts, batter the world with mechanical force, and bring to the shore shells and corals from the depth of the ocean I cannot see. They are the signs of life designed by the hands of a mysterious power. Through this window of illusion I gaze at that mysterious realm, which is dispersed in all. In every form it remains hidden, in every sound it camouflages as vibrations whose frequencies I cannot measure.

The mind is still full of much blood and wounds from that day when I went berserk to get rid of God. It has severely affected the network of

257

the brain and damaged the tissues to the extent that I am unable to re-wire the circuits once again to return to my previous mental state. I do not see any longer what I had seen before; I do not feel the heightened impulses of emotions any longer. The mind seems to have decayed and disintegrated. With it the imagination, feelings, and the capacity to grasp things, which are beyond the human ability to grasp, have also waned. However, to escape further disintegration I am embarked on the task of recreating the one I have destroyed.

My eyes are drawn to one of the canvases lying on the floor and lean-ing on one of the bookshelves. This is the first painting I have made in an attempt to rebuild the image of the man I am trying to depict. The painting shows an artist, who has fallen asleep in despair in front of a canvas. He is holding a brush in his right hand, which is tied with the axons entangled in a complexly knitted neural network of the brain. While painting on a canvas the image of the jumbled network of the brain wirings he has fallen asleep. The hand has become so tightly bound to the neural network that he cannot paint any longer, and therefore, in despair, he has sunk in dream. He is seated on the brain stem, surrounded by the left and right cortex. The artist, the brain and the canvas, where the neural network is painted, are in turn, entangled in a cosmic network, which is formed of galaxies. He is dreaming of the return of the power, who will release him from this captivation in the brain, which, in turn, is entangled in the network of the universe in an incomprehensibly complex way. An angel stands behind the dreaming artist. She holds in her hand a magic wand of creation and directs the dreaming artist to move towards the cosmos.

This painting is the central piece of the project called "The Window of Light". Beside it lies another painting where the man is breaking out of the captivation in a Hall of Time, where slaughtered sheep are hang-ing from the roof. He is making an attempt to escape the Darwinian slaughterer by breaking the glass panes that separate the Time Hall of Illusion from the realm where the Golden Buddha, surrounded by monks, is meditating about the transcendental world. Between these two realms lies a sea illumined by a golden orb. Beside that there is another painting titled "The Window of Light" where a man, sitting

258

in a dark realm, is meditating. The canvas is divided into two worlds separated by a wall. Through the opening of a window existing on the wall, an intense beam of light has entered the realm of the meditating man. It illumines a head that spans the entire dark realm. Through this partially transparent head, the neural network of the brain is visible. The man meditates by sitting in the shadow cast by his huge head. On the other side, from where the light has entered the window, there lies an illumined realm of the senses covered by mountains, fjords and a sky burning in an ethereal sunset. Through the window through light enters to illumine his brain. The meditating monk gazes at the other side of the reality where human beings are swimming in the fjord filled with swirling blood streams.

These are a few paintings of the project that I have started some time ago. The section called "Creativity" is nearly finished by now. This section consists of 22 individual pieces, like the three described above. The project "The Window of Light" is planned to consist of four such sections – possibly around hundred paintings in total. The ideas of the project rose out of the realization that, may be, delusion, what we all possess, is the soundest basis of meaning, if there exists any meaning at all! We are all prisoners of our own experiences and delusions. Without changing the genetic foundation of the individual life, may be, there exists no other way but to accept what one is, as a part of a biological specie, who carries an individual trait. To try to transcend, and seek meaning beyond this biological and existential confinement, may be, is nothing but meaningless.

The first section is about the encounter telling the story how God has entered the consciousness and gradually overpowered the will. It starts with the story of a child listening to the whispering coming from nature, which stirred his imagination to believe that someone "out there" was whispering messages to his mind. Then the imperceptible whisperer appeared as whirling waves stirring the mind and became an integral part of the processes generated by the brain. In this section I want to reconstruct the invisible being, who has appeared as a father, a friend and a guide. I want to go back to the memories and see in more clear details the "face" of that companion, who has baffled and puzzled me, brought experiences of great ecstasies, and walked by my side as an imperceptible shadow.

The paintings of the other section depict the existential drama since that encounter. This confrontation with the spiritual world has unleashed rich fantasies, dreams and imaginations as well as driven the mind to seek answers of the mysteries that surround life with the power of knowledge, critical reflections and scientific arguments. It has led me to search the clue of the mystery of the invisible world into plants, flowers, insects and molecules, in the laws of physics and chemistry, as well in the universe. With the curiosity of a child I have lifted every corner of the mind to look for the hidden world, which may lie outside the domains of science. This hidden realm has been source of creativity. It has inspired me to understand the working of the brain and the material basis of the mind, as well as revealed to me the incomprehensible realms of the artists, the musicians and the poets. It has elevated me to the sphere where I have seen myself as one with the eternal self – as a wanderer searching beauty and love as my way of coming home.

I have started "The Window of Light" by making the paintings belonging to the second section called "Creativity". Here the cosmos is one with the reality of this room. Here I listen to the music where muses play the golden cosmic harp, watch the ballerinas resurrecting from the world of the dead as golden swans while welcoming the mortal eyes to the realm where there is no death and birth. Here winged white horse Pegasus accompanies the muses, who inspire the mortal poet writing about the immortal world. Here the sculptor hews out the face of musicians out of crystals while on the other corner of the crystal studio blood ooze from his torso.

The third section is about the existential crisis that follows the period of creativity. It is the story when the bewildered man rises against God and tries to bring down the spiritual world. The paintings of this section deals with the terror unleashed by a meaningless world. Despair and mental conflicts cloud his paths.

In the last section "Walking inside the Mirror", the cosmos opens and a mirror emerges. The man sees an image of himself as multiple in One. He faces the formless world as himself imaged in the mirror as a man standing in front of God. In the mirror he sees the cosmic ocean flowing through clusters of galaxies in the great cosmic body to which all are parts. As he watches the cosmos, the biological world streams through the cells in the brain, and transmutes into the body. He realizes the presence of the Buddha-body of compassion and love, which encompasses all living beings.

This inner being made me believe that God pervaded everything in the nature and the universe and everything were designed according to the Divine plan driven by the power of love and compassion for all. He inspired me to surrender to the power love and compassion and led me to submit my will to the spirit who moves through all. As said before, I cannot see him clearly anymore. My mind has fractured and disintegrated in different directions: Sometimes the atheist takes abode in my mind; sometimes the healer comes and replaces him; sometimes the "Christian killers" make feast and declare allegiance to Satan instead. My understanding of reality is equally fractured and confused: Sometimes the world that I perceive through the visual cortex, when the rays reach the eyes from outside and trigger sensory perceptions in the brain, appear real; sometimes the brain activities in the state of dream, generating visual images in the mind, appear equally real; sometimes no image appears in the mind, no sound is heard by the brain –only strange waves swirl through the mind and inscribe messages and thoughts. Sometime such phenomenon appear very real; sometimes images appear from the unconscious, without any relation to the rational mind, and through processes, that seem totally accidental, generate scenes that overwhelm the emotions as if they constitute the true foundation of reality. Thus my sense of reality has no fixed base on things in the world or those that lie outside the realm of the material existence. As the days revolve with the spinning Earth, and seasons change with the orbital motions of the planets, Hesus, Osiris, Isis, Christ, and innumerable gods and goddesses of the myths appear in my mind. Age of Taurus moves to the Age of Aries. As the sun again changes constellation at the vernal equinox, Age of Aries follows the Age of Pisces, which is then followed by the Age of Aquarius. With every coming of a new age a new sun/son is born of a virgin mother, who is expected to set the chaos, left by the passing age, into a new order.

I find this new sun standing as Buddha, Krishna and Christ as One in front of me. Where did he come from? In a moment of leisure, while I was playing with colors I suddenly discovered a few figures emerging through my sketches. One resembled the figure of Christ after he was taken down from the cross. He was lying on the ground by the side of a female figure. She reminded Marry Magdalena depicted in a painting from the seventeenth century by an Italian master I had seen. She was lamenting over the death of Christ. The third figure had his face covered. He was watching the sacrifice of Christ.

While Ragne was passing by the room she stopped to watch what I was doing. I explained to her the figures that I saw. She suggested that I should make an inter-religious painting. It ignited my imagination.

I left the colours and brushes and rushed to the computer to visualize such a painting. This has become my way to work, before I start a painting. The computer helps me to visualize the subject before I make the drawings on the canvas. As the process started, Buddha and Krishna also appeared in the sketch and the words "Tamasami Jotirmoyo" reverberated in my mind. These were Sanskrit words which meant "Radiant Light in the Womb of Darkness". The day, which started with a feeling of despair, turned into an exciting journey. Finally the central ideas of Buddhism, Hinduism and Christianity emerged on the canvas. To the left a standing golden Buddha appeared on a lotus with the palm of his right hand thrust forward in the way of assuring the world. On this palm he held the "Wheel of Dharma" with eight spokes connecting the inner and the outer circles and a three armed spiral structure at its centre. To the right of the painting, a mortal was hanging on a cross, while dead Christ leaning on a stone inscribed with the word Santi (peace) was lying on the ground. The lamenting Magdalena was approaching Christ before his resurrection. A triskelion, made of three interacting single spirals, entangled the top of the cross and filled the sky above the crucified man looking towards Heaven. In the middle Arjuna and Krishna were riding a golden chariot. The world around them was engulfed by flames. Above the chariot, Krishna was showing Arjuna his cosmic manifestation. Innumerable galaxies formed his robe. Arjuna with folded hands, sitting on the backseat of the chariot, was listening to his Divine charioteer, and friend.

Thus riding on accidental thoughts the being, whom I was seeking to depict, emerged in the mind.

*"Oh yes! You must be a believer in your unconscious mind, though you claim to get rid of God as a conscious being! You let your mind be influenced by the irrational forces, which a scientifically oriented rational man should not allow ",* Professor Dawkins warns.

"Isn't this unconscious a part of my existence, which I have inherited with my genes? Why have nature implanted these genes that create the realm of the unconscious in the mind from where such phenomena, that seem to be acts of God, appear? How can the unconscious ride the accidents and form a conscious representation of a world that does not exist, though it exists as a part of the brain through my genes? What is existing and what is not existing? Does unconscious exist or not exist in the sense consciousness exists? Is it a part of human reality or just a delusion?"

*"They are not real in the sense that they cannot be explained through the equations of the laws of gravity, electromagnetism, weak forces and the nuclear forces that we know as scientists. Unless things cannot be explained and tested with the laws of nature we know, their existence should be doubted. Unconscious has it reality only when we can affect the unconscious by alternating the sites of the brain, from where the unconscious may arise, with chemical and electromagnetic means",* the Dawkinian argues.

"Does unconscious mind has any special sites in the brain that can be manipulated by electric shocks or magnetic frequencies or changed by pouring in chemical material to those sites? Is that unconscious, which is the source of religious feelings in man, including the feelings of love and compassion for all, the real enemy of man as Dawkins asserts? Has nature conspired against the rational man by not taking away the midbrain and basal ganglia, which is a source of illusion and dream in our brain system? Is evolution leading us to a stage when a new smart species will evolve from Homo sapiens sapiens, who will possess bigger and bigger prefrontal cortex, where the brain process-es rational thinking? Will these species no more dreams and remain always awake against emotions that have no rational explanations in terms of physical equation and laws? Will any day in the future man be liberated from the hallucination of encountering God as it appears to me through this work of art, for example?"

The words "Sambhabami Yugey Yugey" rose and repeated again and again in my mind where Krishna assures the world that he will reincar-nate in different ages to lead mankind to the path of Dharma.

Were those words coming from the Basal Ganglia or limbic system - the more ancient parts of the brain that we have inherited from our pre-mammalian ancestors during hundreds of millions of years of evo-lution? Was it just misfiring of the brain circuits that were producing those words in my left cortex in Wernicke`s and Broca`s areas in the brain, that get activated in the process of recognition of the meanings of languages? Was it a by-product of a particular built-in irrationality in the brain? Is it a sign of a mania as some neuroscientists will say? Or, was it nothing but a disease caused by mental viruses as Dawkins will assert?

As I gazed deeper into the realm from where he appeared, my vision expanded through my brain. I was gripped by a power that rolled in-side me as a force altering the state of the brain, which expands into a formless realm beyond the ordinary visions of seeing and hearing, and lifted me outside the reality of the existence that had surrounded me in the room. I felt being absorbed in an infinite space without time, where the brain was immersed in the state of experiencing a void where a Divine being made its existence felt by affecting the physical nature of the neuronal activities.

He spoke: "Come with me. You will know....

*"Hear from Me the World- and-the Will`s formless movements in forms, and darkened body`s movement from form to the formless Man-God. Knowing Him as Me seek to attain the formless existence that has*

moved among you in form. God has worked miracle through Him. Thus know that I exist, and you exist in Me as a part of Him.

How do I exit out of and enter into the sphere, where the world-and-the will exist, as the power to move the world-and the will in the destined way, is not available to the knowledge of any human being. You must move as I have expressed in forms in the world which is destiny-bound. Your world does not appear as you may will it to appear. His Will is the will of the destiny-bound world. By willing to move He has destined your movement in the matter-bound path. How do you understand this destiny without being a part of Him? How can man seek Him without being a part of Him? How do you make yourself a part of the world-and-the will without being a part of Him? Born and Unborn know that I am Him.

Powerful movement of Man-God is making the mountains move, causing the seas and water of the world to bring torrents and storms. Man and woman! Move with your Savior before the destruction comes!

Hear: The world's mountains are moving, the climate is changing, the forces in nature are warring against each other, and the bodies are being darkened by the will as a great darkness is overpowering the world. Home and the world are moving to the mountains. Man and woman are going to the mountains with Me.

Know what would bring destruction as I move in the world-and-the will. Know Me as the harbinger of the force that will change the world from the matter-bound existence to the spiritual one. Born and unborn I am moving and changing the matter-bound world as willed by Me.

Know what makes me suffer though there is no suffering in Me. Know what is suffering as the movement of the flesh and blood's existence in the will-bound world, that cannot know what is not world-and-will bound. Knowing what is unknown work and act and face the trial as women and men, who are destiny-bound. Crucifixtton of Man-God is the symbol of My exotic existence in the world, that has come as a result of the world's saviour appearing as Man. Crucifixtion is peace and darkened body's salvation from the movement of the will that is fate-bound. Crucifixtion is the work of God as a movement in the world to be released from the matter-bound existence and lifted to the realm of Man-God. Know what I am, and I am not. Seek in Me your soul's movement towards Man-God.

Crucified on the Cross I have existed in time that is death-bound.

*Crucified are the mountains, and the seas; crucified are the men and the women; crucified is the world-and the will as Me. Born and unborn I am Him. Enter me and be a part of the sacrifice.*

*Resurrection of My Son is a fate-bound movement and a formless world's working through Man-God. He is world, and World is Him as I have sent Him to the world assuming darkened form. By darkening himself He has assumed the fate of the world and brought the formless world to women and men. His coming will bring upon the world destruction. Keep faith in Him. Fail not the words I have spoken before you. Enter in Him and offer yourself as a sacrifice to the altar of God."*

When I returned to my senses I wondered "Was it nothing but nonsense and meaningless babbling? Were all these experiences caused by the epilepsy of the temporal lobe in the cortex as the neurologists would say?"

But how shall I call these experiences nonsense when they release a surge of ecstasy and emotion that flood the mind with a supernatural feeling that cannot be measured by any sensory apparatus of any sort? Why shall I believe that this experience of mine is false and others experiences, that the empiricists talk about, are true? What hypothesis shall I use to prove or disprove? Why the understanding that relates existence to the material state will be the only mode of understanding and all other experiences of the existence have to be discarded or accepted with reference to it? What logic is there to reduce the world to the material plane when the human existence may be immersed in many other planes, that most people have not been trained to discover? Why the ones who are not awake and still sleeping in the darkness of the sense-bound world will decide what the language should mean and be allowed to convey? Why the arguments of science that deals with reality in the space-time should also be the foundation to discover the nature of existence that may fall outside its realm?

In this reality, where I am absorbed, "consciousness"(not in the Jungian or the Freudian meaning but a state of awakened awareness as in meditation) of the world is based on the mythical-symbolic realm as well, where thought processes are entangled in a domain that lies outside the boundary of the senses. What is this "consciousness"? What is this awareness? What do I really mean by the self? Is "consciousness" a searching light in the dark universe of the mind that is intricately entangled in many dimensions of reality which we need to explore? Is it a light that evolves and sees greater and greater depth of the mind with the evolution of the brain of the specie? Is it related to the brain or is it a nonphysical entity independent of the brain that sees itself as nothing in an abstract space of thoughts? Is it the inner eye that has another eye behind, which has another eye inside ... yet another beyond... and thus infinitely regressing in to the vast depth of the mind that can never be fully illumined by the brain and be known by the mind of man who finds himself in a particular state of evolution of the species developing for eons!

Is it possible to describe this "consciousness", that will be understandable by all human beings with different capacities to reflect, judge and become aware of themselves? Can it be reduced and translated to the descriptions of the activities of the nervous system in the brain as many neurophysiologists may like to attempt? Although the capacity to be conscious may depend on the development of the brain can it ever be known through neural physiological accounts? Can "consciousness" be understood as algorithms and programmes evolved by the nature through the hundreds of millions of years' process of development of the brain of the mammals from whom man has evolved? Don't we know that the neurological experiments may suggest that the usual physical rules of time, the way it enters our "consciousness", get modified from the time-ordered frame? As the oxford Physicist-Mathematician Roger Penrose have suggested, may be, that the time conceived by the perceptive flow of events do not really "flow" in the linear forward-moving manner by which we are conscious of time and the reality of the world! May be, man imposes the temporal ordering on the way the world is perceived in order to make a sense of them in relation to the physical reality and become conscious of the existence of the self ! Does not this mean that the atomistic logic a la Wittgenstein may make no more any sense? Then what really language should mean? Can the language based on fact and verifiable scientific evidence explain the "consciousness" or anything at all! Is it not still a profound mystery that we are conscious of ourselves and certain of the existence related and perceived by the brain? Is it not a wonder that we think, speak and talk about the world, myth, reality, dream, allegories, symbols, ethics, morals, religions that others may understand? But this understanding in the public space will depend on at what level of the reality man is conscious of and what language man is able to understand by relating the words to the experiences of one's own, that may be extra-perceptible, like the experience of this journey of the man with whom my spirit has wandered through the village, forest and the mountain in the inner hidden reality of the world, through which I have come and gone.

In this "consciousness", where I am awake, I see myself through many lives through "consciousness" of many other human beings who are parts of the One, to whom I belong. The memories, I carry deep within myself, are the memories of the human specie and not the memories of a particular individual body to which my physical existence is bound. Those memories that can be triggered by the electrical signals in the brain are the memories of the particular man who is bound in the sense apparatuses and the activities of the brain. But the memories through which the spirit has travelled are beyond time and space and can only be stimulated by the spiritual waves not moving in time and space. But still the question remains: Do these memories have ultimate foundations in the brain from where they can be retrieved? Can it be that the eternal memories of the whole, which are imprinted in the molecular level from which it is transferred to "consciousness"? Can it be so that, depending on the development of the brains in the evolutionary scale, man develops capacity to construct language and codes to store, and retrieve from the eternal memories of the whole, and communicate information about the higher level of reality? May be, most brains, whose understandings form the public space, are not yet developed to the same extent so that they can form a public understanding of this memory of the eternal journey of the man, who is the whole! Can it be that in that microscopic dimension the spirit is embedded in the matter and able to trigger memories of the existence of the hidden dimensions that lie outside time and space? May be, the brain, developed to certain maturity, functions as a receptor that can retrieve and access the information of the hidden world? How shall we know about it when we know that, at this microscopic level, the functions of such electrical network may function in indeterministic quantum mechanical laws of probabilities and chances, where the observer's existence is intricately enmeshed? How shall I know for sure that I am really who I think I am? Perhaps "me" of today was "consciousness" of another sort than the person, which was conscious of himself yesterday! May be, my consciousness of tomorrow will be of another one of a person who is independent of the "consciousness" of the person who is "me" existing today! How shall I know that I am not living backward in time with all who have died before? Neurologists won't be able to assure me with physical data that will be able to give me any convincing argument or evidence to decide if my "consciousness" is reversing backward in time or not!

Though it seems totally immersed in all, which exist around, the spiritual world seems alien to the sense-bound reality. Is it only a fantasy ridden awareness rising from the unconscious created by the brain, or does it really exist as a being separate from matter? Can it be dissected into parts and made a subject of analysis of the logical mind? Or does it only exist as a whole that cannot be subjected to comprehension by any analytical thoughts? Is it only a feeling, a deep stirring, a delusion, and a reflection of an abnormal mind, which is misfiring signals generated by the chemical reactions in the cells?

Do the creative urges in the mind truly indicate ways to communicate with a world that has a real existence beyond the laws of nature, or do they represent an unnatural way of uniting thoughts behind mental processes that can delude the mind? Is the idea, that it exists in all, fostered by imaginations created by wrong wirings in the brain, and has no reality outside the fantasy of the mind? Or is it really a force that brings unity among all existing beings, while creating plurality of forms held together by an intelligence that brings harmony and order out of disorder and chaos? Does it act behind the grand organic unity, a la Hegel, that nature contemplates, or is it a romantic way to dream about a world that may aid human beings to find ways to live in the world of imperfection and suffering? Does it point to a mystical reality, that is not reducible to conscious appreciation, or is it only a misunderstanding, where the mind glorifies unexamined ideas with a hope to find escape from the suffering and the limitations of the mind? Does this spiritual sphere truly belong to the Platonic realm of beauty that does not provoke the senses but exists as the creation of Demiurge that can be understood and known through contemplative power of the mind? Or is it only, as Freud says, a fantasy and fore-pleasure, and a deceptive web of dreaming that can be reduced and explained in terms of sexual fantasies?

As I ask, I see the spiral moving through the cosmos. It reminds me about the shores, where the mind is making voyage through the multi-layered reality. Here a cosmic mind is radiating compassion and bliss to awaken all to existence in the world, where the psychic energies of the healers and the physical energies of the scientists are flowing. From the physical energy the matter is coming into form and from the psychic energy the will is taking its shape. These matter and will constitute the dual, which move through the world as contradictory aspects united in the same being.

The psychic energy drives the passion and the urges of nature as "id" and unconscious not conditioned by the rational power of the mind. From here the artists, musicians and poets derive their primary power of creation before intellect comes into play. In this domain, unconditioned by reason and idea of the rational world, there exists a vegetative and sleeping world. In these unawakened state lines, forms, patterns exist as chemical signals in the brain. They become line, forms, and patterns of artistic creativity after being organized by the intelligence of the mind. Similarly sounds, rhythms and cadences exist as signals before being awakened to musical sounds carrying the trembling of emotional delight. With this awakening, the will appears in the psychic stream carrying the images of the invisible world.

The world is divided between matter and mind carrying light and darkness. In the domain of reason beauty exists as a bodiless intellective power that brings harmony and order in disorganized impulses and emotions that rise from the darker realm of the mind. In this intellectual realm the beauty exists as the luminous power emanating from a world existing outside the realm of the senses. It is a domain where the mind carries the force of the will, and moves as eddies of psychic energy forming the images in the mirror that moves as the material universe. It is the domain of the intellectual activity that foresees a synthesis and unity of the whole, like a great cosmic symphony holding each individual part in an idea, which transcends the parts and harmonises the whole. It is a transcendental domain uncorrupted by the physical forms, colours and sounds.

In this realm there exists no accident and contingency, or limitations imposed by time and space. Here beauty is self-contained, timeless and sublime like Plato's idea, Kant's reason and Nietzsche's Apollonian force, that reflects the beauty of the mind of the creator. According to Plato it cannot be copied with sounds, symbols, notes, lines, colours and forms pertaining to the world of the senses. In this pure domain beauty is a heavenly vision without any visual and sensual counterparts. Beside this transcendental domain, there exists a realm of the mind that aspires to create copies of this beauty in colours and forms as works of art. As a sculptor chiselling the stones one aspires to create lines and forms that may harmonise with the intellective beauty that exists outside the boundaries of the physical properties inherent in the marbles and stones. Smoothness of the lines - bent and curved, and the intensity of colours spread through innumerable hues, follows the flow of the beauty and light that exist outside weight, touch and visual forms. Mind grapples with the challenge of representing inform the subtle world that exists in the intellectual domain. Mind struggles with matter and the disorganized impulses, which face challenges of the intellect to represent the formless world in forms. Thus when man tries to create an image of the transcendental world in the mirror moving through the sense-bound world, man creates the images of the self in colours and forms that bear the constrains of the  law-bound world. However as Plato believed, given the limitations of the senses, bound to the law-bound sphere, the beauty, seen through intellectual contemplation of the mind, can never be represented by forms existing in the material world.

In this multi-layered reality where so many urges and ideas operate the beauty has a meaning much wider than the so-called Platonic ideas. It has a meaning with reference to the subject appreciating the object of beauty and the level of consciousness that the observer bears. Some find beauty in objects where others find utter chaos of disorganized impulses and thoughts. Similarly where the others may find Platonic beauty and intellectual splendour, one may see a delusive world where mind takes flight in romantic wandering in a non-existing world. While some may glorify the transcendental visionary world as the great realm of arts, the others may defend the petty and banal things of daily life as the true foundation of arts.

Thus in the reality, coloured and formed by the consciousness of the individual minds, order and chaos exist side by side. On one side one is not awakened and born, while on the other side one is awakened by the spiritual power, which moves through the cosmos. The being, I am trying to depict walks in both the born and the unborn realms. He moves through the instinct-bound world of the unconscious where mind is not awakened, walks through the forest where dream and delusion confuse the path, ascends the mountain height, where dazzling lights awaken him from dream and delusion, flies in the cosmos where the cosmic consciousness penetrates the mind, and finally meditates as an awakened and enlightened being in the Time Hall:

*"What a wonderful image! The whole transitory world is moving in it. There are so many wonderful designs being drawn by the movements of the current dragging one part with another that are twisting, turning, circling like eddies, releasing the knots of movements and creating new eddies again. With them feelings are turning, twisting, releasing themselves from eddies and falling into eddies again. The whole Samsara seem to be like this river where moments are fleeing creating such wonderful patterns of colourful thoughts and confusion of feelings. It is Maya - the illusory veil- that is twisting and turning in the motionless river and creating this motion.*

*The will, is it not a river like this? Is not this will make the river move? Or the will is moving with matter that drags the motions of the river? Or are will and matter moving as the same river? The mind seems to be inseparable from the no-mind, that is appearing as the currents, the eddies,* the whirling, turning in the eyes, dissipating and condensing creating the flux of time. Is it carrying emptiness through innumerable structures of thoughts, which are nothing but illusions of the mind, while there exist nothing but the formless void? Is it all void? These rotations, these expansions, contractions, turbulence, tearing apart and taking part into another turbulence, outside and inside , are they only Maya, the transitory reflections of the will into the void or does there exist something concrete, outside the existence of the will, existing by itself?

How marvellous is this image! It is devouring itself, breaking itself into parts, scattering itself in the ripples and waves, distributing itself in many forms and designs without ever vanishing from the sight, and always appearing to be the same. The molecules of water are buffeting on the surrounding matter and evaporating into clouds in order to be absorbed by the tree from the depth of the earth with its roots as well as by the innumerable cells spread across the space as its branches and leaves. How inconstant is this image! Though how unchangeable is this vibrating illusion, that is dissipating without dissipating, falling apart without falling apart, tending to disappear without ever disappearing from the sight. How illusory is this becoming that is always eluding the mind with the vision of the impermanence though always remaining the same!

It is mirroring the void, reflecting the emptiness through which the mind and matter are flowing as two conjoint rivers, which exist to perceptions and feelings and appear to the consciousness only as a result of this unity. In separation they constitute the formless void. Here without the will matter seem to be disappearing and without the matter the will seem to be without its base of existence. Over this river, where the image of the tree is being reflected as an image of the permanent in the stream of impermanence, where wind and air are dragging the matter with it, a spiritual wind is constantly blowing, that is dragging the feelings with it creating turbulence and waves, trying to scatter the image into many small pieces of ideas and thoughts and disperse them in the stream of nothingness. In this nothingness, the world exists as projection of the stream of the psychic energy on the stream of the energy of matter, giving each other form and essence. Here the will is bringing the mind in form and form is bringing the will to its existence. One could not disjoin these two rivers, which is one. From the centre of the mandala they are streaming outside and inside - the world of matter and form as well as *the domain of the mind, that create this marvellous image on the river.*

*Atoms, molecules, gas and clouds are condensing in it. Like this, in the stream flowing in the void clouds of gas are condensing into bigger and bigger units and forming stars, galaxies, cluster of galaxies etc., as burning masses of matter gradually transforming the less organised order into more organised state of solid matter. Energy is being consumed and released in this process, bringing dynamics to the world. Is it not the mind which is bringing an order? Is not the forces attracting the mass into this process is a reflection of a greater mind, that contains the reason and purpose of the beings and becoming? Do not these turning and moving eddies on the river carry the mind that creates the organic cells, vegetation, life and the being that he himself is? Though the image seems to be splitting into pieces by acts of chance in the wind and air driven by the heat and cold, circulating in the currents into different patterns, is not the will impinging on each accident in order to hold the whole into an organised unity ? Does not a unity exist everywhere that transcends the blindness of the chance? Without this can this marvellous image, that is always floating as indestructible projection of this self, be created out of chaos?*

*If this river did not exist, would anything exist? Will not he himself vanish with the disappearance of the river while his own image will disappear? Limbs are dancing in the stream mingling with the branches and leaves- one going over the other with the dancing movement of the rippling waves; mind is waving the wind that is shuffling through the leaves of thoughts and trying to become one with the wind that is shuffling the bits of images of the tree from its root to the crest. There is a beautiful vibration inside and outside. The eyes receiving the images are transforming the sensations into musical vibration in the conscious world. They are changing into notes and sounds as chanting hymn from a greater depth of the mind. The ears, which are collecting the restless reverberations scattered by the excited wind, the flashes of light are breaking on small ripples and waves, seem to be trying to release themselves from the bondage of the sounds and waves. Behind the visible rays and the audible waves there exist strange light and sound, that are moving as the will flowing through the material domain. These strange light and sound are flashing in all corners of the mind while natural light and sound are vibrating on the dancing waves. They are flashing from poles to poles, branches to branches, leaves to leaves, and the marvellous image is growing in his mind to occupy all streams flowing through the void!*

*How marvellous! There seem to exist no boundary between the interior and the exterior! The physical stimuli, the desire, passion, feelings, pain, sufferings, melancholy, thoughts, ideas, conscious reflections and awareness and unconscious exaltations of emotions all have merged with a marvellous beauty! This beauty is emanating from the centre of the mandala, which lies within oneself where the tree also exist as an inseparable part of the whole to which mind and matter are one.*

*How green! How bubbling! How infinitely strange is this beauty! It is sinking, upsurging, rolling with gusts of wind, trilling, spewing, spiting, wheeling, and whirling as the part of the mind itself. It is moving away, and then returning to vision that is near; it is flowing forward and then twirling backward; it is moving upward, and then pouring downwards. In all these motions what is this, which I am looking at? Is it not that I am only staring at myself, and watching the process of living, dying and returning again and again in this stream of life and death? The void that is hanging over the head, is it not too a part of the stream where I exist? Is it not also the part of the void through which this stream is moving carrying me as a being who comes and goes with the perpetual turning of the wheel? And moreover, how can I know that I really exist? Is not my existence an illusion itself? Who is me? Am I matter, will, impulses, feelings, ideas, and knowledge with which as a human being I am gazing at myself? Am I an aggregate of those senses and the reason that are revealed as ideas through the mediation of the conscious mind? Am I ascertainable to comprehension in the world of will and matter, which is constantly in motion and has no meaning except relative to something that only exist in reference to a part? Are not all parts negating my true identity? And what this true identity may be when all knowing are relative to a part and ascertainable in a world of constant material and psychic flux where the knower and the object to be known about have no absolute meaning as such? Am I those feelings of love, pain, suffering and joy, which are twisting and turning and revamping the world as objects of thought? Is not those feelings conditioned such that the feelings, with which I form the concept of the world in images, negates the true nature of himself? Am I not knowable except as negation of all that defines the perceptions, creates logic and the foundations of feeling and emotions?*

*Can I be reduced and reduced by logic without ever being truly reduced but to nothing? Or can I be known as a sum total of these negative descriptions of my being?"*

Tathagata sinks deeper and deeper in the mind and sees the existence of Buddha as the ultimate beauty submerged in the void. In mind's incandescent glow he hears the words: "Sabbe sankhara anicca": All that are constructed and effected by the interaction of the matter and mind are impermanent; "Sabbe dhamma anatta": All conditioned quality is insubstantial; and "Sabbe Sankhara dukkha": All that are constructed and effected by the interaction of matter and mind are the sources of anguish suffering and pain....

With this Tathagata feels a surge of love that has pervaded the universe and spreads his hands to touch the sentient world moving in the stream. The world starts glowing ...

www.ingramcontent.com/pod-product-compliance
Lightning Source LLC
Chambersburg PA
CBHW051726260326

41914CB00031B/1756/J